The High-Tech Potential

The High-Tech Potential

ECONOMIC DEVELOPMENT IN RURAL AMERICA

Amy K. Glasmeier

Published by the Center for Urban Policy Research
New Brunswick, New Jersey 08903

Printed in the United States of America

Library of Congress Cataloging-in-Publication Data

Glasmeier, Amy.
  The high-tech potential: economic development in rural America /
Amy K. Glasmeier.
     p. cm.
  Includes bibliographical references (p.) and index.
  ISBN 0-88285-133-0

  1. High technology industries—United States—Location. 2. United
States—Rural conditions.   I. Rutgers University. Center for Urban Policy
Research.   II. Title.
HC110.H53G53 1991   90-48401
338.6′042—dc20   CIP

Contents

Tables   vii

Figures   x

Acknowledgments   xiii

1   Rural High Tech: Problems and Prospects   1

2   The What, Where, and Why of High Tech   19

3   Regional Distribution of Rural High Tech   47

4   Regional High-Tech Location
        and Rural Industrialization   71

5   Strategic Sectors' Shortcomings Confront
        Rural Communities   93

6   Unmasking High-Tech Location   113

7   Factors Influencing Rural High-Tech Plant
        and Employment Location   135

8   Factors Governing the Spatial Distribution of
        High-Tech Jobs and Plants Among Cities
        and Rural Communities   159

9   Prospects for Rural High-Tech Development   185

Appendix A   194

v

Appendix B   198

Notes   202

Bibliography   207

Index   216

Tables

Chapter 2. The What, Where, and Why of High Tech

2.1   High-Technology Manufacturing Industries   20
2.2   Growth in High-Tech Establishments
       and Employment, 1972–1982   25
2.3   Employment and Plant Change in the United
       States, 1982–1987   26
2.4   Regional Share of U.S. Population, 1980, 1970, 1960   28
2.5   Proportion of High-Tech Employment in
       Four Census Regions, 1972, 1977, 1982   29
2.6   Regional High-Tech Job Change: Absolute
       Difference, 1972–1982   29
2.7   Ratio of High-Tech to Total Manufacturing Jobs
       in Four Census Regions, 1981   30

Chapter 3. Regional Distribution of Rural High Tech

3.1   Modified Shift-Share Analysis of High-Tech
       Employment Growth Across the Urban-Rural
       Continuum, 1972–1982   51
3.2   Distribution of Total High-Tech Jobs Among
       Adjacent and Nonadjacent Rural Counties, 1982   59
3.3   Industries With Greater Than 20 Percent of Total
       National High-Tech Plants in Rural Counties,
       1982 (listed by SIC Code)   60
3.4   Industries With Greater Than 20 Percent of Total
       National High-Tech Employment in Rural
       Counties, 1982 (listed by SIC Code)   61
3.5   Industries That Gained Greater Than 500 Jobs
       in Rural Counties, 1972–1982   63

3.6   Industries That Gained Ten or More Plants in
             Rural Counties, 1972–1982   65

**Chapter 4. Regional High-Tech Location
and Rural Industrialization**

4.1   Percent of Total Rural Manufacturing in the
             Four Census Regions, 1972 and 1982   78
4.2   Occupational Distributions of High-Technology
             Industries by County Group   89

**Chapter 5. Strategic Sectors' Shortcomings Confront
Rural Communities**

5.1   Top Four High-Tech Industry Job Generators,
             1972–1982   94
5.2   Employment Growth in Defense-Dependent
             Sectors, 1972, 1977, 1982   97
5.3   Defense-Dependent Sector Employment and
             Plant Change in Rural Counties, 1972–1982   103

Chapter 6. Unmasking High-Tech Location

6.1   Estimated Employment in High-Technology
             Industry, 1982   114
6.2   State High-Tech Development Programs   125

**Chapter 7. Factors Influencing Rural High-Tech
Plant and Employment Location**

7.1   Adjacent Rural Counties: Absolute Levels
             of Employment, 1982   154
7.2   Adjacent Rural Counties: Absolute
             Employment Change, 1982   155
7.3   Adjacent Rural Counties: Absolute Levels
             of Plants, 1982   156
7.4   Adjacent Rural Counties: Absolute Plant
             Change, 1982   157

Chapter 8. Factors Governing the Spatial Distribution of High-Tech Jobs and Plants Among Cities and Rural Communities

8.1   Expected Signs of Coefficients Indicating
       Spatial Location of High-Tech Industries in
       Rural Adjacent and Metro Areas   165

8.2   Tobit Analysis of Metropolitan-Adjacent Rural
       High-Tech Employment, 1982   169

8.3   Tobit Analysis: Metropolitan-Adjacent Rural
       High-Tech Plants, 1982   170

8.4   Tobit Analysis: Metropolitan-Adjacent Rural
       High-Tech Plants Change, 1972–1982   171

8.5   Tobit Analysis: Metropolitan-Adjacent Rural
       High-Tech Employment Change, 1972–1982   172

8.6   Metropolitan Area Employment: Absolute
       Values, 1982   175

8.7   Metropolitan Area Plants: Absolute Values, 1982   176

8.8   Metropolitan Area Employment: Absolute
       Change, 1972–1982   179

8.9   Metropolitan Area Plants: Absolute Change,
       1972–1982   180

Appendix A. High-Tech Industry Growth Performance: 1972–1982

                                                                       194

Figures

Chapter 3. Regional Distribution of Rural High Tech

Figure A   Comparison of National, Metropolitan,
and Rural High-Tech Job Change,
1972–1982   55

Figure B   Comparison of National, Metropolitan,
and Rural High-Tech Plant Change,
1972–1982   58

**Chapter 4. Regional High-Tech Location and
Rural Industrialization**

Figure C   High-Tech Employment by Census Region,
1972 and 1982   81

Figure D   Location Quotients of Rural High-Tech
Employment by States Within
Census Regions, 1982   85

**Chapter 5. Strategic Sectors' Shortcomings Confront
Rural Communities**

Figure E   Share of Employment and Plants in the
Computer Electronics and Communications
Industries Within Adjacent and
Nonadjacent Rural Counties,
1972 and 1982   99

Figure F   The Share of Total High-Tech Plants and
Employment Growth Accounted for by
the Computer Electronics Communications

(CEC) Sector for the Nation and Rural
Counties, 1982   100

Figure G   Location Quotients (LQs) of Computer-
Electronics-Communication
Employment in Rural Counties by
States Within Census Regions, 1982   102

Figure H   The Share of Defense-Dependent Employment to Total National, Metro, and
Rural High-Tech Employment, 1982   104

Figure I   Regional Shares of Total DDS Employment
and Rural DDS Employment, 1982   105

Figure J   Regional Shares of Total DDS Plants and
Rural DDS Plants, 1982   106

Figure K   Location Quotients (LQs) of Defense-
Dependent Sector Employment in
Rural Counties by States Within
Census Regions, 1982   108

Chapter 6. Unmasking High-Tech Location

Figure L   States' Share of National Rural High-Tech
Employment, 1982   116

Figure M   States' Share of National Rural High-Tech
Plants, 1982   117

Figure N   States' Share of Rural Defense-Dependent
Sector Employment, 1982   118

Figure O   States' Share of Rural Defense-Dependent
Sector Plants, 1982   120

Figure P   States' Share of Rural Computer
Electronics and Communications
Sector Employment, 1982   121

Figure Q   States' Share of Rural Computer
Electronics and Communications
Sector Plants, 1982   122

Acknowledgments

Numerous people have contributed to this book. First and foremost, I wish to acknowledge the financial assistance of the Ford Foundation and the Aspen Institute's Rural Economic Policy Program (REPP), which provided the resources to begin the project. The program has been important in providing me access to scholars in the field of rural development through its various conferences and seminars. I wish to especially thank Susan Sechler, program director, for her consistent support of my work. Norman Collins and Mildred Duncan also deserve credit for supporting the original study.

This book reflects the culmination of my experiences in trying to understand the spatial evolution and regional development implications of high-technology industries. The project really began with my dissertation, which was generously supported by Ann Markusen and Peter Hall through vigorous discussions and joint research efforts. The grant I received from the REPP's original competition allowed me to extend this early work into what is now this book. I would also like to thank Mary Beth Pudup, who commented on earlier drafts of this work on high technology.

The University of Texas Research Institute provided financial assistance for the completion of the manuscript. Along with the Mike Hogg Endowment, the University of Texas provides important assistance to young faculty members early in their careers. I am grateful for their help. I also wish to thank Terry Kahn, program director, for his support in the completion of this project along with his helpfulness during the various stages in the statistical analysis. I would like to acknowledge the support of the Center for Urban Policy Research at Rutgers University for the publication of the book, and to Norm Glickman, who provided encouragement along the way.

This project has had a long life, starting when I began teaching at Pennsylvania State University. Many students, but particularly Kurt Patrizi, assisted me in the initial data compilation efforts, and I wish to thank them for their help. Henry Ruderman, of Lawrence Berkeley Labs, built the original data set. He lent his considerable knowledge of such arcane items as FIPS codes to this project. Upon my arrival at the University of Texas, I had the exceptional opportunity to employ Gayle Borchard as my programmer, mapmaker, and statistical wizard. She learned the ins and outs of the mainframe computer with remarkable speed and mastered complex details associated with managing large data sets. Gayle also researched and wrote the first draft of the state policy response section of this book. Gayle and Rolf Pendall built the data base used in the regression analysis, and Rolf and James McCaine also provided graphics assistance for the final product. The initial report was typed by Margie Henning and Jenell Scherbel. Once the report became the basis of this book, Amy Kays took the helm by guiding it through many drafts while providing expert editorial and content suggestions along the way. She also provided important moral support during the journey. Jeff Thompson deserves special mention for his tireless efforts to piece together high-tech industry categories after the 1987 SIC code revision occurred.

Various colleagues provided important intellectual guidance during the completion of this project. Early research results were reviewed by members of the geography and planning faculties at the University of Toronto, Pennsylvania State University, and the University of Michigan. Unbeknownst to them, David Barkley of Clemson University in South Carolina and Steve Smith of Penn State gave important and detailed comments about the manuscript's overall argument. Chandler Stolp kindly assisted in the final statistical analyses of high-tech location. While technical consultants were essential in the completion of this book, any errors are mine and are not attributable to others.

Finally, my family deserves enormous credit for patience and understanding during the life of this book's writing. My husband, Tom, is my most ardent fan and has been a constant supporter throughout the project. My son, Andrew, who was born on the eve of the project's journey, brought countless hours of joy and diversion to me during the book's creation. This book is dedicated to my mother, whose love, understanding, and encouragement instilled in me the belief that anyone could succeed with hard work and dedication.

1

Rural High Tech: Problems and Prospects

Rural America is at a crossroads in its economic development. Like peripheral regions of other First World nations, the traditional economic base of rural communities in the United States is rapidly deteriorating. Natural resources, including agriculture—the long-standing bedrock of rural economies—show little prospect for generating future job growth, and manufacturing, which once heralded the antidote to overdependence on natural resources, is a new source of instability. Faced with these changes and an increasing vulnerability to international economic events, rural communities seek high-technology industries and advanced services as candidates for job growth and economic stability. What, though, is the likelihood of these sectors developing outside America's cities?

High-technology industries are major components of local economic development wish lists. Across the nation, and increasingly worldwide, communities line up to bid for new plants. In the past, rural places had some chance of competing for manufacturing jobs as products matured and plants shifted out of cities, but what of high tech? Do these newer industries follow the path of prior generations of manufacturing? Do the most labor-intensive, low-skilled aspects of production filter down to communities along the spatial hierarchy, or are rural communities in danger of being passed over for more profitable operations in low-wage countries of the Third World? Answers to these questions form the core of this book.

The prospects for rural high-tech development can be understood only by examining the spatial evolution of high-tech industry across America's urban-rural geographic continuum. Explaining the contemporary spatial distribution of high-tech industry further requires that we acknowledge the convergence of two distinct periods of industrialization: premicroelectronics and postmicroelectronics. For reasons largely related to production skill requirements, a spatial division of labor within these industries has formed that flows unevenly across America's urban and rural regions.

Prior studies of high-tech location have repeatedly attempted to model high tech. By focusing on intermetropolitan decentralization, previous analyses have mistakenly expected that the division of labor could be demonstrated strictly by comparing high-tech industries across cities. Yet cities are primarily the domain of the most complex aspects of new product development, process-related research and development (R and D) and advanced manufacturing. Therefore, these empirical efforts to explain high-tech location have largely compared places whose experiences with high-tech development have been roughly similar. Only by incorporating the rural dimension has the spatial division of labor in high-tech industry been clearly revealed.

Emphasizing intermetropolitan development has also ignored the convergence of two distinct industrial eras — premicroelectronics and postmicroelectronics — and two different modes of production organization. Both experiences have played out precisely among America's major geographic regions. Technology-intensive industries of the premicroelectronics era were part of the nation's midwestern industrial complex of chemicals, electrical apparatus, and premicroelectronics communication equipment. The spatial distribution of this employment reflected a pattern of early postwar manufacturing decentralization. This explains why traditional manufacturing regions still boast large shares of the nation's employment in industries classified as high tech. Postmicroelectronics industry location both overlaps and diverges from the previous era. The most obvious results of this interweaving of industrial eras are the formation of new agglomerations of industrial employment and the penetration of routine production functions into America's lower-cost and growing southern region. The contemporary pattern of high-tech location reflects the convergence of these two experiences.

The driving force behind the spatial evolution of high-tech development is evolving modes of premicroelectronic and postmicroelectronic production that have alternately emphasized labor cost and labor skill; yet although the market circumstances governing the two are fundamentally different, both premicroelectronic and postmicroelectronic modes of production reflect mandates of demand-driven manufacturing decentralization. Premicroelectronic production primarily seeks low-cost labor and occurs when market conditions are characterized by stable or declining demand and product standardization enables the decentralization of routinized forms of manufacturing. Postmicroelectronic production coincides with expanding markets, increasing international competition, and rising global production. These circumstances embrace periods of shortage and surplus as new product generations are churned out and the rate of product maturation accelerates (Taylor 1986). Simultaneous with periods of overproduction and underproduction, the industries face rising skill requirements as products become increasingly complex. During periods of accelerated demand, firms decentralized production to areas of low cost but, more importantly, qualified labor. The conversion from premicroelectronics to postmicroelectronics corresponds with this transition from a focus on labor costs to a focus on the labor skills required in modern manufacturing.

Without recognizing the complex interplay of industry and technology development and spatial evolution, public policy has emerged with a central goal of enhancing and spreading the benefits of high-tech growth. Since the early 1980s, virtually every state has enacted programs to encourage high-tech development. However, by ignoring the driving forces of high-tech regionalization, policies have incorrectly concluded that emphasizing R and D will have impacts on all aspects of America's economic fabric. As the following summary of my findings indicates, to the extent that existing public policies can be successful, achievements may well be at the cost of development in more peripheral regions.

The spatial behavior of high-tech industry provides little or no assurance that rural areas will share in the growth and maturation of high-tech industry employment; nor is there any guarantee that traditional rural industries will experience technology upgrades making them more competitive worldwide. During a period of rapid national-level, high-tech development, rural communities

experienced below-average rates of new-job formation. The existing base of rural high-tech jobs reflects primarily older vintage
technology indicative of premicroelectronics industrialization.
While rural communities have had some success in attracting new
types of product manufacturing, this growth has occurred in a few
labor-intensive and often environmentally damaging industries.

The spatial distribution of rural high tech reflects the regional
realization of this technological convergence. The Midwest and
South embrace the largest base of rural high-tech jobs. Like rural
manufacturing generally, high tech in the Midwest is characterized
by decentralized employment associated with the nation's consumer
and auto electronics industries. The South embraces both older
industries situated specifically to reap labor cost advantages and a
few isolated cases of microelectronics, labor-intensive assembly
locating near new markets and pools of appropriate labor. This
latter type of employment remains tied to metropolitan areas and is
predominantly located on the fringe of cities.

The West, despite its ranking as the nation's premier high-tech
region, in absolute numbers of jobs and plants, boasts little rural
high-tech development. This is explained by the fact that much of
the mundane aspects of microelectronics employment has never
been deployed within the United States. Starting in the early 1960s,
first American electronics firms and later consumer and producer
electronics-dependent firms shifted labor-intensive production
offshore to compete with lower labor costs of the newly industrializing countries (NICs).

While high tech embraces a large number of industries, the
truly dynamic ones—electronics, communications, computers, and
defense-dependent sectors—are only weakly represented in rural
communities. These industries remain fundamentally metropolitan. The nation's defense-led industrial policy has generated few
gains for rural communities. Defense industries situated in rural
areas are the least glamorous and lowest skilled. They are often also
environmentally the most harmful. Eschewing rural communities is
not wholly surprising given that technically sophisticated defense
sectors are largely insensitive to labor costs. Only the more sinister
side of defense high tech escapes to rural areas to avoid population
concentrations.

The vast majority of state-led high-tech development policy is aspatial in orientation. These policies are premised on the belief that state investments in R and D will trickle down to communities along the urban-rural continuum. However, the probability that rural communities will benefit from high-tech development policy depends fundamentally on their spatial proximity to metropolitan areas where qualified labor resides locally or where labor can be attracted to the community. Given diverging rationales for rural high-tech decentralization over the postwar period, recipients of strictly cost-sensitive manufacturing employment may not qualify as future winners of jobs requiring higher skills. Even the few lucky recipients of microelectronics-based high-tech development cannot be sure that job shifts to rural communities will continue unabated. Increasingly, peripheral regions of advanced industrial nations are competing with lower cost yet higher skilled labor of NICs. Rural development policy has yet to address this most powerful and evolving prospect.

Design, Organization, and Methodology

Using a highly detailed data base of manufacturing plants and employment estimates, I examined the location of high-tech employment in 1972 and again in 1982.[1] These years embraced a period of particularly rapid high-tech growth. To assess how appropriate are targeted high-tech development policies, the types of high-tech industries commonly found in rural areas were observed to determine which industries experienced significant job growth over the ten-year period.

This book begins by reviewing the basics. Chapter 2 discusses the problems of defining "high-tech" industries. After commenting on definitional problems, a commonly used working definition is presented. From here, I review the growth experiences of high-tech industries and highlight the variable growth over the ten-year period. I assess the extent that high-tech growth has followed national shifts in population and manufacturing employment over the ten-year period. Given that population was shifting southward and westward with manufacturing, were high-tech jobs exhibiting similar spatial patterns of change? Were high-tech job growth rates in line with, or in excess of, these overall population changes? Such findings could indicate possibilities for high-tech–led development in rural areas.

Subsequently, chapters 3 and 4 blend industry and place analysis to examine high-tech industries across the urban-rural continuum of counties in the United States. This analysis sets the stage for studying the spatial location of high-tech industries within rural counties of the four large census regions — the Northeast, Midwest, South, and West. High-tech growth and other regional aggregates, such as population size and manufacturing employment, are compared.

The most glamorous and sought-after high-tech industries — computers, electronics, communications, and defense-dependent sectors — are the subject of chapter 5. These dynamic sectors bear the fruits of the microelectronics revolution and have precipitated the formation of entirely new industrial agglomerations. What has been the experience of rural areas in garnering a share of this new employment source? What will be the likely effects of state and national policy designed to encourage their development? Does a rural region's success depend on proximity to a seedbed of innovation? Chapter 5 provides some answers to these important questions.

Chapter 6 further descends the geographic hierarchy and examines the role of high-tech industries in rural counties of individual states. At this level, spatial concentration of high-tech employment in rural areas becomes readily apparent. The focus is then shifted to analyze high-tech job growth in rural counties located near or adjacent to metropolitan counties. Both older periods of industrial decentralization from America's manufacturing heartland to her hinterlands and more recent shifts in industrial location south toward the Sunbelt help explain current rural high-tech location. This chapter reviews current state high-tech development policies but finds no emphasis on rural economic development. As illustrated in chapter 3, state policies focus on newly emerging industries that are overwhelmingly found in cities. Thus, by observing high-tech industries commonly found in rural areas, we assess rural areas' potential gains from existing state policy. The discussion clearly shows that government efforts are not designed or intended to address the special problems of rural areas. In fact, most policy assures inhibition of rural high-tech development, given an emphasis on select industries and preexisting research facilities. This is clearly an area where more thought is needed to improve the competitive prospects of rural America.

A unique facet of this study is the attempt to assess exactly where high-tech industries are located and why. The overwhelming majority of high-tech jobs in rural areas are in counties immediately adjacent to cities. A number of tests that identify metropolitan characteristics important in explaining both the absolute number and absolute change in number of high-tech jobs in rural adjacent counties are developed.

Chapters 7 and 8 analyze factors associated with nonmetropolitan high-tech plants and employment and changes over the 1972–82 period. Chapter 7 lays out a theoretical argument about the nature of contemporary high-tech location. Building on previous work, high-tech industries are said to follow two paths of recent industrial development. The earlier period was characterized by firms seeking low-cost locations within existing industrial regions. A more recent era of high-tech development encompasses industries' needs for both low-skilled and high-skilled labor. The convergence of the two eras has resulted in the existing spatial fabric of high-tech industries.

Chapter 8 provides empirical verification for these patterns. The discussion begins by evaluating factors associated with the absolute share of rural adjacent high-tech jobs and plants. This analysis clearly shows that the historically constructed job concentrations reflect shifts of high-tech jobs into the rural periphery— away from cities where unions were strong. This historical accumulation indicates that industrial filtering/product-cycle forces were at work, and firms decentralized production to reduce manufacturing costs. The advent of microelectronics modified the locational calculus of high-tech firms. By examining the absolute difference in rural adjacent plants and employment, it is apparent that the industries' location decisions were made under new circumstances. Rural adjacent communities that gained jobs and plants were near cities with characteristics matching labor requirements, and environmental conditions worked to constrain technical branch plant locations.

To further demonstrate the differences between rural high tech and that found in America's cities, I then compare regression analyses of factors associated with urban high-tech concentrations that have high tech in their adjacent rural counties. It is at this level that the peripheral position of rural communities becomes readily apparent. Finally, in chapter 9, I conclude this book with a discussion of the policy implications of this study.

The Context

In beginning to understand rural America's prospects for high-tech development, this analysis acknowledges the global nature of modern production. The last two decades have witnessed a dramatic change in the spatial distribution of manufacturing industry. Metropolitan areas of traditional manufacturing regions experienced an unprecedented exodus of jobs both to the nonmetropolitan periphery of industrial nations and, perhaps more importantly, to low-cost Third World sites.

Since the late 1970s, public debate and policy initiatives have been directed toward understanding and stemming a tide of job loss in the manufacturing belt cities and states. Only ten years earlier, states in the Midwest (including Ohio, Illinois, Wisconsin, Indiana, and Michigan) and in the Northeast (including Pennsylvania, New York, New Jersey, Massachusetts, and Connecticut) had accounted for 64 percent of the nation's employment in manufacturing (Perloff et al., 1960). Rather dramatically, an almost complete reversal has occurred since then. Now western and southern states harbor almost 50 percent of the nation's total manufacturing employment (Markusen and Carlson 1989). Similar statistics can be cited for other advanced industrial nations whose manufacturing bases have experienced unheralded restructuring and geographic rearrangement of production.

Manufacturing decentralization occurred not only among regions but also between regions, from metropolitan to nonmetropolitan (rural) areas (Lonsdale and Seyler 1979).[2] Between 1962 and 1978, rural areas gained 1.8 million manufacturing jobs. Urban areas grew by only 1.4 million jobs during the same period. Not only was manufacturing job growth in rural areas higher than in cities but rural areas actually increased their share of total national manufacturing employment. Rural's share rose from 23.5 to 28.8 percent between 1962 and 1978 (Haren and Holling 1979).

In addition to employment increases in resource-based industries, such as timber and chemicals (traditional rural industries), rural areas also gained jobs in furniture, electronics, fabricated metal products, and textiles. The much-heralded rural renaissance of the 1960s and early 1970s was, therefore, largely attributable to rural gains in manufacturing employment.

Then came high technology. It arose like a phoenix from the ashes of traditional manufacturing industry's decline. However, this newly expanding complex of science-based industry was blossoming *outside* core manufacturing areas with traditions of industrial innovation. Technological advances such as the semiconductor promised to add new chapters to modern American industrial history; and virtually overnight, tranquil suburbs—the site of new high-tech complexes—began grabbing the attention of national press.

What of rural regions? Were they garnering a share of this new font of economic growth?

Most discussion of high-tech industry development in the United States focuses on metropolitan areas, for example, the wild successes of Silicon Valley in California and Route 128 in Massachusetts (Saxenian 1985a). Rural high-tech industries are paid scant attention, but they are not neglected simply because there are an insignificant number of rural high-tech jobs.[3] Rather, the literature's urban bias can be attributed to both the relative prosperity of rural areas compared to cities of the 1970s and the fact that despite rural participation, high tech is largely a metropolitan phenomenon.

This emphasis on cities is detailed in a rather extensive literature focusing on the locational factors that determine high-tech geography; but instead of explaining the locational tendencies of high-tech industries, contemporary theory has remained content to describe high-tech location after the fact. It is difficult to establish causality; thus, it is simply not known what drove high-tech industries to their present locations. Existing studies are also unsatisfactory at linking high-tech developments with industrial evolution occurring around the world. Rather than studying the processes of change, high-tech analysis has mostly emphasized local peculiarities. Hence, little generalization is possible. Perhaps more significant, this lack of concrete theoretical resolution about the meaning of high-tech location has forced public policy to operate from lists of place factors. Policy cannot recognize the structural constraints that may make high-tech development elusive for most communities.

High Tech and the Spatial Economy

To understand the development significance of high-tech industries, it is necessary to observe high-tech location across a nation's urban *and* rural regions. Absent the rural component of high-tech location, prior studies have been reduced to describing place-based characteristics in lieu of explaining high-tech location. However, rural high tech cannot be treated in isolation either. It must be observed in conjunction with its urban counterpart. In order to understand the development prospects of high-tech industries for any community, we must acknowledge the locational behavior of these industries across America's urban-rural spatial continuum. Increasingly, we must also recognize the forces of change evolving within high-technology industries in Third World nations. Thus, the spatial continuum must necessarily be expanded to include *global* development of high tech.

Much research exists documenting the spatial behavior of high-tech industries within the urban hierarchy of First World countries. There is ample basis to theorize the implications of high-tech development among cities based on theories of urban agglomeration. We expect cities to be the source point for new innovation. Given their access to highly skilled labor, telecommunications infrastructure, and significant internal markets, they are best situated to benefit from developments in new technology. Similarly, research is also relatively abundant theorizing the significance of high-tech industries in Third World development (Castells and Tyson 1988; Henderson 1988, 1989). Starting in the late 1970s, with the now well-known new international division of labor thesis, it was expected that the manufacture of standardized high-tech products would occur in the Third World where an abundance of low-wage, docile workers can be found.

However, recent developments in several NICs question the broad applicability of labor costs as the sole determinant of Third World high-tech locations. As high-tech industries have taken root in Singapore, Hong Kong, and South Korea, domestic industrial capacity and component markets have evolved. Thus, while firms may have initially located for low-cost reasons, the environment has adapted to support the industry in significant ways.

Peripheral Regions of High Technology

Despite the accumulation of knowledge about the extreme ends of the high-tech development spatial continuum, there is a singular absence of theory about the behavior of high-technology industries in peripheral regions of First World countries. Most discussion of the issue relies on product-cycle theory to explain the geography of rural high tech. However, this model has decreasing applicability as new high technologies entirely restructure manufacturing processes and in the process diminish the comparative advantage of low wages as determinants of industry location.

Rural communities are therefore very much at an important crossroad. Starting in the late 1960s, they lost out to low-cost Third World countries for labor-intensive aspects of production. Now several NICs have the capacity to leapfrog to the next technological frontier, leaving behind other low-wage and peripheral regions less well endowed with existing high-tech industries (Castells and Tyson 1988).

What then can rural communities hope for? Much will depend on the base of industries found in peripheral regions. Unlike Third World countries, America's rural communities have none of the advantages of political and economic sovereignty that govern the ability to trade, buy technology, initiate joint ventures, attract foreign investment, and engage in technology diffusion. These activities have been important for the development of high-tech industries in NICs. Rural communities are often small and isolated, with deficient infrastructure and limited skills. In many ways, rural areas are powerless to affect the sea of change surrounding them.

Like countries in the Third World lacking newly industrializing status, the impact of high-tech industries on peripheral regions depends on decisions made at control centers. As corporations are headquartered in metropolitan areas and R and D operations are clustered tightly in a select few American cities, it is from these centers of control that decisions about the nature of high tech in rural areas will be decided. Existing public policy that emphasizes the first stages of product development will serve to reinforce the existing spatial distribution of high-tech industry unless directed otherwise. The ability to obtain and use high-tech industries will further differentiate rural areas—those with the best and least chance of incorporating new technologies in existing industry.

Why Rural?

Aside from the theoretical significance of studying high-tech industries in rural areas, the emphasis here derives from the almost total collapse of rural economies in the latter part of the twentieth century. Whereas the 1960s were the renaissance years of peripheral regions, since the end of the 1970s, things have changed dramatically. America's rural communities have fallen back to pre-1970s conditions of population outmigration, a declining job base, and increasing rates of poverty. As it did in the first half of the twentieth century, rural America is again suffering disproportionately from a lack of opportunity to achieve the benefits of an industrialized nation (Center on Budget and Policy Priorities 1989; Population Reference Bureau 1988). The rural renaissance that appeared to be uplifting this segment of the United States economy is over. The economic balloon seems to have burst (Garnick 1985). The Rural Coalition, a Washington rural advocacy group, reports that in 1986, four years into the national economic recovery, 91 percent of counties showing unemployment levels double the national average were rural (*Business Week* 1986). These statistics have changed little over the intervening years (Parker et al. 1989). Although more recent figures show some improvement, they still follow the same pattern. Rural areas have unemployment rates substantially above the national average.

    Income growth in rural communities has once again begun to lag behind that in urban areas (Garnick 1985). More troubling for the near future, many core nonmetropolitan manufacturing industries—such as textiles, food processing, agriculture, and mining—are in advanced states of restructuring. International competition and cheap labor locations have cut into the market share of traditional rural industries. Surviving firms have slashed payrolls, added new equipment, and sought lower cost production locations to remain competitive. They are not likely to add significant numbers of new jobs. Recent research using Dun and Bradstreet enterprise-based data only confirm earlier trends. Analyzing the 1976–86 decade, Phillips, Kirchhoff, and Brown (1990) show that nonmetropolitan job growth was lower than national and metropolitan averages. Over the ten years, employment in the United States grew at 32.2 percent. Employment in urban areas grew at the fast rate of 34.2 percent. Rural areas experienced a much slower rate of employment growth, at 22.8 percent. Thus, there is a critical need to explore alternative sources of economic development for rural areas.

Historically, rural America's economic fortune was intimately tied to the exploitation of raw resources (especially agriculture and mining) and the decentralization of manufacturing production from cities, but according to some experts, both resource development and mature manufacturing are currently much less significant (Bloomquist 1987). For example, the declining price of oil coupled with a worldwide energy glut has substantially curtailed growth in rural areas of the intermountain West (Glasmeier 1988). Other minerals, such as copper, also experienced price declines and oversupplies leading to mine closures in western rural areas. Even agriculture is not expected to provide its previous level of employment—particularly in the wake of recent farm foreclosures and consolidations—and manufacturing sectors traditionally found in rural areas, such as textiles, apparel, and machinery, have experienced significant import penetration (Glickman and Glasmeier 1989b; Stone 1986). In response to this threat, companies are automating their domestic operations and increasing purchases of goods manufactured in the Third World.

Problems facing rural areas are not unlike those confronting older industrial cities where long-established sources of employment are contracting and in some cases have simply disappeared. Plant closures and significant job loss were the hallmarks of many industrial cities that could do little more than stand by watching as bulldozers tore down idle factories. Rural America has also had its share of plant closures.

The industrialized regions of the Midwest and Northeast responded to the consequent large-scale job loss with efforts to develop new industry, especially that considered high tech (Markusen and Carlson 1989). Programs emphasized industrial recruitment, investigation into new technologies, venture financing, and development of research consortia (Plosila 1987). To date, there have been limited efforts to evaluate the success of these activities. Nevertheless, high-tech industry funding is a prominent component of local and state development policy (Wilson and Schmandt 1987).

Given this emphasis, it is important to ask whether high-tech development is an option available to rural counties. Will high-tech industries operate like traditional manufacturing (which decentralized into rural communities over the last twenty years)? Are there special characteristics of high-tech industries that locate in rural areas that might make them amenable to further growth, or are rural high-tech industries simply modern versions of mature manufacturing industries—with their inherent limitations? This book attempts to answer these questions by examining the spatial location, industrial composition, growth experience, and locational factors associated with high-tech industries in rural counties of the United States.

Unique Characteristics of High Tech

A realistic assessment of potential rural high-tech development requires recognizing that high-tech industries differ from manufacturing industries historically attracted to rural communities. High-tech industries employ many scientific and technical personnel. Traditionally, this has been a critical variable in explaining their predominantly metropolitan locational tendencies (Glasmeier 1986b).

Additionally, American firms enjoyed an early monopoly in many high-tech industries, but today they face intense competition from foreign corporations and they have given up considerable market share (Prestowitz 1988; Semiconductor Industry Association 1989). Thus, firms in the United States have instituted and continue to adopt a variety of production strategies to remain competitive.

During the early development of key industries, firms shifted the most labor-intensive aspects of production to Third World locations where quantity but, more importantly, quality low-cost labor was available. It was not just low wages that enticed firms to Asia. Work force discipline and laborers' willingness to work long hours for no benefits were also attractive. Some of the countries where high-tech manufacturing lodged were little more than dictatorships in which workers had no input or control over their economic circumstances. Many high-tech jobs traditionally equated with a process of "industrial filtering" have simply never been done in the United States (Erickson 1978).[4] Employment shifts were partly determined by high-tech production processes that until recently defied automation and thus remained labor-intensive (Gordon and Kimball 1987). Rapid product changes also discouraged large cash outlays for labor-saving capital equipment. Companies chose instead to invest in new product development while relying on low-wage labor for assembly.

However, the countries in which these industries relocated were not content to remain low-wage assembly locations. Massive education efforts in Korea, Singapore, and Taiwan improved workers' skills. American firms greatly benefited from this development. They now take advantage of not just lower wages, but better-educated workers. This has only exacerbated the gap between United States rural areas, where education levels are generally lower than in metropolitan communities, and Asian production locations.

Another distinguishing characteristic of America's high-tech industries is their long-standing link with the United States Department of Defense (DOD). The DOD was a critical market early in the life of such high-tech industries as semiconductors and communications equipment. Today these industries still sell large portions of their total output to the military, but defense requirements differ from those of commercial markets, affecting the locational behavior of many high-tech industries. Unlike commercial goods for which price and market considerations influence production location, military manufacturing is primarily concerned with quality. The technical nature of these goods limits production to areas with highly skilled labor (Markusen et al. 1991). Furthermore, the various military branches are the end market for many defense products, so defense manufacturing often clusters near military installations. Equally critical is the high degree of interfirm purchasing among defense contractors. There is little evidence of decentralization of military production from major concentrations in Los Angeles, Boston, and Dallas. Therefore, debaters contend that the technical nature of defense products and their unique market orientation have slowed industrial filtering and reduced the number of jobs that might otherwise have reached rural areas (Markusen 1985; Markusen et al. 1991).

Thus, perhaps the most important requirement regulating the location of high-tech industries is the availability of skilled labor — always a limiting factor for rural economies. Analysis of the potential for high-tech development in rural communities must focus on how labor requirements may regulate locational behavior.

Limits to High Tech:
The Low-Wage, High-Skill Contradiction

Dependence on several distinct types of labor means that firms producing high-tech products face both choices and constraints in selecting production locations. The focus on low-wage labor as a locational factor therefore must be qualified. Superficially, high-tech industry's low-wage production employment would seem a perfect job source for rural communities, but this ignores another facet of the spatial division of labor and its relationship to high technology: *quality* of the labor force. My definition of quality encompasses both workplace skills and political and cultural circumstances that provide employees with levels of education and workplace habits. High-tech companies might prefer to use low-skilled and thus low-wage labor, but their production processes are necessarily complex — even for the most labor-intensive operations (Glasmeier 1986a). As a consequence, these firms seek educated but low-paid labor to perform relatively routine tasks. Manufacturers have historically shifted production to the NICs because laborers are well-trained and docile compared with America's low-wage workers. For example, a high school graduate in Singapore, Taiwan, or South Korea can usually perform calculus, a capability far beyond most American students with similar levels of education.[5]

Both high-tech industries' continually changing occupational structures and the declining role of low-wage, low-skill production jobs limit development in rural communities. Just ten years ago, 40 percent of the semiconductor industry's occupations involved skilled labor. Today, more than 60 percent of semiconductor workers are classified as skilled workers (Sieling 1988). Also, the absolute number of *unskilled* jobs within the industry is rapidly declining. This suggests that potential employment in less skilled occupations is also disappearing; hence, the number of jobs that might decentralize to rural areas is further limited.

If technical industries increasingly upgrade their skill requirements, what then are rural communities' long-term prospects for receiving high-tech jobs? In the absence of jobs in the most technical industries, are there other high-tech industries that may provide employment in rural areas? Are there specific characteristics of rural areas that might be more attractive than others for drawing high-tech industries? How is current development policy likely to affect the location of high tech? More importantly, what are the prospects that rural communities will benefit from high-tech growth? With these questions in mind, we review the experience of high-tech industry development among America's rural communities.

2

The What, Where, and Why of High Tech

A Working Definition

My working definition of high tech is based on the human capital component of the labor process (Glasmeier, Hall, and Markusen, 1983; Malecki 1984; Richie, Hecker, and Burgan, 1983; Vinson and Harrington 1983). Using occupational statistics for all manufacturing industries, high-tech industries are defined as those with greater than the national average of engineers, engineering technicians, computer scientists, mathematicians, and life scientists, including chemists and geologists. Twenty-eight industry groups produce high-tech products. These are further disaggregated to include their constituent parts. Table 2.1 lists these detailed industries, which broadly range from explosives to scientific instruments. In this chapter, I will first examine problems associated with defining high-tech industries and then discuss the instrument used to measure them. I will conclude with a review of the theoretical framework used to study high tech.

Early attempts at defining "high tech" resorted to such imprecise measures as industry employment growth, pretax R and D spending, and numbers of patents per industry (see Glasmeier, Hall, and Markusen 1983 for a review of other definitions). Using these measures, there is a consensus that computers and microelectronics are high tech, but there is still some question about industries such as chemicals and portions of machinery. Computer and

TABLE 2.1

High-Technology Manufacturing Industries

SIC	Product Line
2812	Alkalies and chlorine
2813	Industrial gases
2816	Inorganic pigments
2819	Industrial inorganic chemicals, not classified elsewhere (n.e.c.)
2821	Plastic materials, synthetic resins, and nonvulcanizable elastomers
2822	Synthetic rubber
2823	Cellulosic man-made fibers
2824	Synthetic organic fibers
2831	Biological products
2833	Medicinal chemicals and botanical products
2834	Pharmaceutical preparations
2841	Soap and other detergents
2842	Specialty cleaning, polishing, and sanitation preparations
2843	Surface-active agents, finishing agents, sulfonated oils, and assistants
2844	Perfume, cosmetics, and other toilet preparations
2851	Paints, varnishes, lacquers, enamels, and allied products
2861	Gum and wood chemicals
2865	Coal, tar, crudes and synthetic intermediates, dyes, and organic pigments
2869	Industrial organic chemicals n.e.c.
2873	Nitrogenous fibers
2875	Fertilizers, mixing only
2879	Pesticides and agricultural chemicals n.e.c.
2891	Adhesives and sealants
2892	Explosives
2893	Printing ink
2895	Carbon black
2899	Chemicals and chemical preparation
2911	Petroleum refining
3031	Reclaimed rubber
3511	Steam, gas, hydraulic turbines
3519	Internal combustion engines
3531	Construction machinery and equipment
3532	Mining machinery
3533	Oil machinery
3534	Elevators and moving stairways
3535	Conveyors and conveying equipment
3536	Hoists, industrial cranes
3537	Industrial trucks, tractors, trailers, stackers
3541	Machine tools, metal conducting types
3542	Machine tools, metal forming types
3544	Special dies and tools, die sets, jigs and fixtures, and industrial molds

TABLE 2.1 (continued)
High-Technology Manufacturing Industries

SIC	Product Line
3545	Cutting tools, machine tool accessories, and machinists' precision measuring devices
3546	Power-driven hand tools
3547	Rolling mill machinery and equipment
3549	Metalworking machinery n.e.c.
3561	Pumps and pumping equipment
3562	Ball and roller bearings
3563	Air and gas compressors
3564	Blowers, exhaust and ventilation fans
3565	Industrial patterns
3566	Speed changers, industrial high-speed gears
3567	Industrial process furnace and ovens
3568	Mechanical power transmission equipment
3569	General industrial machinery
3573	Electronic computing equipment
3574	Calculating and accounting machines
3576	Scales and balances
3579	Office machines
3612	Power, distribution, and specialty transformers
3613	Switchgear and switchboard apparatus
3621	Motors and generators
3622	Industrial controls
3623	Welding apparatus
3624	Carbon and graphite products
3629	Electronic industrial apparatus
3651	Radio and TV receivers
3652	Phonograph records and tapes
3661	Telephone and telegraph apparatus[1]
3662	Radio-TV transmitting[1,2]
3671	Electron tubes
3674	Semiconductors[1]
3675	Electronic capacitors[1]
3676	Resistors for electronic apparatus[1]
3677	Electronic coils, transformers[1]
3678	Connectors for electronics
3679	Electronic components n.e.c.[1]
3721	Aircraft[1,2]
3724	Aircraft engines and engine parts[1,2]
3728	Aircraft parts and equipment n.e.c.[1,2]
3743	Railroad equipment
3761	Guided missiles and space vehicles[1,2]

TABLE 2.1 (continued)

High-Technology Manufacturing Industries

SIC	Product Line
3764	Guided missiles and space propulsion units[1,2]
3769	Guided missiles and space parts and equipment n.e.c.[1,2]
3795	Tanks and tank components
3811	Engineering, lab, science research instruments
3822	Automatic controls for regulating residential and commercial environments
3823	Industrial instruments for measuring, display, and control of process variables; related products
3824	Totalizing fluid meters and counting devices
3825	Instruments for measuring and testing of electricity and electrical signals
3829	Measuring and controlling devices
3832	Optical instruments and lenses
3841	Surgical and medical instruments
3842	Orthopedic and surgical supplies
3843	Dental equipment
3861	Photographic equipment

Notes: 1. Innovative high-technology manufacturing industries.
2. Defense-related high-technology manufacturing industries.

semiconductor production is based on the application of scientific principles in the development of new products; they also necessarily employ large numbers of scientific personnel in the manufacturing process. It has been taken for granted that the chemical and machinery industries are similarly dependent on scientific skill, but these latter industries are much more mature. Thus, the unifying quality making both sets "high-tech" industry is the application of science and engineering principles in product and process developments.

Problems of defining high tech really originate with measurement and data availability.[6] Ideally, I would identify high-tech industries based on product qualities and make distinctions among products being manufactured at different locations. Unfortunately, companies are not required to make public details about the occupational composition of production in individual plants. This problem is compounded by the broad array of products manufactured in individual plants, of which only a portion require oversight by technical staff. More critical, a key qualitative attribute of high tech is "innovativeness" so I would prefer to identify products and processes at very early stages in their development. However, by the time a product receives a Standard Industrial Classification (SIC) code from the Office of Management and Budget, it has been in existence at least five years. Absolutely precise and timely data are regrettably not available to contend with these limitations. Consequently, researchers use a definition as rigorous as possible yet amenable to policy analysis.

Most high-tech industries are classified based on SIC codes, a numeric classification system developed by the federal government. This scheme orders industries at increasingly fine levels of disaggregation. The most general categories, such as agriculture, mining, and construction, are represented by one-digit industry codes. Very specific products, such as microprocessors or passive devices (subcomponents of the semiconductors' four-digit industry SIC 3674; see Table 2.1), are represented by five-digit and seven-digit level product classifications. Using an SIC code-based classification system, a definition of high tech includes parts of industry groups such as chemicals, nonelectrical machinery, electrical machinery, transportation equipment, communications equipment, and engineering and scientific instruments. I analyzed high-tech industries on the basis of three-digit and four-digit SIC codes. Both levels provide detailed information on industry and product group behavior.

Industries examined here are confined to the broad category of manufacturing. In similar analyses of high tech, other researchers have included key high-tech services, such as software production (Armington, Harris, and Odle 1983; Malecki 1985). Although this study would have been significantly enhanced through examination of such service industries, these data were unavailable. Nevertheless, it is important to note that high-tech services are even more spatially concentrated than is high-tech manufacturing. Service industries are far more dependent on other service firms than are manufacturing establishments; thus, they tend to cluster in cities (Capellin 1988; Glasmeier and Borchard 1989). While rural areas maintain a complement of services, jobs are primarily associated with personal consumption expenditures and sometimes manufacturing. The exclusion of high-tech services is unfortunate, but I would not expect their spatial incidence to demonstrate a rural orientation.

The Growth of High-Tech Industries

The 1970s were golden years for high-tech industry growth. Basic sectors — steel, chemicals, and autos — were drastically contracting in terms of both jobs and productive capacity. In their place, rising from the ruins of America's industrial past, high-tech industries emerged as a symbol of the nation's continuing industrial prowess.

One need only ponder the problems of America's manufacturing cities to understand why high-tech industries garnered such attention. As Detroit collapsed under the weight of its dependence on autos, San Jose and Boston could scarcely contain their burgeoning populations and the job growth associated with high-tech industry. General Motors and the Ford Motor Company competed fiercely with Japanese automakers to maintain market shares while United States-based Digital Equipment Corporation and Intel boasted seemingly unlimited markets and production plants working at capacity.

The great difference in the growth experiences of total manufacturing and high-tech manufacturing contributed to high tech's elevated status. Between 1972 and 1982, manufacturing jobs in the United States declined by almost 500,000. During the same period, high-tech manufacturing grew by 1.22 million (Table 2.2). This rate exceeded the national job growth (27.9 versus 21 percent). As the years passed, high-tech industries became more and more important to the overall manufacturing base, finally accounting for 29 percent of all manufacturing jobs in 1982 (up from 24 percent in 1977).

More recent data verify earlier trends of substantial job growth in high-tech industries. Using Dun and Bradstreet data, Phillips, Kirchhoff, and Brown (1990) show that high-tech industries increased 40 percent over the 1976–86 decade. This was seven percentage points above total job growth in the national economy.

Few Industries Make Impressive Gains

America's high-tech base is made up of more than electronics industries. Contrary to popular press accounts (which hint that high-tech industries are unmitigated job generators), the high-tech

TABLE 2.2

Growth in High-Tech Establishments and Employment
1972–1982

	Establishments	*Employment*
1972	44,147	4,379,777
1977	52,101	4,760,507
1982	56,131	5,601,503
Difference (1972–1982)	11,984	1,221,726

Percentage Change, High-Tech Employment and
Establishments 1972–1977, 1977–1982, 1972–1982

	Establishments	*Employment*
1972–1977	18.0	8.7
1977–1982	7.7	17.7
1972–1982	27.1	27.9

Source: Bureau of the Census, 1986, *Census of Manufactures, Plant Location Tape* (1972, 1977, 1982).

industries analyzed in this book display highly variable growth experiences. Thirty-two high-tech industries actually *lost* jobs between 1972 and 1982, and fifty-seven grew at a rate less than the national average (21 percent) for all nonagricultural employment. For example, twelve of twenty-eight chemicals industries lost employment. Similarly, within machinery (including computers), ten of twenty-nine industries experienced negative changes in employment. (See Appendix A for a table of industry growth rates for 1972 to 1982.)

The extraordinary growth experience of high-tech industry came to an abrupt halt by 1987. New figures from the Census of Manufactures indicate that between 1982 and 1987, high-tech industries declined by almost 150,000 jobs and 2,155 establishments (Table 2.3). In the mid-1980s, high-tech industries con-

TABLE 2.3

Employment and Plant Change in the United States, 1982–1987

	1982	1987	Absolute Change	Percent Change
High-Tech Employment	4,668,200	45,24,400	−143,800	−3.08
High-Tech Plants	54,611	52,456	−2,155	−3.95

Source: Bureau of the Census, 1987, *Census of Manufactures*, Preliminary Statistics, Washington, DC.

fronted significant overcapacity and a series of supply gluts as foreign competition invaded domestic markets. Deregulation of the telecommunications industry coupled with rapidly changing technology and greater capital intensification of formerly labor-intensive processes (such as printed circuit board manufacture) contributed to diminished job growth.

Reclassification of the SIC code system in 1987 makes individual sector comparisons between the two years difficult. Still, while overall high tech declined over the five-year period, a few sectors, such as electronics, aerospace, and instruments, helped offset declines in once rapid growth sectors, such as computer equipment and peripherals (37 and 16 percent growth, respectively, versus a decline of 21 percent).

Nonetheless, there were a few spectacular cases of dramatic job growth. Eight high-tech industries, including semiconductors, more than doubled their employment over the ten-year period, and six others increased by 80 percent. This rise to prominence certainly occurred because, in comparison with overall manufacturing (which was declining), computers, semiconductors, electronic components, and communications equipment all experienced dramatic growth.

Interest in high-tech industries extends beyond their recent growth performance. For regions and communities, the questions become: What attracts high-tech industries to different locations, and what type of development unfolds in a place that has developed a base of high-tech jobs? A few spectacular growth experiences have led communities to believe that with high tech comes the type and scale of industrialization experienced in Santa Clara County, California (Silicon Valley), and the Greater Boston area's Route 128. In fact, as I will demonstrate in later chapters, the path of most high-tech development does not substantially differ from that of other types of manufacturing. Most high-tech plants are not locally owned, supplier links are relatively few, and decisions about what to produce, for which markets, and why are largely made at remote corporate headquarters.

The development consequences of high tech are crucial for rural areas, but will rural communities gain any of the fruits of high-technology growth? High-tech industries are markedly international (products are manufactured and consumed by industries globally), and companies follow geographic production strategies that maximize access to markets and skilled labor (not rural areas' strengths). Will high-tech jobs that develop in rural areas deviate from previous rounds of rural industrialization?

Historically, industries with the greatest proclivity to locate in rural areas were mature, slow growing, and operated in highly competitive, price-sensitive markets. Some authors contend that high tech represents an alternative to the mature industry phenomenon emblematic of rural manufacturing. Others see high tech as little different from rural manufacturing's mainstay—the mature industry.

Finally, will advances in manufacturing technology trickle down to rural areas, or will the production operations that locate there consist of highly automated operations?[7] Does lack of exposure to modern manufacturing techniques ensure that rural areas will fall even further behind in the high-tech race? Are there fundamental benefits of "learning by doing" that will elude rural areas with their less technical operations?

To consider the implications of high-tech industries in rural areas, I must first situate this analysis within the historical context of United States postwar industrialization. How does location theory address current developments? To explain manufacturing patterns, the location literature offers valuable insights about the possibilities of rural industrialization and high tech. Based on this information, I developed a series of hypotheses that will guide the analysis presented throughout the remainder of this book.

Recent Trends in the Location of High-Tech Manufacturing

Like the population and other industries as a whole, high-tech industries have been broadly decentralizing since the early 1970s (Table 2.4). The southern and western regions of the United States have apparently been gaining high-tech employment at the expense of northeastern and midwestern states (Table 2.5). From 1972 to 1982, distribution of high-tech jobs became more evenly divided among regions. Starting in the early 1970s, the Northeast and Midwest together accounted for 60.8 percent of high-tech jobs while the South accounted for 22.6 percent and the West for only 16.6 percent. Over the ten-year period, the South (with 26.4 percent of total national high-tech employment) emerged as the dominant high-tech region. The South was followed by the Northeast with 26.0 percent, the Midwest with 25.1 percent, and the West with 22.5 percent.

While this shift in high-tech job shares seemed to favor the South, western states actually gained the largest number of new high-tech jobs created between 1972 and 1982 (Table 2.6). Major changes occurred in the distribution of high-tech industry; thus, it is important to point out certain underlying trends. Despite a rapid increase in the number of high-tech jobs in the South's manufacturing base, in 1986 the region was still dominated by nonhigh-tech

TABLE 2.4
Regional Share of U.S. Population
1980, 1970, 1960

Region	1980	1970	1960
Northeast	21.69	24.13	24.91
Midwest	25.99	27.84	28.79
South	33.28	30.97	30.66
West	19.06	17.14	15.64

Source: Bureau of the Census, 1986, *State and Metropolitan Data Book,* U.S. Government Printing Office, Washington, DC.

TABLE 2.5

Proportion of High-Tech Employment in
Four Census Regions
1972, 1977, 1982

Region	*1972 % of Nation*	*1977 % of Nation*	*1982 % of Nation*
Northeast	29.72	27.79	25.95
Midwest	31.03	29.97	25.21
South	22.63	24.23	26.25
West	16.63	18.00	22.59

Source: Bureau of the Census, 1986, *Census of Manufactures, Plant Location Tape,* Washington, DC.

TABLE 2.6

Regional High-Tech Job Change
Absolute Difference, 1972–1982

Region	*Absolute Difference 1972–1982*
Northeast	151,975
Midwest	53,058
South	479,639
West	537,054

Source: Bureau of the Census, 1986, *Census of Manufactures, Plant Location Tape,* Washington, DC.

manufacturing industries (Glickman and Glasmeier 1989b). When measured as the ratio of high tech to total manufacturing employment, only the Northeast and West exceeded the national average (29 percent) of high-tech jobs (Table 2.7). The Midwest and South both lagged behind, with 26 and 25 percent, respectively, of manufacturing employment in high-tech industries; nor did the

TABLE 2.7

Ratio of High-Tech to Total Manufacturing Jobs
in Four Census Regions, 1981

Region	Percent High-Tech Jobs
Northeast	30
Midwest	26
South	25
West	41
Nation	29

Source: Bureau of the Census, 1986, *Census of Manufactures, Plant Location Tape,* Washington, DC.

South's rapid high-tech growth over the ten-year period match the region's gains in population shares. While the South accounted for 26 percent of all high-tech jobs, this was far less than its 33 percent share of the nation's total population. Only in the Northeast and West did regional shares of high-tech jobs exceed those of total regional populations.

Various explanations have been offered for this development. Regional disparities in government spending have focused defense dollars on the South and West. Traditional centers of innovation have lost their competitive edge due to high wages, powerful unions, and wide swings in exchange rates, hence, volatile export markets (Browne 1989). Also, both population and industry have been decentralizing since the 1950s, suggesting that perhaps high tech has followed broader trends.

Prior to this, in the 1920s, the aircraft industry relocated to the Los Angeles area. With the onset of the war in the Pacific, the industry became particularly significant economically (Markusen et al., 1991). The airplane played a strategic military role, resulting in the manufacture in Los Angeles of thousands of vehicles for the Air Force branch of the U.S. Armed Services. Postwar, as national defense shifted from a reliance on munitions to more technical rocket and missile technology, the Air Force succeeded the Army in charting national defense strategy. As the location of Air Force R and D, the West Coast area was primed to become the birthplace of the electronics industry necessary to support new mandates for aerospace technology. While the L.A. basin built up tremendous capacity in aerospace hardware and metal working, miniaturized electronics were innovated in Northern California's nascent Silicon Valley (Saxenian 1981). Although other factors were important in establishing the Silicon Valley and the new electronics industry in the early 1950s, DOD purchasing policies encouraged, and in some cases sustained, a number of semiconductor suppliers for the missile program (Borrus 1988). This in part gave the valley firms a protected status. The technical seedbed of California's Silicon Valley is directly attributable to DOD spending.

Defense spending in the South and West contributed to a process of regional realignment, but other factors were also important in creating conditions for the successful shift of economic activities. Federal investments in infrastructure were critical in positioning the South and the West for development. For example, the Tennessee Valley Authority (TVA) provided badly needed electricity and flood control for the East South Central census division, and the West was mostly desert until a complex set of federally funded dams allowed irrigation of California and other parts of the region. The interstate highway system provided access to remote southern and western areas of the nation. Local and state boosterism hustled northeastern and midwestern headquartered firms to relocate manufacturing plants to the South (Cobb 1984).

Overall population migration trends were particularly critical. In the 1950s, for the first time since the turn of the century, the South began to gain population. Increases were largely attributable to return migration, a decrease in out-migration, and new in-migration of nonsoutherners (especially to Texas and Florida; Glickman and Glasmeier 1989b).[8] As population shifted, markets followed. Firms set up production to cater to the needs of burgeoning new southern and western communities.

Southward and westward drifts of high-tech jobs mirror the national population shift over the last twenty-five years. To begin to explain this pattern of high-tech industry and general population distribution, I must review theoretical insights that have developed to explain the distribution of economic activity in modern industrial economies.

Explanations for Shifts in Manufacturing

A number of theories have been proposed to account for the spatial shift of U.S. manufacturing employment. One explanation links employment filtering and the product-cycle model of industrial development (Erickson 1978).[9] This model, by pointing out that as industries mature the location of their employment changes over time, offers observations to help explain manufacturing decentralization.

Spatial applications of the product-cycle model have emphasized three stages of industrial development: innovation, growth, and maturation. Across all three, demand-led growth of industrial output drives an industry through successive states of technological development, from unstandardized, single-unit output heavily dependent on highly skilled labor to capital-intensive, routinized mass production employing less skilled workers. Dependence on qualified labor in the early stage of the model serves to concentrate production in "industrial agglomerations" (Markusen, Hall, and Glasmeier 1986; Norton and Rees 1979; Rees 1979).

As production becomes more standardized, hence routinized, increases in scale of output decrease the per-unit transaction cost of acquiring inputs. Thus, locational flexibility of production increases. The product-cycle model predicts spatial clustering in the early stage of a product's life and spatial decentralization as it reaches mass production and maturity. As an industry changes over time, the organizational structure of firms also evolves from single to multiunit branch plants. These new production facilities are often relocated, or "spun off," to low-cost locations.

Therefore, manufacturing employment shifts away from traditional industrial centers and from metro to nonmetro areas as mature phases of production seek low-cost manufacturing sites. The product-cycle theory has been widely accepted as the explanation for much of recent industrial development. Rural manufacturing growth that occurred in the 1960s and 1970s is typical of the model's mature industry decentralization stage (Bloomquist 1987; Park and Wheeler 1983).

The product-cycle model, however, has been used to explain more than just the decentralization of mature manufacturing from urban to rural areas (Norton and Rees 1979). Some authors,

heralding new high-tech manufacturing accumulations, have concluded that these locations have become candidates to spawn industry agglomerations and new manufacturing complexes. According
to this perspective, a bad business climate and high production
costs drove more than mature manufacturing out of the traditional
industrial heartland. During the growth phase of new products,
branch plants were spun off to southern and western locations
where wages were low and labor pliant. Over time, high-tech
manufacturing complexes displayed the characteristics of industrial
accumulations that would indicate a capacity to act as a seedbed
capable of autonomous innovation.

   Although buildup of high-tech industries in the Sunbelt over
the postwar period has been viewed as creating environments conducive to further high-tech development, this argument seems to
dictate that both technical and nontechnical aspects of high-tech
industries shifted southward; but with the exception of a few major
metro areas (for example, Dallas–Fort Worth, Phoenix, and
Atlanta), new high-tech concentrations have not demonstrated the
characteristics of Silicon Valley and Route 128 innovative
agglomerations. Corporate headquarters remain primarily in the
Midwest and Northeast and secondarily the West, and production
facilities are mostly branch plants manufacturing high-volume
products. These plants encompass engineering functions, but
technical labor is primarily concerned with process, not product-
related scientific operations. Few high-tech industries are present,
and most employment is concentrated in one or two industries and
large production facilities (Glasmeier 1986a).

   In contrast, in a core center of technical activity, the employment base consists of large numbers of technical and highly skilled
workers, such as engineers and technicians, who are necessary in
the design phases of production. Additionally, autonomous core
manufacturing centers display high levels of interfirm linkages, new
firm spin-offs, and new product development. These interdepen-
dencies and new independent firm formations are indications that
industry is responding to unique circumstances that call for innovative solutions.

   Thus, new metropolitan centers of high-tech accumulation do
not have the seedbed attributes that make a complex capable of
spawning new industry on its own. Although new firms are often

created within these industry clusters, product designs are usually imitative of preexisting products. In cases where new products have been developed within these new clusters, the innovating firms tend to relocate to existing technical centers in search of markets, capital, and industry know-how. For example, a small semiconductor firm was started in Albuquerque, New Mexico, with significant assistance from state and local economic development authorities. Upon successfully innovating a new product, the firm's principals shifted production to Santa Clara, California, in search of access to venture capital and markets. Certainly, for some industry segments, it is simply difficult to achieve market success outside the confines of dominant industrial concentrations. Therefore, it is even less likely that rural areas will attract these industry segments. In fact, findings decisively support product-cycle model anticipated outcomes. Rural areas receive low-wage, capital-intensive branch plants in relatively slow-growing, mature industries administered primarily from remote corporate headquarters (Rosenfeld, Malazia, and Dugan 1988).

The Spatial Division of Labor

While the product-cycle model is valuable for explaining the spatial decentralization of manufacturing, it is rigid and linear in its prescription for industrial development and location. Not all industries follow such a direct three-stage route of concentration and decentralization (Taylor 1986); nor do modern industries inexorably succumb to maturation and capital intensification. It is even questionable to contend that each branch plant embodies the same type of production technology assuring economic development predictions based on this industrialization. Perhaps the strongest criticism of product-cycle theory is its time dependence (Storper 1985). While immediate postwar plant relocation might resemble the product-cycle theory, the model is incapable of characterizing branch plant location imperatives of the late 1970s. It overlooks other strategic factors that shape the spatial distribution of industry. In particular, the model underestimates the constraints that firms face when production requires a technical labor force accompanied by a need for low-cost, low-skilled labor. The model fails to recognize that one solution to this problem is the creation of a spatial division of labor. This is especially important for high-tech industries. By adding this dimension, we can begin to understand the contemporary spatial location of high-tech industries in the United States.

Historically, location decisions of single-unit firms were constrained by excessive transportation costs and firms' need to be near suppliers and markets. Most authors suggest that the spatial division of labor evolves as firms seek locations that meet their logistic needs and also have supplies of appropriate workers. The early watch industry is characteristic of this model (Glasmeier and Pendall 1989). While research, development, and design of watches remained embedded in Switzerland's dominant cities, Geneva and Zurich, manufacture and assembly were separated and shifted to a remote rural region of the Jura Mountains. A network of highly specialized and fragmented firms operated in geographic proximity within a complicated web of interfirm exchanges. The production chain was quite interconnected, and because transportation was expensive and inconvenient, the industry concentrated spatially. Watch components manufactured disparately were brought together by assemblers who coordinated their finishing.

Thus, location decisions of early single-unit firms were dependent upon methods of production (Storper 1982). America's first manufacturing cities consisted of tightly linked firms producing and selling goods within a regional geographic market. Early agglomerations, such as Baltimore and Philadelphia, epitomize this development. Trade among cities and regions was facilitated by merchants who spanned the distances between America's formative urban areas (Vance 1970). The dawn of the Industrial Revolution brought with it larger and more vertically integrated production.

As the American system of mass production took hold in a key set of industries, manufacturing practices became increasingly capital-intensive — applying single-purpose machines to crank out huge volumes of goods to meet burgeoning consumer demand (Hounshell 1984). In many industries, rigid, mechanically integrated production methods also restricted manufacturing location (Storper 1982). No example better reflects this pattern than the American automobile industry. Autos were manufactured by single-purpose production equipment woven together with miles of conveyor belts that moved automobiles along as they were manufactured from the metal frame up. America's industrial heartland was literally built upon this model of manufacturing.

In recent years, though, firms' locational choices have increased dramatically due to changes in corporate organization from single to multiestablishment firms (Hymer 1979). Telecommunications advances allowing real-time communication between far-flung production operations have facilitated this decentralization, and transportation developments, such as air freight, have further decreased shipping time and costs. Finally, the application of microelectronics to manufacturing processes makes production capacities more flexible, hence more divisible (Dicken 1986).

Locational choices of high-tech firms are, however, still constrained by the need for different categories of labor. In design stages, firms employ high proportions of technically trained engineers and technicians. As a product becomes stable and production standardizes, design engineers and technicians become less important and other classes of more production-oriented labor take over. This dependence on different types of labor means that firms producing high-tech products face both choices and constraints in selecting production locations.

Firms can and do operate vertically integrated production facilities with technical, production, and assembly workers in one location, but increasingly employers finely tune location decisions to match the need for skills associated with different phases of production. Firms also attempt to separate technical and nontechnical workers. Some product characteristics may encourage or impede this spatial segregation.

Clark (1981) argues that differences in bargaining power among workers encourage this separation of technical and nontechnical employees. Employers have the option of moving technical activities outside core industrial areas to restrict skilled workers' interfirm mobility, but anecdotal evidence suggests this is dysfunctional because it is difficult to attract highly trained workers to remote locations. On the other hand, unskilled production workers can ill afford to be choosy. Therefore, employers are more apt to successfully decentralize low-skilled production activities to rural outlands.

The nature of products and production technologies can influence the feasibility of this spatial division of labor (thus regulating decentralization). Case studies of the semiconductor industry indicate that although firms maintain technical activities in industry cores, production work is often spun off to satellite centers, while assembly work is shifted to low-wage, low-skilled locations (Massey 1984; Saxenian 1981; Storper 1982). The effect is a manufacturing pattern that reflects highly automated production primarily shifting to the Sunbelt beyond the core centers of technical activity (Glasmeier 1986a; Sayer 1984).

Even this more elaborate skill-based description of the spatial location of industry does not adequately embrace advances in high-tech industry. The mix of skills needed for product manufacture has changed. As industrial products and manufacturing processes have become more complex, intermediate centers of skill-dependent manufacturing have evolved. Much of the branch plant creation associated with high-tech growth of the early 1980s consisted of factories combining their needs for process engineering skills and low-skilled assembly (Glasmeier 1988). Communities such as Austin, Texas, Colorado Springs, Colorado, Tucson, Arizona, Burlington, Vermont, and Portland, Oregon, became recipients of the technical production phase of high-tech industries. In contrast to the outcome that a literal interpretation of the product-cycle model would predict (decreasing need for technical skills and pure emphasis on manual technique), a new tier of production competency evolved relocating process-oriented production to midsize communities with the requisite skill base. Rural communities have largely been cut out of these industrial transformations of high-tech manufacturing.

Explaining High-Tech Industry Location

The literature on the location of high-tech industries in the United States has expanded rapidly over the last five years (Armington, Harris, and Odle 1983; Glasmeier, Hall, and Markusen 1983; Malecki 1985, 1986), but although numerous studies exist, it is difficult to generalize about high-tech industry location because authors have addressed varying levels of spatial aggregation, worked with different time periods, and utilized numerous data bases. Nevertheless, even without a common framework, a review of available work reveals several significant patterns.

With few exceptions, high-tech industries grow in places that have existing bases of business support services. Thus, while one might argue that, prior to 1950, Silicon Valley was a fruit orchard, in fact, this benchmark industrial cluster is a subregion of the Greater San Francisco Bay area. Capital, business services, social infrastructure, and, importantly, markets were all available within a thirty-mile radius.

Defense spending constitutes another important factor in high-tech industry's location. Since World War II, high levels of defense spending have been key to the development of science-based industry (Shapiro 1964). The DOD served dually as the major source of R and D funding and the market for resulting high-tech products. Areas that were awarded high levels of defense spending also gained large numbers of high-tech jobs.

The Barkley, Dahlgran, and Smith (1988) seminal multistage study of high-tech industry in rural counties of the western United States is a baseline for research on high-tech industries in rural areas (Barkley 1988; Barkley, Dahlgran, and Smith 1988). The early analysis by Barkley of enhanced *County Business Patterns* data noted the dual tendency for high tech in rural western areas to reflect a large base of slow-growing industries concomitant with high rates of change in fast-growing high-tech industry (1988). Another facet of the multistage study surveyed a complete census of 321 high-tech firms and a sample of 160 low-tech firms in rural counties. Statistical analysis of high-tech location included all establishments of ten or more employees. The results suggest that western rural high technology was attracted to relatively large rural communities (35 percent of the establishments were located in towns with a population greater than 25,000 and 57 percent of the firms surveyed were in counties adjacent to metropolitan areas). Furthermore, branch plants and single-unit establishments were attracted to similar communities, with a few notable differences. Employment levels in single-unit and branch plant manufacturing facilities were positively associated with county population, population growth rates, and adjacency to a metropolitan area. Both establishment types eschewed counties with a narrow economic base (for example, military, manufacturing, or agriculture-dominated counties). This research further suggests that single-unit establishments prefer communities with significant amenities, an educated population, and good public infrastructure. Branch plants, alternatively, are not as sensitive to communities with universities or high-quality public services (as measured by proxy, the local per capita income). As Barkley and coworkers note, this dual pattern is consistent with product-cycle expectations of branch plant behavior (Barkley, Dahlgran, and Smith 1988).

Research on the spatial location of high-tech industries in rural areas suggests a dual pattern of employment decentralization alternatively emphasizing labor cost and labor skill. Barkley's (1988) research suggests skill-dependent high-tech jobs locate in adjacent rural counties within the Northeast and West with easy access to metropolitan amenities. On the other hand, slow-growing high-tech industries locate in nonadjacent rural counties in southern and midwestern states where wages and skill levels are low (Barkley 1988).

High-tech industries are attracted to places with existing technical work forces. New high-tech firm formation has been highest in these areas. In the early years, high-tech industries created their own labor market by hiring engineers from universities across the nation. Over time, as high technology rapidly expanded, it became necessary for firms to find suitable locations to undertake technical production. Thus, a new tier in the spatial division of labor was created. Starting in the mid-1970s, firms began making location decisions that explicitly sought places where both technical and nontechnical labor could be found. Over time, a number of medium-size American cities became centers for technical branch plants (Glasmeier 1988). Key to these new industrial clusters was access to universities where technically trained workers could be found and existing employees could upgrade their skills over time. Evidence of this evolving spatial division of labor can be seen by examining the organizational structure and spatial distribution of these corporations.

Understanding contemporary high-tech industry location also requires that we view the formation of labor markets dynamically. Initial placement of branch plant facilities resulted from earlier eras of standardized technology that allowed branch plant spin-offs to occur; but many of these establishments, once in place, did not remain static. As the technology of products evolved and became increasingly sophisticated, firms phased in new products as permitted by both the original technology and the evolving local labor market of branch plant facilities.

The IBM branch plant in Austin, Texas, represents the convergence of two eras of technology. In 1968, Austin's Chamber of Commerce president, John Gray, successfully recruited an IBM typewriter plant. Personal contacts were important in the coup, but IBM also needed a Southwest regional production facility to serve the rapidly growing Southwest market. The product manufactured at the plant, IBM's Selectric® typewriter, found its way onto almost every secretary's desk, and several additional generations of office products were manufactured at the site.

Because of the plant's size and vertically integrated structure, IBM had millions of dollars of fixed capital invested in Austin—too much to abandon with their market's transition to office automation products. Thus, in the early 1980s, the plant was upgraded to produce components and subsystems for personal computers. Simultaneously, computer manufacturing in IBM's Boca Raton, Florida, plant was slowing. The plant is now being downsized, and production is being shifted to Austin and Raleigh, North Carolina.

The Austin plant currently operates as the technical component of IBM's desktop computer production line and manufacturing system. Advanced engineering stations are also produced in Austin. R and D activities have gradually but clearly evolved as important in the Austin plant. Now this once-peripheral typewriter production plant is the facility logging the most patents of any manufacturing facility in the corporation.

Like the Austin IBM site, some branch plant locations have evolved from single production facilities to major process-oriented technology entities; but these gifted locations are not inherently seedbeds capable of engendering new firms poised to create autonomous industrial complexes. Instead, they are the homes of a new generation of branch plants manufacturing very sophisticated products with a trajectory within the confines of a preexisting technological paradigm. Therefore, a place such as Austin remains a center of technical branch plants surrounded by small firms selling into specialized product markets. Regional innovation consists of existing technical know-how applied to the development of products and processes. The complex still exhibits little internal integration. Both large and small firms buy inputs from distant sources and sell output to national and international markets. Unlike better-known high-tech complexes, Austin remains a center of isolated technical production units selling to world markets. Only a handful of locally based establishments have grown beyond the small-firm stage.

The Organizational Structure of
High-Tech Small Firms and Branch Plants

The meteoric rise of high-tech industry in the early 1970s was characterized by the creation of two key industrial centers, Silicon Valley and Route 128. The emergence of Silicon Valley has been characterized as the overnight sprouting of a new industrial complex from the fertile ground of valley prune orchards. Although subsequent treatments have tied the complex's development to the convergence of factors ripened within the Greater San Francisco Bay area of California, a whole new industrial complex emerged with the development of the semiconductor. High-tech manufacturing followed a unique path to preeminence.

Route 128 is a by-product of New England's industrial past based on textiles and shoe production. Early investments in electronics were fueled by World War II defense spending, which created technical giants like Raytheon. Along with defense-related scientific development, the region prospered with the emergence of computers. Route 128 eventually excelled as the nation's leading center for minicomputer and early office automation.

Emblematic of both regions, early high-tech trajectory was the base of small firms that grew into large firms and formed the core of the new complexes. Now well-worn tales of new firms launched from the garages of engineers are the model of this new industry. Companies such as Intel, Data General, and Shockley Semiconductor—rebel offshoots of older established firms, such as Fairchild Semiconductors, Digital Equipment, and Bell Labs—are only the most vivid examples of this development; and while the origins of Silicon Valley and Route 128 can be partly attributed to small entrepreneurial firms, the growth of these regions and their base industries was coupled with the likes of very large national corporations, such as Lockheed and Ford Aerospace, which lodged early in the fabric of these new high-tech regions.

The importance of small firms in the creation of new centers of innovation leads to the general perception that high tech is made up of small, innovative establishments. This component of industrial formation is critical to the structuring of high-tech development, but it is somewhat time dependent.

High-tech industries are comprised of large, multilocational corporations. Almost 90 percent of high-tech employment is found in establishments employing one hundred or more employees (compared with total industry, of which only 75 percent of employment is in large establishments). Although much has been made of the entrepreneurial component of high tech, tiny firms (less than twenty employees) account for only slightly more than half (53.4 percent) of all establishments (compared with other industries in which small firms make up more than 76 percent of all firms) and contribute only 4.2 percent of total industry employment. The residual 6.8 percent of employment was contained in establishments with between twenty-one and ninety-nine employees. While small-firm growth was impressive, it was lower than that of both total manufacturing and service industries.

Belying the image of high-tech firms as entrepreneurial start-ups, high-tech establishments consist primarily of multiunit corporations. Eighty-eight percent of high-tech employment is concentrated in multiestablishment firms. (Only 73 percent of other manufacturing and service firms employ multiunit organizations.) A majority of high-tech facilities are owned by nationally headquartered firms (Armington, Harris, and Odle 1983; Malecki 1985).

The composition of corporate organization varies across regions. The Northeast and Midwest (historic centers of corporate headquarters) maintain the largest shares of high-tech corporate headquarters. These regions also have the largest concentrations of employment in headquarter establishments. The highest numbers of single-location firms are found in the West and Northeast. The South has the highest concentration of national affiliate branch plants. In 1985, 88 percent of all southern high-tech jobs were in branch plants (Malecki 1985). High-tech industries have spread jobs (and secondarily plants) across the nation (but primarily within the South) while new firm formation rates have remained high in the Northeast and West.

Thus, high-tech industries have created their own spatial division of labor (Glasmeier 1986b). Because few states have high numbers of engineers and engineering technicians, a large portion of high-tech development occurring outside the primary technical centers consists of branch plants. Process R and D has been important in a number of places (for example, Austin and Colorado Springs), but little product-related R and D occurs in these outlying facilities. Overall, regions that received branch plants have experienced low levels of new high-tech firm formation; so, while branch plants have produced significant numbers of direct jobs, there has been relatively little innovation resulting in new products that form the basis for an integrated high-tech agglomeration (Malecki 1985).

Accordingly, a pattern of contemporary high-tech industry location emerges. High-tech industries are likely to be found in states with traditions of innovative manufacturing and within major metropolitan areas where business services and other urban amenities are ample. The size of both a state industrial base and an individual metropolitan area is a key factor in explaining concentrations of high-tech employment, and locations experiencing rapid increases in new firm formation are those with pools of technically trained labor. Thus, states and cities with high-tech manufacturing bases (including corporate headquarters and R and D labs) have the highest rates of new firm formation.

However, the majority of locations have simply received branch plants of national high-tech corporations. These findings suggest that the composition of high-tech industries differs across locations. Some places are clearly centers of R and D and advanced manufacturing. Others have gained highly automated production. Still others have received the more mundane, least technical, and most labor-intensive aspects of high-tech industries.

Decentralization of manufacturing in the United States has long produced shifts in jobs both across regions and between metropolitan and nonmetropolitan areas. Explanations for this development focus on product maturation, which leads firms to shift production to low-cost locations. In high-technology industries, the division of labor facilitates such decentralization. High-tech products can be segmented; that is, firms locate technical activities of production in core regions but move manufacturing and assembly to regions with appropriate pools of labor.

This does not mean that products or processes have stabilized to the point where skilled labor is no longer an important criteria in plant location decisions. Indeed, the need to tap more and varied pools of technical labor made plant locations of the 1980s more difficult. The emphasis on technically trained workers in no way denies the importance of direct unskilled laborers. If anything, this component has become more important because these workers are less mobile than technically trained labor, their skills are directly related to the preexisting economic base, and firms are therefore often in competition. Therefore, firms must be able to accumulate and retain such labor forces, often in communities where workers are scarce and competing opportunities are numerous. Again, Austin, a successful branch location, demonstrates these conflicts.

Austin has been a major recipient of technical branch plants created by high-tech firms in the 1980s. The city's low-skilled labor market is unusually tight because its economic base is government, which provides relatively equal benefits and occupational mobility. Layoffs in one firm are a boon for other labor-starved establishments, but it is not just a lack of labor pool mass that plagues the region's industries. More critical, entry-level workers lack minimum qualifications. For example, a large semiconductor firm indicated that it interviews fifteen applicants to find one potential employee. Increasingly, the corporate solution to local labor market problems is to shift production to plants completely outside the United States where adequate pools of labor can still be found.

Recognition that the spatial division of labor is an important factor in high-tech industry location is the ingredient most often missing from policy discussions. Consequently, our understanding (or misunderstanding) of the spatial inclinations of these industries tends to be unidimensional. High-tech employment location reflects long-standing tendencies in the distribution of population and economic activity. While shifts in high-tech employment are clearly discernible at a regional level, employment distribution is still greatly influenced by past patterns of industrial development.

As emphasis on technical labor input has increased, so have the requisite skills for low-skilled direct labor. Production-line skills of even the least technically trained employee have increased as precision in manufacturing has been refined. Statistical quality control, packaging automation, and process improvements all necessitate more highly skilled manual workers. Gone are many of the mind-numbing tasks associated with high-tech manufacturing. Increasingly, production workers are expected to intervene at critical moments when automated processes go awry. This requires laborers who can monitor increasingly complex and costly equipment and make judgments about in-process manufacturing. Mistakes are not easily rectified, and their consequences can be hundreds of dollars of faulty, useless production. Thus, although direct labor requirements have declined in numbers, these workers' role is increasing in responsibility and importance.

The growing use of education-based skills for routine production bodes poorly for rural communities. Skill levels and educational attainment in remote communities are among the lowest in the nation. As I will show in later chapters, rural America is in danger of being left behind in the race for high technology. To understand rural America's prospects for high-tech development, I combine insights from both location models. As this book unfolds, it will become apparent that earlier periods of decentralization were probably motivated by product-cycle concerns. Starting as early as the 1950s, companies moved more mundane aspects of production to the rural hinterlands of America's industrial cities. During this era, the critical factor regulating plant location was the desire to escape high-cost production locations. Since the 1970s, both markets and the need for highly skilled and low-wage labor have drawn high-tech production to growing Sunbelt cities. Characteristics of high-tech industries themselves have intervened and newly structured the locational possibilities and site selections of high-tech industries. Therefore, the spatial division of labor thesis is central to explaining rural high technology of a more recent vintage.

3

Regional Distribution of
Rural High Tech

For most Americans, the term "rural" conjures up images of bucolic agricultural communities with green pastures and an enviable pace of life, but a romanticized vision of arcadia truly reflects few of the nation's rural communities. Rural America is surprisingly diverse, taking in vast areas of the arid West as well as many southern counties, and a large portion has undergone dramatic transformation since World War II, necessitating a complex, less idealistic redefinition. More importantly, although we might have once been able to say that rural economies could escape the reality of competition in the modern world, increasingly this is not the case. Regardless of whether they are directly touched by industrial change, rural communities are indirectly affected by global events.

Thus, the concern about high-tech industry growth in rural areas is not simply academic. What defines rural economies is their interconnection with the rest of the world. In the increasingly global economy, no community can remain autonomous. Shifts in international economic patterns cause price changes in the local goods of even very remote economies, and turnover in basic industry, such as agriculture or mining, has occurred in communities that appeared self-contained.

Over the last twenty years, rural America has undergone a convulsive and often wrenching roller-coaster ride, first the 1960s' "rural renaissance," which spurred population and job growth, and now excessive out-migration of young people and economic activity. Manufacturing industries' search for low-wage locations, the unexpected rise of energy prices following the first oil shortage of the early 1970s, and high prices for agricultural and certain industrial commodities contributed to an unnatural uplift of selected rural communities. Changing demographics also advanced the cause of rural areas' renewed growth. Older Americans retiring from years in the nation's urban factories sought refuge in the regions of their youth. Some moved south seeking warmer climates and easier living. The nation's rising standard of living meant more Americans had money to vacation and travel. Rural communities with particularly attractive physical settings enjoyed the growth of tourist industries expanding to serve an affluent and more mobile population.

While portions of the nation's rural communities experienced an unexpected boost over the last thirty years, however, there is a darker side to rural America. A large component remains underdeveloped. Many rural southern counties teeter on the brink of survival, with the largest concentration of the nation's poor, often illiterate population mired in a late nineteenth century sharecropper heritage (Lichter 1988), and economic factors that renewed selected rural areas of the Midwest and South missed the hollows of Appalachia, where labor force participation rates remain more than 20 percent below the national average (Pudup 1989).

Thus, there is still an obvious need to inject new sources of growth into rural economies. The circumstances that momentarily uplifted some rural American communities are again spiraling downward. Agricultural areas of the Midwest (typified by Iowa, which in 1988 experienced population out-migration in excess of natural increase) are struggling back from severe drought and declining commodity prices for farm staples. Land values, although recently rising from earlier crises, remain unstable.

In the West, falling oil prices and an exodus of petroleum workers thrust rural mountain state communities back to pre-1970s population and job levels. Small western towns are suffocating under the weight of infrastructure debt taken on to cope with the boomtown growth of the 1970s. Retirement and tourism dollars, the bright spots of recent rural development, benefit few communities, and hope for future tourism growth depends on local amenities and extraordinary physical settings.

Branch plant production, once heralded as the savior of rural

America, seems poised to snatch back the economic blessings it bestowed upon many communities. America's manufacturing industries are under siege. Starting with the most vulnerable (for example, textiles, apparel, and consumer goods), global competition has forced producers to capital-intensify. In extreme cases, entire plants have closed, with production shifted to low-cost Third World locations. Now even new factories manufacturing products such as consumer electronics, auto parts, and certain high-tech products face cost-cutting pressures leading to increases in automation, employment reductions, and plant closures.

Also, there still remain America's neglected and largely silent rural backwaters—the underdeveloped rural communities of the South. In spite of the region's meteoric rise as the nation's dominant manufacturer, its population remains the least educated and lowest paid. Illiteracy and high school dropout rates are a national embarrassment. While the South has indeed risen again, its advance is based on unbecoming exploitation of cheap labor, docile workers, and probusiness local governments that have sold the region's workers short for the last seventy years (Cobb 1984).

Whether high-tech industries are growing in rural America is therefore not simply academic. As high-tech jobs have some opportunity for expansion, it is essential to know not only if but where and why these jobs are growing in rural communities. If rural America is not to be left behind as the nation propels itself further into the age of high technology, then we must understand when and under what circumstances components of these industries are growing.

Where Are High-Tech Jobs?

Distribution Across the Urban-Rural Continuum[10]

Like manufacturing generally, high-tech industries are predominantly metropolitan. Because of their relative youth, high-tech industries concentrate in cities where needed infrastructure, skilled labor, and markets are found (Glasmeier 1986a). And high tech's dependence on technical labor ensures an even greater metropolitan-area concentration than other mature manufacturing industries. The two key centers for American high-tech—Boston and Santa Clara — are premier concentrations of technical talent. The skill pool is so dense in these areas that companies come from all over the world (for example, Germany's Siemens and Japan's National Electronic Corporation {NEC}) to recruit specially trained workers.

Nevertheless, there is evidence of some employment decentralization over the ten-year study period. Hewlett-Packard and NEC operate production plants in rural communities adjacent to metropolitan areas in California and Oregon. Even predominantly rural Nebraska benefited from high-tech growth. The Dale Corporation, America's largest capacitor producer, located plants in small towns in that state. Just how representative are these anecdotal examples, though?

Understanding the distribution of high-tech industries requires defining the geographic unit of analysis used throughout this study (see Table 3.1 for a description of the urban-rural continuum). Counties are the most consistent, convenient, and frequently used unit of geographic analysis. Boundaries are defined by the federal government and rarely change. I differentiated among counties according to their 1980 population size, commuting patterns, and adjacency to a metropolitan county. For rural counties, I further distinguished based on county adjacency to metropolitan areas.

The significance of rural adjacency merits brief comment. A rural county adjacent to an urban area is characterized by benefits derived from urban spillover and access. Individuals and firms operating in adjacent rural counties enjoy the benefits of access to higher quality and more sophisticated infrastructure and amenities without the drawbacks of city life. Adjacent rural areas are also more likely to attract plants decentralizing from urban areas. In this instance, firms can enjoy lower land prices and often lower wage rates yet still be within commuting distance of a metropolitan area. I therefore expect that it is easier for metropolitan-adjacent rural areas to attract high-tech industries than it is for their more remote rural counterparts.[11]

This analysis also considers both total high-tech employment and employment in sectors of the computer, electronics and communications equipment complex, and defense-dependent sectors. The shift-share calculation compares the actual number of jobs created in each urban-rural county category with the number of

TABLE 3.1

Modified Shift-Share Analysis[1] of High-Tech Employment
Growth Across the Urban-Rural Continuum[2]
1972–1982

Urban-Rural Continuum	Absolute Employment 1972	Regional (R) Expected Employment 1982	National (N) Actual Employment 1982	R-N Difference 1982
01				
HT Emp*	1,604,524	449,267	33,199	–416,068
DDS*	316,341	82,248	2,114	–80,134
CEC*	266,703	240,032	280,032	40,000
1				
HT Emp	782,067	218,978	336,271	117,292
DDS	100,584	26,152	40,983	14,831
CEC	164,332	147,898	132,024	–15,874
2				
HT Emp	1,013,041	283,651	293,938	10,287
DDS	138,598	36,035	53,366	17,330
CEC	142,022	127,819	110,998	–16,821
3				
HT Emp	. 357,790	100,181	110,353	10,172
DDS	16,133	4,194	41,131	36,936
CEC	41,692	37,523	46,188	8,665
4				
HT Emp	223,133	62,477	24,852	–37,625
DDS	22,699	5,902	6,346	444
CEC	23,966	21,569	3,567	–18,002
5				
HT Emp	98,647	27,621	20,552	–7,069
DDS	629	163	2,614	2,450
CEC	6,729	6,056	2,330	–3,726
6				
HT Emp	144,620	40,494	46,514	6,020
DDS	11,194	2,910	3,241	331
CEC	6,551	5,895	5,939	43
7				
HT Emp	130,351	36,498	49,390	12,892
DDS	3,204	833	5,761	4,928
CEC	4,061	3,655	8,206	4,551

TABLE 3.1   (continued)

Modified Shift-Share Analysis[1] of High-Tech Employment Growth Across the Urban-Rural Continuum[2] 1972–1982

Urban-Rural Continuum	Absolute Employment 1972	Regional (R) Expected Employment 1982	National (N) Actual Employment 1982	R-N Difference 1982
8				
HT Emp	11,979	3,354	4,072	717
DDS	160	42	481	439
CEC	636	572	3,387	2,814
9				
HT Emp	11,995	3,359	4,953	1,594
DDS	96	25	398	373
CEC	437	393	379	−314

*HT Emp = High-Tech Employment; DDS = Defense-Dependent Sectors; CEC = Computer, Electronics, Communications Complex.

Notes: 1.   The computation performed in this table reflects the national component of shift-share analysis in which the total change in regional employment in industry is compared with the change in employment that would have occurred if the industry in the region had changed at the national rate.

2.   The urban-rural continuum used in this study was designed by Calvin Beale of the U.S. Department of Agriculture. The criteria for designating a county to be urban or rural are based on population size, commuting patterns of residents in individual counties, and the county's spatial position relative to a metropolitan area. Urban status is that announced by the Office of Management and Budget in June 1983 using 1980 census population figures. Each county is coded based on its population size and spatial orientation.

The classification scheme consists of ten urban-rural categories. Categories 0-3 identify counties that are metropolitan in nature. Metropolitan is defined as counties with populations between 50,000 and 1 million or more. Both central counties and fringe counties of a metropolitan area are separately identified.

Rural counties are classified based on population and adjacency to a metropolitan area. Categories 4-9 classify counties on the basis of population size—20,000 or more, 20,000 or less, and completely rural—and on the basis of whether they are adjacent to a metropolitan area.

TABLE 3.1 (continued)
Modified Shift-Share Analysis[1] of High-Tech Employment Growth Across the Urban-Rural Continuum[2] 1972–1982

Urban-Rural Continuum	Absolute Employment 1972	Regional (R) Expected Employment 1982	National (N) Actual Employment 1982	R-N Difference 1982

Metropolitan Counties
0   Central counties of metropolitan areas of 1 million population or more.
1   Fringe counties of metropolitan areas of 1 million population or more.
2   Counties in metropolitan areas of 250,000 to 1 million population.
3   Counties in metropolitan areas of less than 250,000 population.

Nonmetropolitan Counties
4   Urban population of 20,000 or more, adjacent to metropolitan area.
5   Urban population of 20,000 or more, not adjacent to metropolitan area.
6   Urban population of less than 20,000 adjacent to metropolitan area.
7   Urban population of less than 20,000 not adjacent to metropolitan area.
8   Completely rural, adjacent to a metropolitan area.
9   Completely rural, not adjacent to a metropolitan area.

Metropolitan status is that announced by the Office of Management and Budget in June 1983, when the current population criteria were first applied to results of the 1980 Census. Adjacent was determined by physical boundary adjacency and a finding that at least 2 percent of the employed labor force in the nonmetropolitan county commuted to metropolitan central counties.

Code prepared in Economic Development Division, Economic Research Service, USDA.

Source: Bureau of the Census, 1986, *Census of Manufactures, Plant Location Tape* (1972, 1977, 1982).

jobs that would have been established if the industries had grown at the national rate. Shift-share analysis is essentially an accounting technique frequently used to express the relative growth performance of industries or population across different geographic units. Here I used the technique to explain the relative growth performance of high-tech industries in urban and rural counties.

To begin to understand the locational tendencies of high-tech industries in metro and nonmetro counties, it is convenient to examine both the expected and actual growth of high-tech employment in urban and rural areas (see Table 3.1). Overall, metropolitan counties gained 1.07 million high-tech jobs and grew at a rate of 29 percent over the 1972–82 period. This job growth was unevenly distributed across different size counties. Metropolitan areas with more than 1 million people, such as New York, Los Angeles, and Dallas, grew more slowly than the national average. Had large cities grown at the national rate, they would have added almost 420,000 additional jobs.[12] The difference was partly due to slow growth in defense sectors somewhat offset by higher-than-average growth experiences in the computer, electronics, and communications (CEC) sectors. All other metropolitan counties posted significant *gains* over those expected, with one exception — employment in the CEC sectors (given the employment base) was lower than expected in counties on the fringes of large metropolitan areas.

In contrast, rural counties experienced high-tech job growth below the national average, 24 versus 29 percent (Figure A). Between 1972 and 1982, high-tech jobs in rural counties added approximately 150,000 jobs, increasing from 620,725 to 770,477. Had rural counties grown at the national rate, 23,111 additional jobs would have been created.

Low growth rates occurred in the largest rural counties both adjacent and nonadjacent to metropolitan counties. Rural counties also performed below average in the high-growth CEC sectors. Clearly, these results indicate that between 1972 and 1982, similar to their overall manufacturing industry experience, rural areas were simply not adding as many high-tech jobs as metropolitan areas were. Some of the difference is probably attributable to plant closures and employment reduction. While in a previous era marginal firms may have moved to rural areas, they now find it difficult to stay in business at all. Smaller and more remote rural counties posted impressive gains in both total high-tech manufacturing and in the CEC and defense-dependent sector (DDS) sectors. Above-average growth no doubt reflects the limited original high-tech base of many of these communities. While significant increases are clearly a positive sign of remote rural development, the small initial base overstates the significance of what are actually modest absolute changes. For example, in 1972, a small rural Texas county might have had seven jobs in high-tech industries. By 1982, this figure

FIGURE A

Comparison of National, Metropolitan, and Rural
High-Tech Job Change
1972–1982

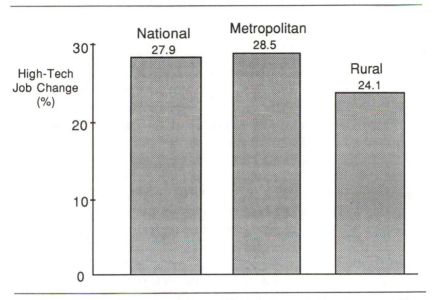

Source: Bureau of the Census, 1986, *Census of Manufactures, Plant Location Tape* (1972, 1977, 1982).

could have increased to twenty-one jobs. Change in this instance would be 200 percent, yet only fourteen jobs would have been created. In spite of impressive percentage changes in rural America's small and more remote communities, the total of this investment was not enough to counteract the losses of the larger rural counties.

The rather poor showing of high-tech employment growth in rural areas remains the status quo. Analysis of Dun and Bradstreet data illustrates continuing slow growth of high-tech jobs in rural areas through the latter half of the 1980s. Breaking employment into three categories, high tech, low tech, and other industries, Phillips, Kirchhoff, and Brown (1990) show that over the 1976–86 period, national high-tech job growth was 39.8 percent. Cities grew rapidly, experiencing a 43.7 percent increase in high-tech jobs.

Rural areas continued their previous poor showing with only a 15 percent increase in high-tech jobs over the decade.

Urban areas gained jobs in both large and small high-tech establishments. Rural areas, however, experienced high percentage job gains (though below national average) predominantly in small firms. Based on these results, Phillips, Kirchhoff, and Brown conclude that small businesses can be major players in rural high-tech growth; but this conclusion is misleading. Overall, rural areas turned in a dismal performance, with high-tech job change comprising only 3 percent of all new jobs created in rural areas. High rates of change for small high-tech establishments, although impressive, mask an otherwise unhealthy rate of overall high-tech job growth. Less than 10 percent of all high-tech jobs were created in rural areas.

The structure of high-tech job growth in rural areas deviates significantly from national trends. At the national level, high-tech job creation occurs predominantly in large establishments. Fully 73 percent of all high-tech establishments are large firms. In contrast, high-tech job creation in rural areas occurs almost exclusively in small establishments. Given that high-tech establishment formation rates are highest in larger firms, it seems that rural communities are being sidestepped by corporations seeking more profitable locations to establish branch plants. Furthermore, the absence of large plant growth suggests that small communities are proving unattractive to the more mature and perhaps more stable phases of high-tech development.

Another sign that high-tech firms have a difficult time "surviving and then growing up" in rural areas is the low rate of branch plant formation by firms headquartered in rural communities. Of 14,324 new branch establishments created in the United States over the decade, only 452 were created by firms headquartered in rural areas, and while rural firms located proportionately more of these plants in rural communities (compared to metropolitan-headquartered firms), nonetheless, rural firms located the majority of their branch plants in urban areas (53 percent). Successful rural firms obviously find it necessary to establish branch plants in urban areas (presumably to gain access to markets and enjoy the benefits of agglomeration economies).

Over the decade, rural areas lagged behind national growth rates in all industry categories, high tech, low tech, and other industries. Rural high-tech industry grew at a marginally faster rate than low-tech industry. Overall, however, manufacturing jobs in rural areas grew below the national average. Only industries such as services grew at respectable rates, yet this rate was also below national and metropolitan averages.

More ominously, rural areas are lagging in job creation within their traditional manufacturing mainstay—low-technology industry. Low-tech small-firm creation occurs almost exclusively in urban areas. Rural areas also lagged in large low-tech firm job creation. Thus, even product-cycle forces that previously brought branch plants to rural areas diminished in the late 1980s.

Plant Gains in Rural Communities

While rural high-tech job growth was below the national rate of employment change, high-tech plant gains in rural communities, both absolutely and on a percentage basis, were far more substantial (Figure B). Between 1972 and 1982, 2,250 new plants were added in rural counties. Unlike employment, percentage change in rural plant growth exceeded the national rate (45 versus 30 percent). Therefore, rural areas were experiencing the beneficial effects of plant decentralization.

The distribution of high-tech jobs and plants among nonmetropolitan counties shows a clear bias toward rural counties located adjacent to metropolitan areas. In 1972, 61 percent of all rural high-tech industry employment was found in adjacent counties. In 1982, this figure was reduced by only 2 percent—a vivid contrast with the distribution of population in rural counties (Table 3.2). Fifty-one percent of the population live in nonadjacent counties.

High-tech job growth also was not evenly distributed. During a period of rapid expansion, nonadjacent counties gained only 31 percent of new high-tech jobs, less than their relative share of rural manufacturing employment or population. On the other hand, plant growth in nonadjacent counties grew at approximately the rate for total rural high-tech job change (29 percent).

FIGURE B

Comparison of National, Metropolitan, and Rural
High-Tech Plant Change
1972–1982

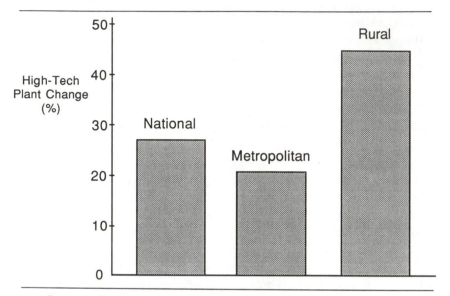

Source: Bureau of the Census, 1986, *Census of Manufactures, Plant Location Tape* (1972, 1977, 1982).

Above-average plant growth in rural areas is clearly a positive sign of future high-tech development, yet it is important to speculate about the significance of this development. Most of the increase is manifest in adjacent rural counties. Thus, no doubt a process of industrial filtering is occurring. Plants needing proximity to but not location within metropolitan areas are moving to adjacent rural counties. Perhaps the need for land and the desire for freer land use attracts plants to remote communities. Despite the hopes for rural high-tech growth that these findings may encourage, industries in which plant growth was most pronounced were generally associated with rural industrialization. Machine tool and die firms are prevalent. Therefore, while plant growth was impressive, the majority of new establishments are likely to be engaged in routine manufacturing operations. They are not applying scientific skills to complex production processes.

TABLE 3.2

Distribution of Total High-Tech Jobs Among Adjacent and
Nonadjacent Rural Counties, 1982

	Rural Adjacent Metropolitan Counties	*Rural Nonadjacent Metropolitan Counties*
	(percent of total)	
1982 High-Tech Employment[1]	59	41
1980 Population[2]	49	51
1972–1982 High-Tech Job Growth[1]	50	50

Sources: 1. Bureau of the Census, 1986, *Census of Manufactures, Plant Location Tape* (1972, 1977, 1982).
2. Bureau of the Census, 1986, *State and Metropolitan Data Book*, Government Printing Office, Washington, DC.

Which Jobs and Plants Locate in Rural Counties?

Rural counties have had some success in attracting high-tech industry plants and employment. These gains raise questions about the composition of industrialization—particularly its relationship to factors such as the traditional economic base of rural communities (for example, agriculture and mining) and manufacturing industries that decentralized to rural areas over the postwar period. Because a number of high-tech industries are chemicals (many of which are used in agriculture or are dependent on raw resource mining), I expected chemicals industries to constitute a significant portion of rural high-tech jobs and plants. Furthermore, given rural communities' tendency to attract mature, often slow-growing industries, a similar pattern would be expected to prevail in relation to high-tech industries. For the most part, this is true. Rural high-tech industries comprise only a small subset of the ninety-four industries studied.

Tables 3.3 and 3.4 list industries in which 20 percent or more of an industry's total employment and plants are concentrated in rural counties. As expected, rural communities support a base of

TABLE 3.3

Industries with Greater Than 20 Percent of Total National
High-Tech Plants in Rural Counties
1982 (listed by SIC code)[1]

>20%	21–25%	26–30%	31–40%	41–50%
+3533	+2819	*2812	*2824	−2861
*3612	+3519	−2823	+2874	+2873
+3677	*3621	+2879	*2892	−2875
−3721	*3624	+2911		−2895
*3743	*3675	*3531		+3532
*3769		*3562		

Growth Experience 1972–1982
+ = Above-average industry growth rate.
* = Growth positive but below-average growth rate.
− = Negative growth rate.

Note: 1. For key to industry SIC codes, see Table 2.1.

Source: Bureau of the Census, 1986, *Census of Manufactures, Plant Location Tape* (1972, 1977, 1982).

the more mature, hence slower-growing, high-tech industries and resource extraction activities associated with the traditional rural economic base. A number of observations can be made about these high-tech industries. Only nine of twenty-five industries with 20 percent or more of their plants in rural areas had growth rates at or above the national level for total high-tech plant growth. Of thirty-six industries with 20 percent or more of total employment in rural counties, only seven had growth rates at or above the national average for all high-tech industries. The process of industrial filtering (characteristic of general manufacturing) holds for certain high-tech industries.

As I noted in chapter 2, postwar rural industrialization consisted of manufacturing establishments seeking low-cost production sites. Researchers have characterized this process as industrial filtering. Firms shift manufacturing operations that embody stable production technology for the manufacture of mature products. According to this view, plants filter down the spatial hierarchy from urban to rural communities as they become less dependent on urban agglomerations' skilled labor and high-level business services.

TABLE 3.4

Industries with Greater Than 20 Percent of Total National High-Tech Employment in Rural Counties 1982 (listed by SIC code)[1]

>20%	21–25%	26–30%	31–40%	41–50%
–3536	*2899	–2812	+2819	–2824
+3842	–3531	–2874	–2823	–2861
–3031	+3534	+2879	–2873	–2892
*3631	*3537	*3546	–2875	–2895
	–3542	*3568	*3532	*3675
	–3574		–3562	
	–3651		3563	
	+3822		–3612	
			3621	
			*3675	
			–3676	
			–3677	
			+3824	

Growth Experience 1972–1982
+ = Above-average industry growth rate.
* = Growth positive but below-average growth rate.
– = Negative growth rate.

Note: 1. For key to industry SIC codes, see Table 2.1.

Source: Bureau of the Census, 1986, *Census of Manufactures, Plant Location Tape* (1972, 1977, 1982).

Thus, plants that are found in rural areas show less dependence on their immediate environment for inputs other than low-cost labor and land.

A second observation relates to the type of industries with either plant or employment concentrations in rural areas. Approximately half of the twenty-five industries with plant concentrations, and a third of those with employment concentrations, are in the chemicals sectors. Many of these are tied to other traditional rural industries. For example, organic chemicals are inputs to farming and also depend on raw resource commodities found in rural regions. Gum and wood chemicals are found in proximity to natural resources — in this case timber, used in the production of wood products, such as plywood. Synthetic organic fibers are inputs to textiles, a traditional rural industry. Finally, the explosives industry seems drawn, if for no other reason than public safety, to places with sparse populations.

High-tech industries in the machinery sector are also linked with the economic base of rural communities. Plants in these sectors decentralized in search of low-wage labor and access to markets. For example, the construction, farm, and mining equipment industries are heavily represented in rural counties. Other machinery sector industries are common and produce goods such as ball and roller bearings. With the exception of aircraft production, which requires large tracts of land for both production and testing, industries with high proportions of total employment and plants in rural counties are either tied to agriculture and resource extraction or they are common inputs, such as machine tools and dies.

Tables 3.3 and 3.4 clearly indicate that the high-tech industries that have large shares of their employment or plants located in rural areas (as mentioned earlier) are the more mature, least technical, and, in many cases, the most vulnerable industries within the group. These industries are also related to the traditional rural economic base of agriculture and mining. Thus, a major explanatory factor in rural high-tech industry location is the presence of these traditional sectors. This means that rural high-tech growth is significantly affected by growth in traditional rural industries and neither independent of nor a replacement for them. For example, synthetic fibers are an integral part of the textile industry. It is widely known that developments in synthetic fibers actually impelled the textile industry's greater use of new technologies, making the industry more competitive worldwide. It is possible to conclude that efforts to stimulate growth in the electronics and computer sectors are likely to have little impact on rural economic development *unless* they are tied to concurrent efforts to increase development and growth of traditional rural sectors.

This observation has not gone unnoticed by all rural policymakers. In a few exceptional cases, such as the member states of the Southern Growth Policy Board, political leaders of predominantly rural states support programs encouraging the adoption of new process technologies in existing rural industries, but as later discussion will show, these efforts prove rare. Most state-led high-tech development policies simply ignore the challenges posed by rural economies.

The Select Few: Job Generators in Rural Areas

Table 3.5 lists industries that added more than five hundred jobs in rural counties over the ten-year period. The range of these industries is broad and includes everything from computers and electronic components to photographic equipment. Rural counties gained substantial new jobs in both traditional rural high-tech industries, such as chemicals, and more typically urban industries,

TABLE 3.5

Industries That Gained Greater Than 500 Jobs in Rural Counties
1972–1982

| | Rural Continuum Categories | | | | | |
	4	5	6	7	8	9
	−2812	2819	2821	2819	3573	2819
I	2834	2834	−2824	−2823		
N	2869	2869	2873	2834		
D	2879	−3531	2891	2869		
U	3519	3533	2911	2911		
S	3533	3535	3519	3532		
T	3569	3546	−3531	3544		
R	3621	3561	3537	3545		
I	3661	3573	3544	3561		
E	3675	−3612	−3562	−3562		
S	3679	3674	3563	3564		
	3728	3679	−3612	3568		
	3823	3824	3613	3573		
	3825	3842	3662	−3576		
	3841		3678	3613		
	3842		3679	3621		
			3724	3622		
			3728	3661		
			−3822	3662		
			3825	3679		
			3829	3724		
			3842	3728		
				3841		
				3843		
				3861		

− = Negative growth rate over the 1972–82 period.

Source: Bureau of the Census, 1986, *Census of Manufactures, Plant Location Tape* (1972, 1977, 1982).

such as communications equipment and semiconductor production. It is interesting that the smaller rural counties (those with
urban populations of less than 20,000 persons) experienced the
greatest diversity in high-tech job gains. Having noted this, the two
types of rural counties—urban-adjacent and nonadjacent—had a
mix of high-tech industries consisting almost equally of industries
that lost jobs nationally while gaining them in rural areas and those
that showed substantial job gains above the national rate. For very
small rural communities, regardless of proximity to metropolitan
areas, only one of the ninety-four industries in each case gained
more than five hundred jobs.

Table 3.6 lists industries that added at least ten new plants in
rural counties between 1972 and 1982. The importance of this
finding relates to the role plant growth can play in further expansion over time. Unlike employment growth, which can represent
short-term fluctuations in demand (hence, temporary expansion of
output or employment shifts from one plant to another), plant
growth signifies a commitment on the part of either an
entrepreneur or a corporation to invest in a local area. Thus, the
high rate of plant growth in rural areas is one hopeful signal of
future development potential.

Plant distribution is similar to that of employment with the
following exceptions. First, unlike employment, where almost half
the industries were declining overall, rural plant additions occurred
primarily in industries growing at the national level. At least over
the period studied, a strict interpretation of the product-cycle
model does not reflect the diverse experience of high-tech industries
growing in rural areas. According to the model, industrial filtering,
hence job gains, should occur in mature industries growing slowly
at a national level, yet the analysis suggests plant growth occurred
in many dynamic industries, such as aircraft and electronic components.

Research by Smith and Barkley (1989) and Barkley, Smith,
and Coupal (1990) suggests that entrepreneurial ventures have
taken root in western rural communities. Products produced by
firms range from sophisticated components to labor-intensive and
low-skilled medical equipment assembly. An occupational mix of
rural western establishments revealed high-skill content in high-
tech versus low-tech establishments. High-tech single units (non-

TABLE 3.6

Industries That Gained Ten or More Plants in Rural Counties
1972–1982

	4	5	Rural Continuum Categories 6	7	8	9
	–2813	3569	2819	2869	3544	3544
I	2819	3613	2851	3531		3679
N	–2899	3662	2869	3532		
D	3531	3679	2873	3535		
U	3533	3842	2899	3544		
S	3541	3531	3531	3545		
T	3544	3532	3532	3561		
R	3569	3533	3533	3564		
I	3573	3544	3535	3569		
E	3622	3545	3544	3613		
S	3662		3545	3662		
	3677		3563	3679		
	3679		3569	3728		
	3728		3613	3842		
	3823		3662			
	3842		3674			
			3679			
			3728			
			3842			

– = Negative growth rate over the 1972–82 period.

Source: Bureau of the Census, 1986, *Census of Manufactures, Plant Location Tape* (1972, 1977, 1982).

branch establishments) boasted levels of professionals in the work force significantly in excess of branch plants. Levels of professionals in high-tech branch plants were dramatically higher than in low-tech branch plants. The extent that these results can be generalized to other rural regions of the country is questionable. While the results are promising, the authors note the serendipitous basis for most establishment location decisions and do not generalize their results to the bulk of America's rural counties.

One of the problems facing researchers using occupational data to determine the extent that a firm is innovative is that the use of occupational data to identify technical workers does not link easily to levels of innovation in the firm. For example, firms may have technical workers on staff but essentially be making a product that is a copy of another firm's product. Occupational data provides an indication of the potential for innovation, but it alone cannot be used to prove that a firm is innovative or capable of being innovative.

Another problem is that there are inadequacies in the industrial classification system. Even at a very specific four-digit SIC level, there can be heterogeneity among plants. It is likely that facilities locating in rural areas produce more mature components of high-growth industries, but because high tech is growing overall, it is impossible to detect declining subcomponents within a single industry. For example, the production of discrete semiconductor devices is increasing much more slowly than is that of microprocessors (Scott and Angel 1987), but the industries share a common four-digit SIC code. Therefore, I cannot separate industries whose employment base is either stable or declining. Drawing on Barkley and Smith's (1988) work, it is apparent that in rural areas, even the more advanced high-tech industries defined by industry codes have low levels of technical employees compared to their urban counterparts. The most innovative firms could be performing very mundane tasks in their rural locations.

How Do High-Tech Plants Affect Rural Economies?

New plants in nonmetropolitan areas were primarily in the nonelectrical machinery and electronics industries. Machine tools and miscellaneous electronic components were consistent plant generators across the range of rural counties. These two industries were responsible for 23 percent of total new plant additions. Both contain a wide variety of products with broad applications. For example, machine tools range from one-of-a-kind products designed for a single purpose to those that are mass-produced for many applications. Nevertheless, the broad nature of the category embraces facilities that repair all types of machinery, including agricultural, mining, and construction equipment. Virtually any community with some claim to industrial activity hosts a machine tools plant. The presence of machine tool firms indicates rural areas possess at least some of the technical skills needed to support other related industries, but as further discussion will confirm, this possibility is more illusionary than real. Machine tool industry firms locate in rural communities for many of the same reasons other manufacturing does — low wages and pliant work forces.

The electronic components sector presents a yet different set of issues for rural development. Encompassing the most labor-intensive but fast-growing high-tech industries, this is a particularly heterogeneous group made up of many different components. Some are newly emerging and thus not mature enough to warrant unique SIC codes. Others are mundane apparatus used in everything from air-conditioning system repair to electricity regulation. Products in the early growth phase (but complementary to other micro-electronic-related products) are produced by American and foreign firms in domestic and Third World locations, but increasingly, for quality and cost reasons, it is more economical for firms to manufacture outside the United States. Thus, companies choosing to maintain production within the country are under constant pressure to automate just to remain competitive, and when products are of a mass scale, this product group is vulnerable to domestic job loss or certainly slower employment growth.

More recently, the electronic component industry — particularly the production of printed circuitry — has been suffering from significant overcapacity (United States Department of Commerce 1988). Any product using electronic components is built upon a printed circuit board into which the components are inserted. Printed circuit board production has traditionally been one of the most archaic and marginal aspects of high-tech production (Scott 1983). Until recently, the production process was highly labor-intensive and defied automation. Firms making boards were typically fly-by-night operations. The production process is also dirty, especially in combining laminants to form the raw boards. Therefore, companies no doubt locate circuit board production in rural areas to exploit both low-cost labor and land and relatively lax environmental standards.

Printed circuit board production, though, has succumbed to capital-intensive automation practices. Surface-mount technology (in which components are fused onto the circuit board instead of being hand inserted and then soldered) is becoming the standard practice of circuit board producers (Glasmeier et al. 1987). This capital-intensive, automated process is leading to consolidation of industry firms, a development with serious implications for rural areas. Given that the technology is moving toward greater miniaturization and automation, employment growth in circuit board production is not likely to accelerate at anywhere near past rates, and in the long run, future industry changes will most assuredly include employment reductions.

The AMP Corporation—A Case Study[13]

Thus, the typical rural high-tech plant manufactures products made in long production runs with standard technology. The product market is extremely competitive, and the lowest price determines market share. For thirty years, a rural location has served two purposes for this type of manufacturing: cheap labor and a compliant work force. High-tech industry has largely come to rural areas for the same reasons.

The following example of a typical rural operation points out both the pitfalls and the possibilities of this development. The AMP Corporation, headquartered in Harrisburg, Pennsylvania, is the nation's largest computer connector producer. Connectors are multiple-pin devices used as the interconnection between different electronic subassemblies and components in almost every microelectronic-dependent device, from computers to calculators to radios. The wide application of such products presents particular difficulties to connector producers. Simple connectors for non-technical products may consist of just a few pins implanted by hand in a case of plastic and wires, but some connectors are made of expensive materials and are more sophisticated. These may be manufactured for use in computers and have minute areas between pins. Therefore, there is little tolerance for error, and pin placement must be extremely precise.

Historically, connectors were made by hand. Mostly women sat in front of bins of pins and placed them one by one in plastic sheaths. AMP employed a policy of small-plant production in rural adjacent counties near Harrisburg, other areas of Pennsylvania, and, more recently, near markets (Glasmeier 1987b). Workers were paid relatively low wages for the tedious and mind-numbing work, but as end product requirements became more complex and volumes reached huge proportions, companies such as AMP were forced to automate. Pins got smaller, placement more dense, and material more sensitive to impurities introduced by human contact. In some cases, the tolerances of individual products were simply too minute for human manipulation. AMP's recent strategy has been to shift this still labor-intensive and now increasingly automated production to metropolitan and metro-adjacent rural counties of the South in search of cheaper labor and government incentives. Inputs are shipped in, and the local community presently benefits from wages paid to workers.

AMP represents typical contemporary rural high-tech development. Later examples will only buttress these findings. While product and production process momentarily require engineering oversight, skill-base changes are short-term as the company works out bugs in new equipment. AMP hopes the new plants will eventually run themselves, obviating the need for engineering oversight. Research and new product development still take place in Harrisburg (and increasingly in the laboratories of AMP's major customers).

Does this scenario differ from the last thirty years of rural industrialization? For the most part, the answer is no. Like branch plants of the past, new factories have come to rural America in search of low wages, pliant workers, and a probusiness climate. Also like past experience, products produced in these plants are standardized and manufactured in large volumes. While markets are temporarily flush, the connector industry is internationally competitive, and success turns on quality and price. Already AMP's competitors are producing with identical equipment in Singapore and Hong Kong, which have lower wages and higher skilled production workers than the United States.[14] Thus, while AMP's product vintage may be newer, America's rural communities are not on the verge of developing an economic base substantially different from their past. Indeed, competitive pressures in these industries are only likely to add to the economic instability already present in rural economies.

4

Regional High-Tech Location and Rural Industrialization

Strong historical forces have influenced the current spatial ordering of high-tech jobs and plants, so in determining the locational considerations of rural high tech, it is important to consider its regional distribution. In this chapter, I first outline the significant historical inputs to each region's industrial trajectory. I then examine the characteristics and location of rural America and begin to analyze the regional distribution of rural high-tech employment and plants.

The Northeast Economy: Research, Development, and Technical Education

The literature on the spatial location of corporate R and D activities indicates that a considerable amount of basic engineering and science occurs at the sites of corporate decision making (Malecki 1980). This begins to explain why industry in the Northeast is technical in nature. Although there has been some decentralization of R and D functions over the post–World War II period, an enormous number of corporate headquarters, hence research labs, are still found in the region (Malecki 1980). The dense concentration of universities and colleges contributes to the Northeast's technical base of R and D labs and corporate research centers.

The region's high-quality engineering and science-based institutions annually regenerate a labor pool of engineers and technicians (Browne 1983; Deutermann 1966; Dorfman 1983). In fact, New England has the highest proportion of engineers and scientists of any U.S. census division (U.S. Department of Commerce 1986). Universities and the available labor pool create a number of dynamic environments supporting both private industry research labs and government-funded basic research too risky and long range for private firms (Saxenian 1985a).

Still, contemporary success of northeastern high-tech development should be viewed in light of longer term changes in the region's manufacturing industry base. As late as 1975, when the end of the Vietnam War led to a decline in defense spending, Massachusetts's unemployment rate was actually 2.5 percent higher than the national average (Dorfman 1983). Earlier, during the 1940s, when the textile and shoe industries were shifting production to the South and overseas, unemployment was also a serious problem (Estall 1972; Harrison 1982; Hekman 1980). Thus, the transformation of New England's economy was particularly painful for communities whose sole sources of employment were either defense production-dependent or these maturing industries.

As the mills declined, however, electronics manufacturing began to infiltrate the region (McCluskey, Jagger, and Dahl 1985). R and D contracts left over from World War II provided local companies with a market for sophisticated surveillance and reconnaissance equipment. Massachusetts's nascent Route 128 complex benefited from labor pools left by retreating watch and textile industries. Unemployed but experienced precision workers from the Waltham Watch Company and Lawrence and Lowell mills had great finger dexterity. They seemed poised to participate in seedbed high-technology industries (Rand 1964).

Yet despite the region's strong tradition of R and D and concentration of universities, high tech is not monolithic. Eroding markets for many of the Northeast's major firms have resulted in work force reductions and plant closures. Even Route 128 is no longer immune to the effects of competition and technical change.

The Midwest: Metal Bending and Machine Tending

Rich in natural resources and fertile farmland, the Midwest was also the nation's manufacturing center for steel, agricultural implements, consumer electronics, metal fabricating, and food-processing equipment (Resek and Kosobud 1982). It was here that many early inventions in these industries—the railroad engine, woodworking and metalworking machine tools, and consumer electronics, such as the radio and phonograph—were first mass-produced.

The Midwest stands out as the region where tremendous technical advances occurred in heavy industry and durable manufacturing. Much of this innovation focused on improvements designed to grow, process, and speed up the movement of agricultural commodities and natural resource-based products over longer distances for the rapidly expanding U.S. population (Pudup 1986). The amalgamation of large and highly integrated process and product-based industries created a massive industrial complex.

However, the Midwest appears to have been passed over by high-tech industries. This may stem from the region's reliance on durable goods industries, which have undergone serious restructuring during the last fifteen years. The make-over has engendered a spatial-industrial structure of company towns tied to large, vertically integrated corporations headquartered in major manufacturing belt cities.

Such vertical integration may have exacerbated the Midwest's inability to succeed in new product development. For example, engineers in the steel industry have been preoccupied with labor-saving improvements oriented toward process innovation. This has been at the expense of development of new product technologies and investment in capital improvements, such as new plants (Markusen 1985).

The Midwest also suffers low proportions of independent and local affiliate establishment employment. Midwestern states' share of small manufacturing establishments has been declining since 1969 (Starr 1982), yet despite an inability to concretely explain the Midwest's lack of vigor in small business, the revitalization of the northeastern economy provides a model with some hope. Could the Midwest, through development of high-technology industries, emerge from its current malaise and dependence on mature industries?

A high-tech–based economic recovery would presume that the Midwest's problems can be solved through the orderly decline or stabilization of mature industries. In reality, the midwestern labor force shows serious deficiencies (such as low proportions of scientists, engineers, and other college graduates), many traceable to the region's historic industrial structure, which provided a good living to employees with only a high school diploma.

The Sunbelt—Two Faces of America's Industrialization

A recently exploding industrial area, the Sunbelt is made up of two diverse regions—the South and the West. Each has a unique production and industrial history that must be considered separately to illuminate individual emerging industrial landscapes.

The South—A Product of Continuing Historic Factors

Despite its "sunrise" image, the present-day South is much a product of its past. The region is characterized by externally owned manufacturing branch plants and mostly low-wage jobs. The South's heritage of slavery and racial discrimination has evolved into a manufacturing structure characterized by paternalistic management and docile workers who, unlike unionized labor forces of other U.S. regions, seem mostly grateful for available low-wage jobs. Even today, some researchers indicate that pioneering investment may go to previously undeveloped areas of the South to avoid work forces that have experienced exploitation and are likely to exhibit militancy rather than grateful pacifism (Johnson 1988, 1989).

The South's capital structure still suffers vestiges of early industrialization patterns. Historically, assets were concentrated with members of the "planter class." Rather than investing capital in their own region, these few elite preferred to export funds to the more industrial Northeast (Pudup 1988). While this "capital flight" may have financed innovative production outside the region, it discouraged in-place economic investment and largely drained the South financially.

Added to this lack of capital for start-up manufacturing investments, the South's history of low-skill commodity production has not required a technically trained or well-educated labor pool. Low-value–added industries, such as textiles, shoes, auto parts, and furniture production, traditionally relied on exploitation of low-wage workers to produce mostly consumer goods (Glasmeier and McCluskey 1987; Glasmeier and Patrizi 1985; Hansen 1980). An educated labor force was neither necessary nor desirable for this type of production, and with few exceptions, southern public school systems have yet to catch up with their counterparts in other regions.

Some economic changes occurred in the 1930s with the implementation of New Deal legislation (Wright 1986). Policies such as the National Industrial Relations Act, the Works Progress Administration, and the Fair Labor Standards Act forced the South into the national labor market by requiring firms to pay higher wages, but even these programs designed to improve laborers' conditions and stimulate local economies exempted many traditional southern enterprises from participating. Farmers were permitted to pay agricultural workers less than the national minimum wage, and industries such as textiles were not included in otherwise sweeping industrial reforms. With southern workers remaining largely underpaid, the negative economic conditions of the Great Depression in the South have outlasted those of other regions.

Later wartime industrialization did benefit the rural South. Munitions factories and military bases were established, which led to increases in population and employment, but southern defense spending is largely in the form of military and civilian personnel. Except in Texas, Florida, Georgia, and Virginia, few weapons are actually being produced compared with other regions. Concomitantly, there are few sites where basic research, which can lead to proximate production, is occurring.

Postwar improvements in transportation, such as the interstate highway system and increasing commercialization of air travel, have opened up largely inaccessible areas of the South, and improvements in air conditioning have made it more feasible to operate manufacturing facilities in that part of the country.

Additionally, traditional southern activities in agriculture and extraction of other natural resources have joined to form the base for a number of chemicals sectors. These are characterized by their need to be either near sites of extraction or away from major population centers. Chemical employment is unusual because much of the production uses continuous process technology requiring large numbers of engineers to operate production plants (Freeman 1982). Unlike durable manufacturing operations, the primary raw materials conversion process cannot be broken down and shipped out to maximize marginal site-specific savings. This bodes well for advancements in the quality of the South's employment pool.

Still, neither technology-intensive chemicals nor defense-related complexes are concentrated in more than a handful of states, and the majority of southern production that can be considered high tech is centered in primarily low-skill branch plant assembly locations. In fact, many of even the much-wooed defense-related high-tech jobs turn out to be largely low-skilled production (Schlessinger, Gaventa, and Merrifield 1983). Despite the South's "sunrise" imagery, the characteristics of most industries moving into the region are not primarily high tech but instead are as assembly-oriented as activities of the past (Johnson 1988, 1989).

The West—America's Newest Region

The West has largely enjoyed a different industrial trajectory. Contrary to the South's legacies of paternalism and capital flight, the region's capital structure is characterized by entrepreneurialism and in-place reinvestment of capital. Early settlers were prospectors, farmers, and business entrepreneurs who succeeded in establishing a thriving and varied export-based economic system in a region of brutal but mineral-laden mountains, unyielding deserts, and fertile farmland and timber forests (McWilliams 1949).

The debilitating labor patterns of the South's slave heritage were not repeated in the West. Initially, the region's abundant mineral resources drew innovative migrants seeking better economic conditions, and yet the West, too, has always had a reserve army of workers. First Chinese and later Hispanic workers provided a critical labor base for the region, but unlike the South's economy, which was largely dependent upon a single crop— cotton—the West's natural resource wealth was both more diverse and more abundant. Also, exploitation of this natural resource endowment often required the development of innovative technologies and major infrastructure investments in the form of highways, dams, and factories.

Distance from the industrial heartland succeeded in attracting branch plants of manufacturing firms headquartered in the American Midwest. The West's year-round temperate climate also facilitated the creation of consumer industries catering to a life-style free of cold harsh winters and blistering summers (McWilliams 1949).

The West's high-tech manufacturing history is closely linked with the fortunes of the aerospace industry. Preceding World War II, and greatly accelerating during the Cold War era, California's high-tech industrial structure rooted in this defense-dependent sector. The state was well along the path of industrialization before many of its emerging high-tech industries even reached a commercial stage. Government R and D contracts nurtured this nascent industry. Thus, California can be properly considered both a traditional manufacturing center and an innovative core.

Other western states have similar industrial roots predating World War II. For example, the first airmail system evolved in Washington, the site of fledgling wooden aircraft construction, and Utah's desert has been a strategic site for nuclear and other missile weapons systems testing.

Federal mandates to shift defense production into interior states shaped the industrial trajectory of states such as Arizona and Colorado. Motorola's earliest transistor and semiconductor development operations took place in Phoenix (Safer, Leaf, and McCaine 1986). Colorado's high-tech seeds were similarly sowed back in the early 1950s.

Thus, the West is the rising star of American high-technology industrial development. The region boasts the state with the largest high-tech base, California, as well as Arizona, which has the highest proportion of high tech to total manufacturing. Perhaps more importantly (as illustrated in the Northeast), the West is the home of growing numbers of corporate headquarters, rapidly expanding service sectors, and huge markets for high-tech products (Cohen 1981; Mollenkopf 1984; Noyelle and Stanback 1982).

Where Is Rural America?

Because rural manufacturing largely reflects the irregular pattern of American rural community distribution, it is now imperative that we examine the regional distribution of rural areas in the United States. With almost half of the nation's rural population residing within its seventeen-state area, the South is America's most rural region. The Midwest's share of rural population is also substantial—30 percent. The populations of the Northeast and

West, by contrast, are quite metropolitan — only 17 and 12 percent, respectively, of the nation's rural population live in these regions.

In both the South and the Midwest, almost a third of total populations reside in nonmetro counties. Again, the Northeast and West are more decidedly urban in character, with only 21 and 16 percent of their respective populations in rural counties.

A similar pattern exists in the distribution of rural manufacturing employment (Table 4.1). In 1982, 52 percent was located in the South. The Midwest also had a significant share, approximately 29 percent of the total. By contrast, the West had only 8 percent of the nation's rural manufacturing, while the Northeast had a slightly larger, yet still modest, 11 percent.

Jobs in the South and Midwest stand out with large shares of rural manufacturing. In 1982, the South had 32 percent of its manufacturing jobs concentrated in rural counties, followed by the Midwest with a small yet substantial share (22 percent). The Northeast and West had comparable shares of their manufacturing in rural areas (10 percent each).

Significantly, changes in this pattern reflect increasing concentrations of rural manufacturing in the South. Between 1972 and 1982, regions except the South and the West declined in shares of rural manufacturing. The Midwest experienced the most profound negative shift of manufacturing jobs. Over the period studied,

TABLE 4.1

Percent of Total Rural Manufacturing in the
Four Census Regions
1972 and 1982

Census Region	1972	1982
Northeast	12.4	11.0
Midwest	30.3	29.0
South	49.4	52.0
West	8.0	8.0

Source: Compiled for the Economic Research Service, 1986, Bureau of Economic Analysis, U.S. Department of Agriculture, Washington, DC.

national manufacturing growth was essentially static. Hence, these changes were reflected as absolute increases in the South's share of the nation's rural manufacturing employment, from 49 to 52 percent. This pattern of high-tech location clearly follows larger trends in the distribution of population, markets, and jobs. Although it is difficult to prove conclusively, high-tech jobs appear to follow rather than lead major changes under way in the structure of the nation's spatial economy.

Overall, America's postwar regional growth experience consists of many factors. Since the 1960s, population has been shifting away from the Northeast and Midwest toward the South and West. Once under way, population flows created demand for goods and services, and firms responded by setting up production facilities closer to new markets. The location of high-tech industries clearly reflects these larger trends.

In part, this general shift represents life-style preferences of America's elderly population. Military spending and base placement also contributed to population shifts over the period studied. During the 1970s, 15 percent of the migrating population consisted of military personnel (Weinstein, Gross, and Rees 1988), and population increases in the South and West created expanding consumer markets. Companies producing consumer goods added many plants to serve the growing regions' populations. This in turn attracted additional migrants in search of employment. Moreover, a portion of manufacturing growth consisted of new plants shifting southward to take advantage of low-wage workers and lax regulation (Cobb 1984).

Rising oil prices in the 1970s greatly contributed to the dramatic growth of Texas, Louisiana, and Oklahoma (Glasmeier 1987a; Glickman and Glasmeier 1989b). Domestic oil and gas production expanded significantly, and workers displaced from factories in the industrial heartland flooded into these southwestern states in search of work. The South's manufacturing base further expanded as foreign firms set up plants in the chemical and auto parts industries (Glickman and Glasmeier 1989b).

High-tech industries have also been important (though often overstated) in the Sunbelt growth experience. In 1972, total high-tech employment was concentrated in the Midwest and Northeast, but by 1982 (after shifts in employment patterns and population migration), the South had joined the Northeast as the nation's dominant high-tech region (Figure C).

Regional Shifts: Regional Distribution of Rural High-Tech Employment

With few exceptions, the location of rural high-tech jobs follows general manufacturing locational patterns. In 1972, rural high-tech employment was almost evenly divided between the Midwest and South, with the Northeast and West capturing the residual. Nevertheless, at the end of the study period (1982), the Midwest had lost this position of prominence, falling significantly behind the South as the locus of U.S. rural high-tech manufacturing employment.

The South contains 42 percent of the nation's rural high-tech employment. This number has increased substantially from 1972, when the region accounted for only 37 percent; and while clearly below the region's share of rural manufacturing, the South's share of the nation's *rural* high tech is nonetheless substantially above its share of *total* high-tech employment (42 versus 26 percent).

The late 1970s — a convulsive period of industrial restructuring — left America's traditional manufacturing communities reeling from massive job loss and industrial contraction. Employment in high-tech industries was not immune to these larger economic changes. Midwestern industrial cities lost high-tech jobs at a dramatic rate. During the same period, the Midwest's share of rural high-tech jobs also declined by almost four percentage points (from 37 to 33 percent). The region's share of rural high-tech jobs is still slightly above its share of rural population (32 percent). Importantly, given these shifts, the Midwest's share of national rural high-tech jobs is above its regional share of all high-tech employment in general (33 versus 25 percent). Unfortunately, this simply indicates that the region's urban areas lost jobs at a faster rate than did midwestern rural communities.

The long-term consequences of this pattern are worrisome. That both metropolitan and rural high-tech employment in the Midwest have declined since 1972 indicates just how intimately rural high tech is tied to overall regional trends in high-tech employment. Rural communities in the Midwest enjoyed growth in

FIGURE C
High-Tech Employment by Census Region
1972 and 1982

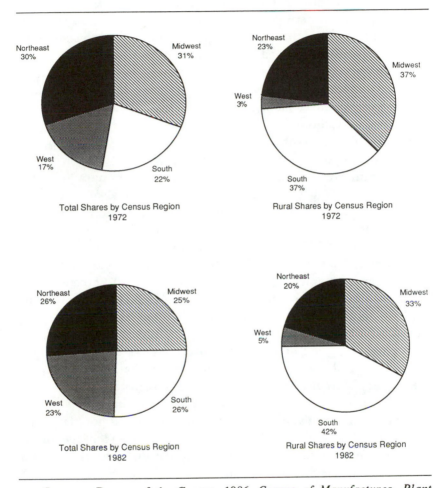

Total Shares by Census Region
1972

Rural Shares by Census Region
1972

Total Shares by Census Region
1982

Rural Shares by Census Region
1982

Source: Bureau of the Census, 1986, *Census of Manufactures, Plant Location Tape* (1972, 1982).

high-tech industries as companies fled their historic metropolitan locations. Auto and consumer electronics-related producers set up huge plants to provide components for the region's assembly industries. Companies such as Delco, Champion, and subsidiaries of the Big Three assemblers (GM, Ford, and Chrysler) found rural midwestern communities especially receptive to branch plants.

Many towns were interested in trading their dependence on agriculture and related manufacturing industries for newer growth-oriented sectors.

Initially, high-tech jobs were seen as antidotes to declines in traditional midwestern industry, but the development masks the dependent nature of the region's high-tech jobs. As many communities have painfully learned, rural midwestern high-tech industries are intimately tied to the region's industrial base. Ohio, Indiana, Illinois, and Michigan have historically had the nation's most integrated regional economy. Interdependence meant that as major employers in traditional industries declined, so did high tech. The decline of high-tech jobs is therefore directly traceable to the fortunes of the region's dominant industries.

This interrelationship between a region's dominant economic base and the growth of high-tech industries is also seen in the experience of rural areas in the Northeast. Over the ten-year period, northeastern states lost manufacturing jobs overall, falling from a 27 to a 23 percent share of the nation's manufacturing employment. A similar but less dramatic shift occurred in rural manufacturing, which declined from 12.4 to 11.0 percent. Given the overall decline in manufacturing, the Northeast's manufacturing base actually became proportionately more high tech (up to 31 from 28 percent). That is, declining jobs in traditional industries were partly replaced by high-tech industry growth. The same can be said of rural manufacturing within the region, which declined overall yet experienced rising shares of rural high-tech jobs.

The percentage of rural high-tech jobs in the Northeast approximately equals that of the region's total rural population (10 percent). This is essentially the same as the percentage of the region's share of total national rural population. Over the ten-year study period, the Northeast consistently accounted for about 11 percent of high-tech employment.

There appears to be a fair degree of interdependence between northeastern states' economic base and the changing composition of rural manufacturing. High-tech companies headquartered in the region set up new branch plants in rural areas where labor and land were available. New York–based IBM expanded into Vermont while Massachusetts computer companies opened plants in New Hampshire. Because many of these facilities are branch plants, fluctuations in product markets affect local employment levels. Peripheral plants in Massachusetts are now undergoing contraction, and in some extreme cases closure, in response to competitive pressures within the computer and component-related industries (*New York Times,* August 11, 1989).

The experiences of rural areas in the Midwest and Northeast highlight the significant link between a region's economic base and the growth of rural high-tech industry, yet this trend is not monolithic. The West represents a stark contrast to America's traditional industrial regions.

The West has a much larger proportion of total high-tech jobs to population. With only 18 percent of the population, the region garnered almost 23 percent of the nation's high-tech jobs—the majority (80 percent) concentrated in one state, California; but the same pattern is not reflected in *rural* high-tech job shares. Sixteen percent of western population is rural, but the West's share of total rural high-tech employment and plants is a meager 5 percent. This figure showed very modest change over the ten-year period. In 1972, the West had 3 percent of the nation's rural high-tech jobs, and by 1982, this figure had increased by only 2 percent. Thus, there is a great divergence in the West's share of rural high tech in comparison with the region's rural population.

Even more remarkable, only 3 percent of the West's total high-tech jobs are in rural counties. In comparison, these areas account for 8 percent of the region's total manufacturing jobs, far below what would be expected based solely on manufacturing distribution. The absence of rural high tech is particularly noteworthy because the West contains more than 20 percent of the nation's total high-tech jobs and gained 45 percent of *all* new high-tech jobs created between 1972 and 1982.

Despite the West's prominence as America's premier high-tech region, the region's rural communities experienced limited high-tech gains. There are several explanations for this pattern. First, western wages are high relative to those of other regions' rural areas. The existing economic base is largely made up of resource-extracting industries, such as timber and mining, which are highly unionized and provide good incomes and working conditions. However, there is more to the region's existing economic base.

High-tech companies in the West grew rapidly over the period

studied. Many Silicon Valley (Santa Clara County) companies were
landlocked in their headquarters' locations and experienced pressures to expand into branch plants, yet relatively few moved to
western rural counties. Branch plant activity has occurred mainly
in areas of the South where wages are lower, markets are expanding, and sufficient technical workers can either be attracted or
found on location. Most of these plants required process engineers
to tinker with the manufacturing of high-tech products. Their presence, though significant, does not reflect an emphasis on new product development. Engineers monitor the production process and
oversee setups required during product changeovers.

Western high-tech companies also established a policy of locating plants in Asia, where wages are low, labor is comparatively
well-trained, and governments maintain rigorous control over work
forces (Henderson 1988). This shift of western firms' production
operations to both U.S. and foreign locations has been under way
since the early 1960s. Only in the last ten years have New England
manufacturers followed suit, locating plants in the South and
increasingly in Asia. The result is that many jobs that might have
otherwise filtered down to western rural communities simply found
equal or better locational alternatives.[15] Although branch plants
were established in the region, they primarily consist of facilities
within a reasonable commuting distance of headquarters' locations.
While some authors examining the exceptional experience of a few
communities in rural California and Colorado predicted a postin-
dustrial pattern of development, this has not occurred for a majority of the West's rural communities (Blakely and Bradshaw 1979).

These results underscore the fact that success of rural areas
cannot be discerned from the region's mix of industries. Although,
as Smith and Barkley (1989) note, the West's high-tech job base
grew rapidly in the period studied, the underlying numbers are
small and in no way indicate the region's rise to high-tech status.
Indeed, in relative terms, rural areas in the West are only a small
component of the evolving spatial division of labor in high-tech
industries.

Figure D provides a graphic summary of the importance of
high-tech jobs in rural counties of the four large census regions. I
calculated location quotients for total high-tech jobs to account for
industry specialization relative to some aggregate—in this case,

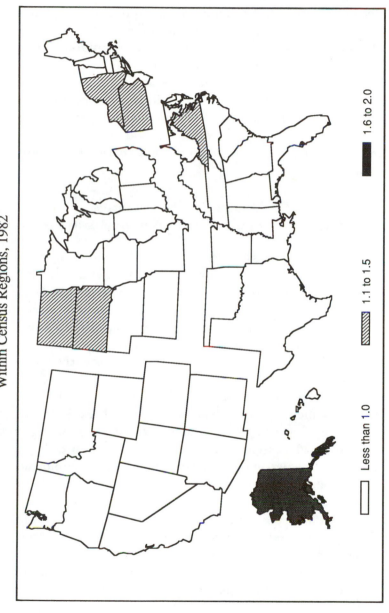

FIGURE D

Location Quotients of Rural High-Tech Employment by States Within Census Regions, 1982

Less than 1.0   1.1 to 1.5   1.6 to 2.0

rural population. Of note is the rare instance in which a state's rural high tech is above its share of rural population. These cases are attributable more to the states' overall populations, which are decidedly rural, than to an inordinate number of high-tech jobs in rural areas. For all high-tech industries, only North and South Dakota, Pennsylvania, New York, North Carolina, Delaware, and Alaska have more rural high-tech jobs than the specific state's share of rural population. This only reiterates what has been said about the modest presence of high-tech jobs in rural communities of the United States. In part, the rather poor showing reflects the idiosyncratic nature of new firm formation and the fact that larger segments of high-tech production have never been domestically deployed.

Where Are the Factories?
High-Tech Plant Distribution in Rural Counties

Contrasting patterns between the distribution of high-tech plants and measures of regional population and manufacturing employment are also apparent. The West has far fewer rural plants than expected based on either population or manufacturing. In contrast, the Midwest and Northeast have plant levels close to their population shares. The Northeast's and Midwest's plant levels accord with these regions' historic positions as early sites of decentralization.

By this measure (plant distribution compared to population and manufacturing employment), the South exhibits the greatest divergence between plants and other measures of regional size. With only 20 percent of the nation's rural high-tech plants, the South has 42 percent of total rural high-tech employment. This means that, on average, high-tech plants are much larger in the South than in other regions. The pattern is characteristic of southern manufacturing, which has consisted predominantly of modest plant growth and significant employment change. Over the last twenty years, the South has been a primary target of branch plant location (Armington, Harris, and Odle 1983: Glasmeier 1986a; Malecki 1985). This suggests that the South has emerged as the quintessential national production region, and high tech has tended to mirror aggregate trends rather than set new ones.

Still, branch plants are a peculiar problem for rural communities. Despite the fact that they have historically represented plants in established industries seeking low-cost locations, they are sought as a welcome addition to a rural economy; and they do bring jobs, but because of their mature vintage and ownership status, branch plants develop few links with a local economy. For the most part, they receive inputs from distant locations and sell their products to national and international markets. Previous research indicates that high-tech branch plants exhibit even more limited linkages than their low-tech counterparts (Barkley, Dahlgran, and Smith 1988; Porterfield and Pulver 1988; Smith and Barkley 1988). Additionally, high-tech firms rarely have local markets and have a significant tendency to use distributors, as opposed to local suppliers, to acquire inputs, further reducing the positive economic effect on a rural economy.

There is also limited evidence suggesting that remote branch plants located far from parent headquarters have a propensity to shut down during periods of economic decline. High-tech branch plants are especially notorious for this. Thus, America's rural communities may be but way stations in high tech's increasingly global pursuit of low-cost locations and expanding markets.

Data used in this study are not detailed enough to verify the maturity of products produced in rural high-tech branch plants, nor can we ascertain the extent that plants are integrated into a local economy. Nonetheless, given the historically limited skill base of rural residents, we can conclude that plants in rural areas are not manufacturing complex products. More likely, the majority of rural high-tech plants locate to take advantage of low-cost labor. In addition, given the increasingly competitive nature of high-tech products worldwide, rural areas are vulnerable to pressures for automation to further reduce labor costs, and their plants are candidates for shifts to even lower cost locations (Rosenfeld, Malazia, and Dugan 1988). Examining the skill base of rural high-tech industry in one region confirms these statements about the composition of this employment.

Low Expectations and Low Returns:
The Skill Base of Rural High Tech

For the past sixty years, state governments of America's most rural region, the South, have been active recruiters of branch plants. Companies headquartered in the Midwest and Northeast were lured southward by industrial incentives and favorable labor conditions. Economic historian James Cobb (1984) carefully documents the results of these policies and convincingly shows how local and state officials sold out the South on the basis of low wages, docile workers, and lax environmental standards.

High-tech companies have been a major target of these efforts. Under the guise of higher-quality economic development, state officials woo high-tech plants with promises of union-free climates and generous tax incentives. For workers, offers of better jobs and advancement prospects generate community support, often cinching such deals. As early discussion points out, rural communities of the South are a major recipient of these new high-tech production plants, but does this new job base differ significantly from that of the past?

A recent book by sociologists William Falk and Thomas Lyson, aptly titled *High Tech, Low Tech, No Tech* (1988) documents southern rural communities' experience with new high-tech development. Their results are not encouraging. Using a number of different data sources, Falk and Lyson find that high-tech job growth in southern rural counties is not altering the existing industry skill base. Jobs are primarily in low-skilled, blue-collar occupations (Table 4.2). By comparing the high-tech occupational profiles of firms in both metro and nonmetro areas, it is clear that high-tech jobs in rural areas are overwhelmingly low skill. For example, in southern metropolitan areas, 30 percent of jobs in firms of one hundred or more employees are in professional, technical, and managerial occupations. In contrast, only 20 percent of rural high-tech jobs are in these occupations. Furthermore, whereas 31 percent of metropolitan high-tech jobs are unskilled production work, 52 percent of rural high-tech jobs are comprised of low-skilled occupations. As Falk and Lyson suggest, when high-tech plants move into rural areas, they often bring with them only the

TABLE 4.2
Occupational Distributions of High-Technology Industries by County Group

	County Groups			
Occupations	SMSA[1] %	Other Urban %	Rural White %	Black Belt %
Managers and Officials	14.8	11.3	10.2	10.2
Professionals	14.7	7.5	5.1	8.2
Technicians	8.7	4.6	3.8	4.9
Sales	1.9	0.9	0.5	0.6
Office and Clerical	20.6	12.9	9.2	7.6
Craftsmen (Skilled)	16.5	22.9	20.2	14.8
Operatives (Semiskilled)	19.2	34.2	41.8	41.3
Laborers (Unskilled)	2.4	4.4	7.9	10.6
Service Workers	1.2	1.3	1.3	1.8
Total	100.0	100.0	100.0	100.0

Note: 1. SMSA = Standard Metropolitan Statistical Area.

Source: Equal Employment Opportunity Commission, EEO-1 Reports, 1982.

popular designation of "high tech"—not the much-sought high-tech occupational structure.

Smith and Barkley's (1988) study of high-tech firms in the western United States provides some indication of high-tech industry skill levels in other regions. Data from a 321-firm survey show there are skill differences between both high-tech and low-tech plants and between high-tech single-unit firms and branch plants. The survey population consisted of 76 percent single-unit establishments with a size range from five to fifty-two employees. On average, single-unit, high-tech firms employ approximately 11 percent more technical and professional workers than do their nonhigh-tech counterparts. There is also evidence that skill levels are on average 6 percent higher in high-tech, single-unit firms than in high-tech branch plants. As the results of this study indicate, adjacency to metropolitan areas is important in explaining significant high-tech employment levels. The largest establishments are branch plants of multiunit firms located in adjacent rural counties.

These results are somewhat difficult to interpret given that branch plants still provide the majority of rural high-tech employment — confirming product-cycle expectations that the more mature phases of high-tech production are attracted to rural areas. Given the dominance of branch plants, rural communities need to develop a basis to evaluate strengths and weaknesses of individual establishments. Branch plants are not all the same. As the following case study points out, occasionally, a high-tech branch plant can provide more than just low-wage, low-skilled jobs. Over the long run, a branch plant can make positive contributions to a community's skill base and development potential.

Gore and Associates—A Case Study[16]

In 1986, Gore and Associates selected a site for production outside Austin, Texas, in rural Bastrop County. There the company employs about one hundred people with a modest variety of skills to make cable harnesses for the electronics industry.

Selection of the Bastrop site provides additional insight about competitive qualities of rural communities. Bastrop was picked for its bucolic setting, availability of relatively low-cost skilled and unskilled labor (including graduating engineers recruited from the nearby University of Texas), cheap land, and access to a metropolitan area. Industrial incentives, though not decisive, were mentioned by the plant manager as a positive attribute associated with the site. At the time, Austin was one of several hot spots for high-tech development in Texas.[17]

Gore's success in locating in a rural county is related to its product, production process, and market. The product is lightweight and somewhat customized to the final user's needs, and the company's major western market is Dallas. Since materials are received primarily through intracorporate purchases, local inputs are unnecessary. Perhaps most important, product design is stable, so a large cluster of engineers is not required for the operation to run smoothly. Thus, markets can be easily served from Bastrop, where labor of a variety of skills and qualities is readily available.

Also, Gore and Associates uses the services of manufacturing representatives and distributors to sell the product.

Rural skills largely match the firm's requirements, but, more important than skills, workers have a positive work ethic and respond well to Gore's incentive system. The company undertakes significant employee training and offers the equivalent of lifetime employment. Proximity to Austin provides access to a labor pool qualified for general engineering tasks; management is imported from corporate headquarters.

Gore's Bastrop location is an example of enlightened rural high-tech development. Few if any local linkages exist, and the firm operates autonomously in a largely agricultural community. While generally satisfied with the site, the plant manager indicated that the region's high-tech complex is short on management and entrepreneurial skills. He would like to hire locally, but the plant has so far been unsuccessful in developing local managerial talent. Evidently, while a rural community can provide a production work force, it is less successful in generating many highly skilled and experienced employees.

Summary

Distribution of rural high tech among regions—concentrated in the Midwest and South, but almost completely absent in the West—has numerous explanations. First, there were early attempts to decentralize manufacturing, including high tech, in traditional manufacturing regions of the Northeast and, more importantly, the Midwest. Midwestern manufacturing has been decentralizing toward the region's rural counties for some time. While general manufacturing employment levels are high in southern rural counties, the region's relative underrepresentation of high-tech plants indicates it is primarily a production location. This fact, coupled with Falk's and Lyson's (1988) study of high-tech skill levels, indicates that high-tech firms come to the region bearing low-skilled production jobs in search of relatively inexperienced labor pools.

The West, despite its role as the nation's premier new high-tech growth region, contains little *rural* high-tech employment or plants. Companies have obviously chosen among several location options for conducting low-skill production. Firms shift low-skill jobs abroad or between regions (most notably between the West and South) and capital-intensify production processes to reduce their need for low-skilled labor inputs. These alternatives partly explain the poor showing for high tech in western rural areas.

In the aggregate, rural counties' share of manufacturing employment continues to be below its share of the nation's population (20 versus 25 percent). Nevertheless, rural areas *have* added manufacturing jobs over the ten-year period. For example, their share of national manufacturing employment increased from 18 to 20 percent, and over the ten-year period, employment filtering was still occurring, as indicated by a 9 percent increase. This change is particularly significant given that manufacturing declined overall on a national level. Still, rural areas did not receive the lion's share of new manufacturing jobs. On the contrary, rural shares of both population and manufacturing job increases were approximately equal. These figures clearly reflect the end of rural areas' meteoric rise of the 1960s and early 1970s. Although growth in manufacturing employment occurred, it was not out of line with other economic indicators. High-tech job gains in rural counties, while slightly above percentage changes in overall manufacturing employment (12 versus 9 percent), were considerably less than comparable gains in total manufacturing. While rural counties gained 30 percent of the increase in total manufacturing jobs, they received only 12 percent of total high-tech job gains during the same period. Thus, in comparison with both national population and manufacturing shares and with gains in these indicators over the same period, rural high-tech job shares and growth between 1972 and 1982 appear meager. Later analyses, discussed in the following chapters, confirm this trend.

5

Strategic Sectors' Shortcomings Confront Rural Communities

Growth Industries

At an aggregate level, high-tech industries mirror changes under way in the overall organization of the nation's population and economic activity, but what of the truly dynamic or outstanding sectors within high-technology industries? Has location of these industries followed the course of high-tech industries overall, adding to the preexisting base of rural communities, or do these high-growth industries respond to different stimuli?

I will now examine in detail the rapidly expanding rural electronics-related and defense-dependent high-tech sectors. This discussion will then be extended to the individual state level. It is apparent that rural high-tech jobs and plants are concentrated in a distinct minority of states.

The Electronics–Computer Complex

The electronics sectors are the group of dynamic industries regularly referenced in the business press—computers, semiconductors, communications equipment, and electronics components. These four industries added almost half of all new high-tech jobs created (580,000) over the ten-year study period (Table 5.1). The recent rapid growth of the electronics industry is attributable to a number of factors. Among these, commercial application of products is perhaps the most important, and semiconductors are the most obvi-

TABLE 5.1
Top Four High-Tech Industry Job Generators
1972–1982

| | Total National Employment | | Percentage Change 1972–1982 |
	1972	1982	
Computers 3573	144,661	348,821	141
Communications Equipment 3662	317,556	491,821	60
Semiconductors 3674	97,389	184,019	89
Miscellaneous Electronic Components 3679	98,340	226,362	130
Absolute Difference	593,077		
Percent of Total National High-Tech Job Gains 1972–1982	49%		

Source: Bureau of the Census, 1986, *Census of Manufactures, Plant Location Tape* (1972 and 1982).

ous case. Semiconductors consist of two types of products—discrete devices that perform only one function and integrated circuits performing multiple functions. Increases in industry output since the 1960s are due to developments in integrated circuitry. In the 1950s, integrated circuits contained fewer than ten discrete devices. By the late 1960s, chip computational capacity had increased one hundredfold. Since then, capacity has doubled every two years. Sheer volume of chips available helps boost demand, but a far more important factor is the delivery of chips at constantly decreasing prices per unit of computing power. With each new generation of chips, prices fell as firms advanced along the learning curve and improved manufacturing. Succeeding generations were not just more powerful, they were also cheaper. A "bit" of memory (one piece of stored information) fell from 1/10 to 1/1,000 of a cent between 1973 and 1986.

As chips became more powerful, they found wider application in a multitude of industries and products. Prior to the late 1960s, the majority of semiconductor output was used in military applications. Demand for semiconductors was modest but stable, and prices for products were high. With the advent of the microprocessor and its commercial application in other industries, demand increased exponentially. Over the period studied, products such as semiconductors and computers gained wide acceptance in both American and worldwide markets. Because these industries are highly interconnected, growth in one industry influences growth in other related electronics industries. This characteristic also partly explains CEC industries' rapid expansion. Growth of the computer and communications industries was made possible by advances in semiconductor design. Smaller and more powerful chips allowed computers to shrink in size while expanding in power. In turn, computers facilitated increased yield for semiconductor production. By allowing chip producers to automate production, computers increased yield and decreased per-unit production costs. As costs of semiconductor and computer industry products fell, more industries made use of the new devices, and as the use of computers and semiconductors penetrated other *non*electronic industries, such as autos, scientific instruments, and machinery, demand for these products also increased. Today the automobile industry is the single largest consumer of semiconductors in the country. In all cases, further innovation required heightened levels of electronic componentry. Thus, expansion in the four industries had a snowball effect. Increasing demand for one sector's output produced positive and reinforcing levels of demand for other high-tech products. As demand for microelectronic components and computers increased, production became more standardized. Products of these four high-growth industries entered an expansion phase accompanied by spatial decentralization of employment and plants over the 1972–82 period.

The Defense Connection: Military-Dependent Sectors

A second subset of high-tech industries is tied to national defense expenditures. Over the postwar period, the DOD has functioned in a dual capacity as sponsor of high-tech research and product development and as provider of a critical and protected market for high-tech products. Perhaps there is no better example than the DOD's influence on the semiconductor industry. After World War II, national armaments policy moved strongly toward a missile defense system. This required considerable miniaturization of electronic components, and the development of semiconductors was the logical outgrowth. So in the early years, the DOD provided R and D funding to generate these miniaturization capabilities. Once the product could be successfully manufactured, the DOD acted as a captive market for the new output. Importantly, the DOD deviated from past policy of funding only large defense contractors and purposely split the market to support the development of numerous firms with sufficient production capacity (Saxenian 1981). Even today, the DOD performs this dual role. For example, the department both funds the majority of research on artificial intelligence and is the primary market for computer systems using the innovation (*New York Times*, March 5, 1989).

Defense dependency has both positive and negative effects on domestic high-tech industry. Government involvement in R and D reduces private firms' costs of high-risk research. Companies might otherwise retreat from product areas where high cost, long lead times, and considerable uncertainty are evident. Yet some critics argue that defense expenditures siphon off personnel from new product development efforts in consumer goods. The defense connection also orients high-tech company research toward areas that may have limited commercial application.

The DOD was a critical market during the initial development of many high-tech industries. It continues to play a major role in high-tech industry growth by supporting selected R and D (Borrus 1988). DOD R and D spending translates into new product development and protected markets for specific high-tech products. Of the ninety-four high-tech industries studied, only a few are primarily dependent on federal defense spending. Seven high-tech sectors sell more than 20 percent of total output to the DOD (see

Henry 1983 for the method used to identify these sectors). These industries include aircraft, aircraft engines, missiles, space vehicles, space vehicle parts and equipment, and scientific and professional instruments.[18] Six of the seven defense-dependent sectors gained new jobs (Table 5.2). I examined defense-dependent industries separately because their geographic location is at least somewhat responsive to national policymaking. There have also occasionally been federal efforts to relocate defense production from the previously concentrated Northeast. As part of this analysis, I will address

TABLE 5.2

Employment Growth in Defense-Dependent Sectors
1972, 1977, 1982

Industry	1972	1977	1982	% Change 72–77	% Change 77–82
Aircraft 3721	231,919	220,800	264,295	–3.9	18.6
Aircraft Engines 3724	99,563	106,200	134,530	11.1	26.7
Aircraft Parts and Equipment 3728	102,414	101,934	137,201	–0.5	34.6
Guided Missiles Space Vehicles 3761	118,309	93,929	112,417	–20.6	19.7
Tanks 3795	5,319	12,120	16,753	127.0	38.0
Scientific Instruments 3811	36,482	42,197	47,448	15.7	12.4
Optical Instruments and Lenses 3832	19,637	29,906	53,348	24.0	78.4

Source: Bureau of the Census, 1986, *Census of Manufactures, Plant Location Tape* (1972, 1977, 1982).

how successful decentralization has actually been since the early
1970s, but first we return to the experience of CEC industries in
rural areas.

Computer, Electronics, and
Communications Industries (CEC)

In 1972, approximately 42,000 jobs in four key high-tech industries
(computers, electronic components, semiconductors, and communication equipment) were found in rural counties. Of these jobs,
approximately one-fourth were in nonadjacent rural counties.
Plants were more evenly distributed between adjacent and nonadjacent counties. Of the 279 rural plants, 37 percent were located in
nonadjacent counties. By 1982, rural counties had gained approximately 25,000 jobs, and new plants increased by 344 for the four
industries. Both employment and plants became more evenly distributed between adjacent and nonadjacent counties, with 34 percent of employment and 41 percent of plants in nonadjacent counties (Figure E).

During the period studied, growth in rural plants and employment in the CEC sectors exceeded growth in CEC sectors in the
nation. Employment between 1972 and 1982 increased by 59 percent, and plants increased by 123 percent. Growth rates were
highest in nonadjacent counties. This result is not surprising given
that the more remote locations began the period with small
numbers of high-tech jobs and plants. As noted earlier, in rural
areas, a small absolute change represents a substantial percentage
change. However, this development obscures a number of important facts about distribution of the CEC industries. First, rural
shares of CEC employment declined over the ten-year period, from
6.0 to 5.3 percent, and plant shares increased by just 1 percent.
Second, the rate of change in urban-adjacent county employment
was also below the national level. Third, and perhaps more important, changes in shares of national rural employment and plants
were substantially below population change over the same period.

The composition of rural plant and employment growth was
weighted toward less technical industries. At a national level, CEC

FIGURE E

Share of Employment and Plants in the Computer Electronics and
Communications Industries Within
Adjacent and Nonadjacent Rural Counties
1972 and 1982

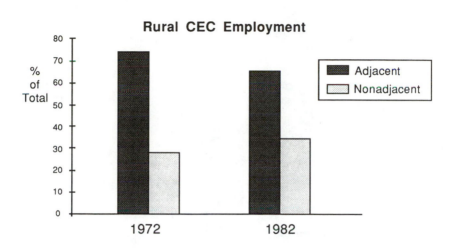

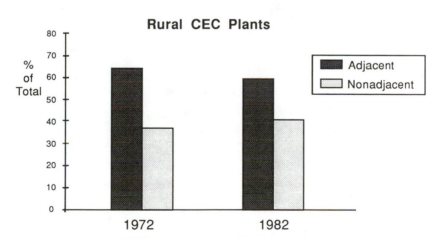

Source: Bureau of the Census, 1986, *Census of Manufactures, Plant Location Tape* (1972, 1982).

FIGURE F

The Share of Total High-Tech Plants and Employment Growth
Accounted for by the Computer Electronics Communications (CEC)
Sector for the Nation and Rural Counties
1982

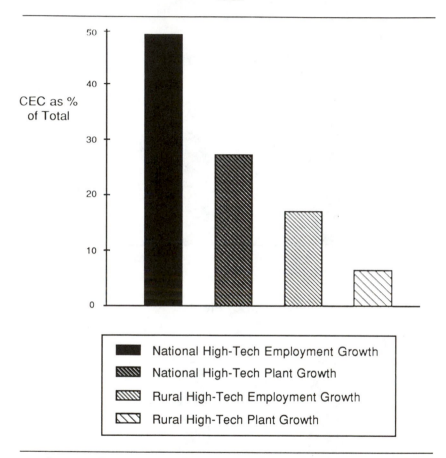

Source: Bureau of the Census, 1986, *Census of Manufactures, Plant
Location Tape* (1982).

industries accounted for 49 percent of employment growth and 27
percent of plant change. Comparable figures for rural areas were
substantially less — 17 and 6 percent, respectively (Figure F). Moreover, in 1982, CEC sectors constituted 22 percent of total high-tech
employment. For rural counties, the comparable figure was only 9
percent.

Where the Chips Fall in America's Rural Communities

Employment in the CEC complex is highly concentrated in the West. Forty percent of national CEC employment and plants are located here, and this concentration has only increased with time. The Northeast, in comparison, contains 27 percent of the U.S. employment and plants in CEC sectors. The residual is shared between the South and Midwest, which have 21 and 12 percent of the nation's CEC sector employment and plants, respectively.

However, the proportion of CEC industries within the rural areas of the four regions is quite low. For example, the Midwest has the highest proportion of rural CEC employment and plants (15 percent), followed by the South with 7 percent and the Northeast with 6 percent. The West's insignificant share of CEC industry employment in rural areas (1.3 percent) suggests that distinct components of these industries are distributed differentially among regions. Management and R and D activities largely occur within metropolitan areas in the West and Northeast. Production branch plants locate in rural adjacent communities of the Midwest and the South. (Figure G identifies states in which the ratio of CEC employment to rural population is greater than the national ratio.) To the extent that there has been region-based decentralization, corporations headquartered in the Midwest and Northeast have shifted lower-skilled jobs into their own rural hinterlands and higher-skilled and lower-skilled jobs and branch plants to the South.

Data analyzed here do not allow confirmation of specific shifts. For this, it would be necessary to track individual company relocation decisions over time. However, other researchers, using data on enterprises, do show that southern high-tech employment consists primarily of branch plants of companies headquartered in the Midwest and Northeast (Armington, Harris, and Odle 1983; Malecki 1985). Anecdotal evidence also substantiates branch plant shifts from companies headquartered in the West. These represent largely intermetropolitan relocations, as opposed to shifts from metropolitan to nonmetropolitan areas.

Still, branch plant attraction is not the only viable means for rural communities to capture some of the fruits of high-tech development. Occasionally, rural communities add jobs and plants in the rapidly growing computer and electronics sectors through nurturance of homegrown firms. Barkley's (1988) work on high-

FIGURE G

Location Quotients (LQs) of Computer–Electronics–Communication Employment
in Rural Counties by States Within Census Regions, 1982

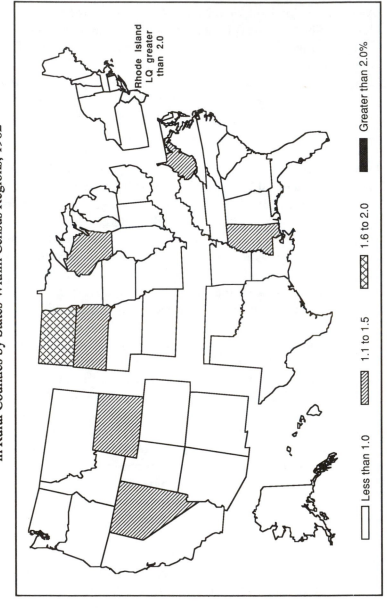

tech firms in the rural West documents such a development. Existing state high-tech development incentives are not designed to help these operations, yet they may provide the most viable means of future high-tech development for rural communities. Such experiences are important teachers because most rural communities cannot hope to attract high-tech branch plants, nor should they necessarily want to.

The Military-Industrial Complex: Rural High-Tech Defense-Dependent Sectors (DDS)

In 1982, rural counties held 56,800 jobs and 296 plants in DDS sectors (Table 5.3). The ratio of DDS employment to total high tech remained essentially constant at both the national level and within rural areas, and like the nation's, rural areas' *share* of DDS employment remained essentially constant between 1972 and 1982 (6 to 7 percent). Rural shares of DDS plants were lower, 3.6 and 4.1 percent for the same two years, respectively.

Over the ten-year period, both DDS rural employment and plants grew rapidly. Employment increased by 50 percent and plants by 63 percent. This constituted 12 percent of the total rural high-tech employment change and 21 percent of total rural high-tech plant change, but it is important to remember that DDS represents only 7 percent of rural high-tech employment (56,800 jobs), as compared with the nation's 14 percent (Figure H).

Like high-tech employment in general, DDS high tech is concentrated in rural adjacent counties. In 1982, 78 percent of rural

TABLE 5.3
Defense-Dependent Sector Employment and Plant Change
in Rural Counties, 1972–1982

	1972	*1982*	*Percent Change*
Employment	37,892	56,825	50
Plants	182	296	63

Source: Bureau of the Census, 1986, *Census of Manufactures, Plant Location Tape* (1972 and 1982).

FIGURE H

The Share of Defense-Dependent Employment to Total National,
Metro, and Rural High-Tech Employment
1982

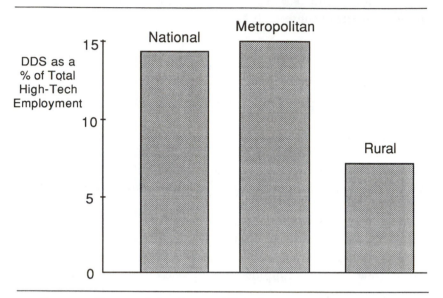

Source: Bureau of the Census, 1986, *Census of Manufactures, Plant Location Tape* (1982).

DDS employment was in these adjacent counties. Conversely, DDS plants were more evenly spread among adjacent and nonadjacent counties. In the same year, 42 percent of rural DDS plants were in nonadjacent counties. Nonetheless, compared with other high-tech manufacturing, rural counties generally perform poorly in attracting defense-dependent sectors.

A regional examination of DDS reveals a highly skewed pattern in which 36 percent of the nation's total employment is concentrated in the western United States. The Northeast is a distant second in terms of national share (24 percent). The Midwest and South have levels far below their shares of total high-tech employment (19 and 21 percent, respectively).

On the other hand, regional shares of total rural DDS employment run counter to the aggregate regional distribution (Figures I and J). The Northeast and South each contain 41 percent of DDS

FIGURE I

Regional Shares of Total DDS Employment and Rural DDS Employment*
1982

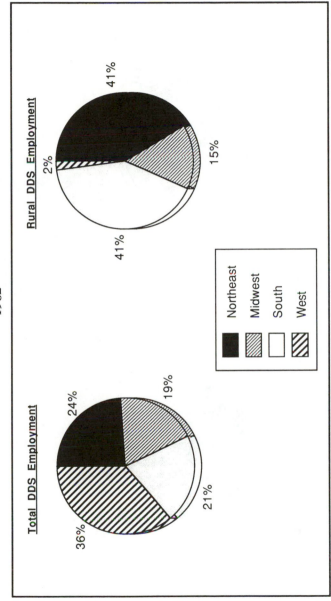

Total DDS Employment

24%
36%
19%
21%

Rural DDS Employment

2%
41%
41%
15%

Northeast
Midwest
South
West

Note: * May not add to 100% due to rounding errors.
Source: Bureau of the Census, 1986, *Census of Manufactures, Plant Location Tape* (1982).

FIGURE J

Regional Shares of Total DDS Plants and Rural DDS Plants*
1982

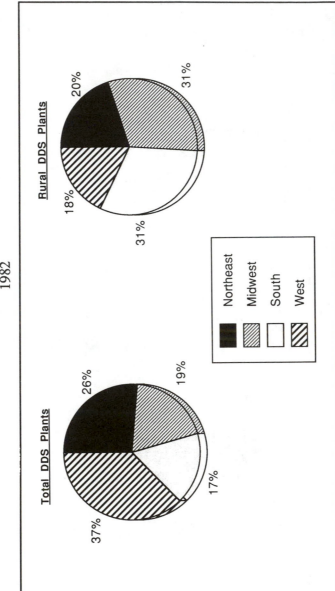

Note: * May not add to 100% due to rounding errors.
Source: Bureau of the Census, 1986, *Census of Manufactures, Plant Location Tape* (1982).

rural employment. The Midwest has a much smaller share, 15 percent, and the West an insignificant 2 percent. Given the concentration of these industries in the western United States, this result is surprising. The divergence—one indication of major regional differences—merits comment.

The West has long been a center of strategic R and D. DDS employment in the region is more likely to be technical in nature compared with that of the Midwest or South. In contrast, the South contains more mature and mundane aspects of DDS employment, a point made by other authors (Schlessinger, Gaventa, and Merrifield 1983). With a few exceptions, such as aircraft production in Georgia and Texas and missile assembly in Alabama, defense-dependent production in the South primarily consists of routine equipment assembly.

Regardless of the regional distribution of rural DDS employment, no more than 15 percent of total regional DDS employment is located in the rural areas of any one region. That is, in all four regions, defense-dependent high-tech industries are a largely metropolitan phenomenon. For example, the Midwest and West each have less than 6 percent of their total DDS employment in rural areas, and the Northeast and South have approximately 15 percent each. So it is unlikely that rural communities can count on this source of employment to offset losses in traditional rural industries. (Figure K identifies states in which the ratio of defense-dependent employment to rural population is greater than that at the national level.)

During World War II and the later Korean conflict, legislative efforts were designed to shift certain components of defense production from concentrations in the Northeast. Cities such as Dallas, Tucson, and Denver received such plants (Campbell 1989). A number of the nation's defense laboratories are also located in largely rural regions of the South and West. For the most part, this development has created enclaves of highly technical workers around which communities have grown up, yet rural areas of states like New Mexico, which has a large concentration of defense weapons labs, have only marginally benefited (if at all) from this type of development.

Despite national policies to decentralize defense-dependent employment and plants throughout the country, rural communities

FIGURE K

Location Quotients (LQs) of Defense-Dependent Sector Employment in Rural Counties by States Within Census Regions, 1982

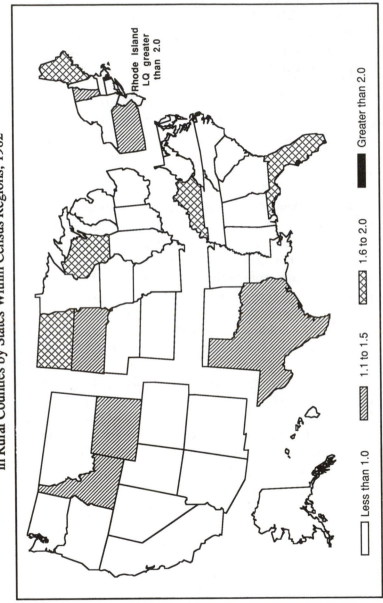

appear to have benefited little. Given that these sectors (at least theoretically) are more amenable to political debate and pork-barrel procedures in Congress, it is particularly surprising that rural areas have gained such a small percentage of the employment and plants in DDS industries.

The uneven distribution of rural defense-dependent high-tech relates to the composition of national defense spending and the long-standing structure of regional military complexes. Defense production is highly urban. Defense-dependent production found in rural America contrasts starkly with the aerospace complex of California and the strategic planning complex of Massachusetts.

Rural DDS industry represents the dirty, least technical aspects of these sectors. The majority of hardware purchased from firms with plants in rural parts of the country consists of mass-produced munitions. Rural plants are heavily concentrated across the South. These plants manufacture products from ammunition boxes to more pernicious materials, such as cancer-causing explosives.

For large parts of rural America, defense spending has been a cruel joke. Most plants produce aging products with outdated equipment (Schlessinger, Gaventa, and Merrifield 1983). Many munitions facilities were explicitly planted in the rural South by the War Industry Board, a New Deal agency, because they were producing dangerous bomb components. Thus, plant location required large open areas and limited population concentrations. Military arsenal plants found convenient homes in many southern rural communities (and, to a lesser extent, in the Midwest).

The federal government and the DOD have not always been good neighbors. Rural communities hosting defense munitions plants have serious pollution problems only now becoming obvious. Defense weapons installations in the South claim the dubious distinction of harboring 17 percent of Superfund sites recently identified by the Environmental Protection Agency. As these facilities are often run by private contractors, health and safety issues may take a backseat to production and profit mandates. In a detailed study of defense spending in the upper South, researchers document the wanton disregard for human life demonstrated by military contractors (Schlessinger, Gaventa, and Merrifield 1983). As they sadly noted, "Aerojet General expands into rural east Tennessee because of the state's reputation for lax regulation and job-hungry hillbillies." Perhaps rural communities should simply be grateful they receive so little of this DOD high-tech employment.

The intimate link between high-tech industry growth and defense spending cannot be denied, but the result does not always have to be negative. An alternative can be seen in the case of State of the Art, Inc., a small capacitor company located in State College, Pennsylvania. The case study of this rural Pennsylvania firm, whose market is in part the federal government's space program, points out the strengths of combining local entrepreneurship with benefits of high technology. It underscores the point that branch plants are not the only alternative for rural high-tech development. As noted by Barkley, Dahlgran, and Smith (1988), Barkley, Smith, and Coupal (1990), and Smith and Barkley (1988), the existence of entrepreneurial ventures provides at least some indication that policies enveloping more than simple branch location assistance may be important to the future success of high-tech industries in rural areas.

State of the Art, Inc.—A Case Study

State College, Pennsylvania, home of the Nittany Lions and Pennsylvania State University (PSU), is the economic focal point of rural Centre County. Although the county experienced rapid growth between 1970 and 1980, it is still quite rural. Nevertheless, because State College is a university town, there are a number of qualities that make the community particularly appropriate for high-tech development. The level of social and cultural amenities is high, the population is well-educated, and the university has a number of programs that lend themselves to discovering technologies that are adaptable to commercial use. PSU has also helped create the context for new firm creation, and, with limited results, a few high-tech firms have developed. Completely separate from the university's influence is one firm that is by any measure an unqualified high-tech success story. The following discussion briefly recounts the history of State of the Art, Inc., a small high-tech company that produces capacitors for the electronics and satellite industries.

State of the Art, Inc. (SAI) was established by Don Hamer, a former employee of Erie-Murata, a large capacitor producer in Erie, Pennsylvania. In 1980, Hamer left the company and moved to State College, where he work for five years as a salesman and technical consultant to Murata customers. By then, he had identified a market niche (variable-size batch production capacitors) unfilled by the big capacitor producers, so he set up production in State College. SAI started out quite modestly, with fewer than twenty employees. Hamer understood the market for capacitors and chose to compete in both the commodity end and the higher-value-added end of military products. Within four years, the flourishing company had become the nation's second largest capacitor producer (on a volume basis). When interviewed in 1986, SAI had one hundred employees (largely local high school graduates and individuals with less than a full four-year college degree) and utilized sophisticated production equipment. The growth of SAI has been steady and solid. Even during a period of industry downturn, the company avoided layoffs. Production was built up carefully—as the firm grew, it wisely invested in new technology—and throughout company development, decisions were made to automate and upgrade workers' skills rather than maintain a labor-intensive production posture, the least costly direction in the short run.

To the extent that geography matters, SAI's success can be partly attributed to locating in a community in which education is highly valued. Local elementary and high schools provide a solid education. Thus, even noncollege-bound students are prepared for success in industry.

Locational isolation is not a problem for SAI because the capacitor product has both national and international markets. Individual units are small and lightweight, easily shipped to customers by overnight delivery. Customer satisfaction and competitive edge revolve around providing quantities ranging from 100 to 100,000. Therefore, the company's success rests not with an extraordinarily technological product per se (though the product is highly sophisticated and meets stringent and exacting DOD standards) but on its ability to supply a wide variety of customer demands that large firms have overlooked.

An important factor in SAI's success, given its isolated location, is the role of distributors and manufacturers' representatives. SAI has only a limited internal sales force and uses sales representatives and distributors to market the product. These individuals and organizations vastly extend the reach of SAI, making a rural location not only possible but profitable.

By being flexible on the market side, SAI continues to gain new customers, but perhaps the overriding factor in the company's success is Don Hamer, the owner, who is innovative, who recognizes that the cheapest way—employing labor-intensive processes—is not always the best way, and who chooses instead to continually upgrade his work force and production equipment as the company grows.

Summary

Glamorous, rapidly growing high-tech industries are meekly known in rural communities. Even being a rural community in a dominant high-tech region does not guarantee receipt of this job source. The West stands out based on its lack of rural high tech. In this sense, high-tech industry behaves much like traditional manufacturing industry, which expands to take advantage of low-wage labor and attractive business climates. Government policy over the postwar period has not appreciably benefited rural communities. Although occasional enclaves of high-tech activity exist in rural areas, these prove the exception to the rule, and such gains have precipitated little secondary development aside from economic activity associated with the high incomes paid to technical workers. In many instances, brain trusts such as Oak Ridge National Laboratory and Sandia National Laboratories have a darker side. Defense weapons production facilities are notorious sites of pollution and lax worker safety regulations. Rural communities do have options, however, that importantly include local entrepreneurship. Although the example cited is somewhat unique (dependent on local levels of amenities and serendipity), still it cannot be discounted. As later discussion of policy will show, funding for this type of development is minimal, and existing high-tech policy is not oriented to encourage it. Thus, rural communities must mobilize local leaders to get their share of the high-tech pie.

6

Unmasking High-Tech Location

Rural High-Tech Jobs, Individual States

In earlier analysis, we have seen that rural high-tech location and change have been similar to larger national developments, but to stop at this would obscure the highly concentrated nature of high-tech location within the United States. Armed with only a regional view, policymakers might erroneously conclude that rural areas within *any* region have an equal chance (or an equally slim chance) of attracting high-tech industries. But by turning to the state level, the really quite specialized location of these industries is apparent.

States

Many of the states with the largest concentrations of high-tech jobs are located in the nation's traditional manufacturing regions. Northeastern and midwestern states account for ten of the fourteen states with the largest concentrations of total high-tech plants and employment (Table 6.1). In 1982, these fourteen states were collectively responsible for 73 percent of total high-tech employment.

The spatial concentration of high-tech employment is even more powerfully manifest in the proportion of both total and manufacturing employment accounted for by these states. Altogether, though comprising three-quarters of all high-tech employment, the fourteen states contain 68 percent of all manufacturing employment and only 64 percent of all nonagricultural jobs. Thus,

TABLE 6.1

Estimated Employment in
High-Technology Industry
1982

States	1982 High-Tech Employment	Percent of Total Manufacturing Employment	Percent of Total Nonagricultural Employment
California	907,512[1]	11[2]	11[2]
Texas	400,276	6	7
New York	366,761	7	8
Illinois	327,096	6	5
Pennsylvania	312,280	6	5
Ohio	284,773	6	5
New Jersey	257,230	4	3
Massachusetts	241,295	3	3
Florida	174,265	2	4
Michigan	173,011	5	4
Connecticut	172,790	2	2
Indiana	138,885	3	2
Wisconsin	125,566	3	2
North Carolina	123,844	4	3
Percent of National Total	73%	68%	64%

Sources: 1. Computed from employment estimates of high-tech jobs using
the *Census of Manufactures Plant Location Tape*, 1982; and
2. Bureau of the Census, 1986, *State and Metropolitan Data Book*,
Washington, DC.

the importance of traditional manufacturing states as centers of
high-tech employment is certain.

States that comprised the largest portion of total national
high-tech employment remained surprisingly constant over the
ten-year study period. While there was some repositioning, the
states that were centers of high-tech manufacturing in 1972 were
still prominent in 1982.

Rural High Tech

Using a broad definition of high tech, each of twenty states has 2
percent or more of the nation's rural high-tech employment. Ten
states in the South and eight in the Midwest make up a majority in

the group (Figures L and M). In fact, only three midwestern states (Indiana, Illinois, and Ohio) account for 16 percent of rural high-tech manufacturing. This strong showing no doubt reflects the Midwest's dominance in auto electronics. Independent auto electronics companies and subsidiaries of the Big Three auto assemblers, Ford, GM, and Chrysler, also remain large production plants within the region. The remaining five midwestern states make up an additional 31 percent. Another ten southern states account for 35 percent of total rural high tech. Clearly, using our broad definition of high tech, the dual pattern of decentralization—from Midwest metro to nonmetro areas, secondarily to the South, and interregional shifts of jobs from the Northeast and Midwest to the South—is apparent.

DDS and CEC Rural Employment, State View

Definitions of high tech that are restricted to the dynamic DDS and CEC industries reveal a far more concentrated pattern of rural high-tech employment distribution. Ten states account for 73 percent of DDS rural employment (Figure N). Of these, Texas, Florida, Rhode Island, Maine, Vermont, Georgia, and Pennsylvania make up 63 percent, and although midwestern states are modestly more represented in this group (numerically), their share of total rural DDS is much less significant (10.6 percent). This mirrors low levels of DDS in the Midwest, and despite the West's clear dominance in overall shares of DDS employment and plants, not one western state contains more than 2 percent of the nation's rural DDS employment.

The absence of high-tech defense production in the Midwest is a subject of some controversy. Various authors contend that a conservative business climate and the burgeoning postwar demand for consumer goods mitigated against firms remaining or entering markets for military products (Markusen and McCurdy 1988). Although companies such as Motorola, a major military electronics supplier and the world's fifth largest semiconductor producer, are headquartered in the Midwest (for Motorola in Schaumsburg, Illinois), postwar plant locations shifted electronics production out of the region. In 1949, Motorola set up its early major transistor research and production laboratory in Phoenix, Arizona. This facility now serves as Motorola's semiconductor division headquarters.

FIGURE L

States' Share of National Rural High-Tech Employment
1982

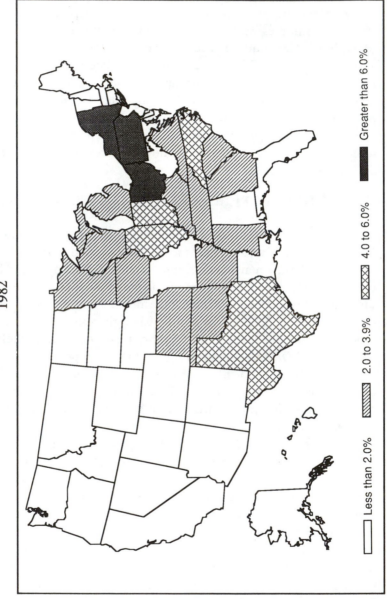

Less than 2.0%   2.0 to 3.9%   4.0 to 6.0%   Greater than 6.0%

FIGURE M

States' Share of National Rural High-Tech Plants
1982

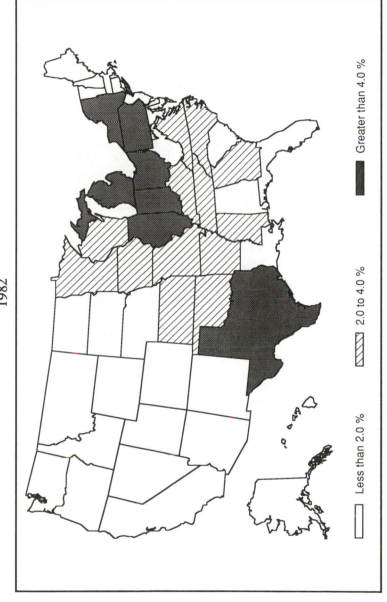

Less than 2.0 %　　2.0 to 4.0 %　　Greater than 4.0 %

FIGURE N

States' Share of Rural Defense-Dependent Sector Employment
1982

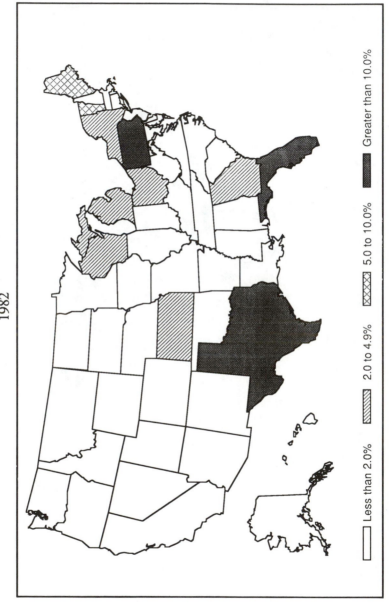

Less than 2.0%   2.0 to 4.9%   5.0 to 10.0%   Greater than 10.0%

Other explanations account for the lack of defense plants and employment in the rural West. The geographic definition of urban and rural areas may conceal the early location of defense plants in areas now considered urban but that were formerly rural (for example, Aerojet's missile propulsion plant outside Sacramento, California). More probable, however, are restrictions associated with the technical nature of defense products manufactured in the region and the availability of large tracts of land within commuting range of the region's largest and most defense-dependent city — Los Angeles. Also important are ties between defense contractors and military establishments. The city of San Diego boasts the nation's second largest naval installation, and many aerospace contractors locate nearby to support base functions. Defense companies literally grew up in conjunction with expansion of naval facilities since World War II.

DDS plant shares are more widely distributed than is employment. Sixteen states account for 59 percent of rural defense-dependent plants (Figure O). As expected, states in the Midwest, Northeast, and South dominate this group. In contrast with employment, three western states, Oregon, Washington, and California, account for 6 percent of the nation's rural DDS plants. Washington's showing no doubt reflects location decisions of one corporation — Boeing Aircraft.

The group of CEC sector industries suggests concentrated distribution of rural manufacturing in northeastern and midwestern states. Sixteen states account for 76 percent of rural CEC employment. Twenty-eight percent of the nation's rural manufacturing in CEC sectors is concentrated in northeastern states (Figure P). New York alone has 11 percent of the nation's total rural CEC employment. Midwestern states comprise 25 percent of all CEC rural manufacturing, half in one state alone (Minnesota). Three southern states account for 15 percent of the nation's rural CEC plants; almost 9 percent of these plants are concentrated in Virginia. Only one western state contains more than 2 percent (Figure Q). California, with 36 percent of the nation's total CEC plants, has only 3.3 percent of the existing *rural* CEC plants.

This highly skewed distribution can be partly attributed to the influence of individual companies. In New York, IBM has long had a policy of locating plants in areas adjacent to metropolitan

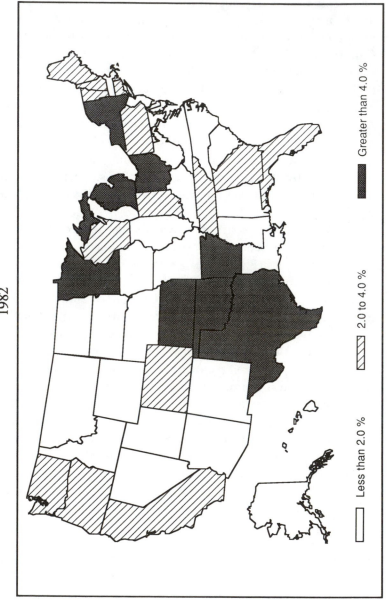

FIGURE O

States' Share of Rural Defense-Dependent Sector Plants

1982

Less than 2.0 %

2.0 to 4.0 %

Greater than 4.0 %

FIGURE P

States' Share of Rural Computer Electronics and Communications Sector Employment
1982

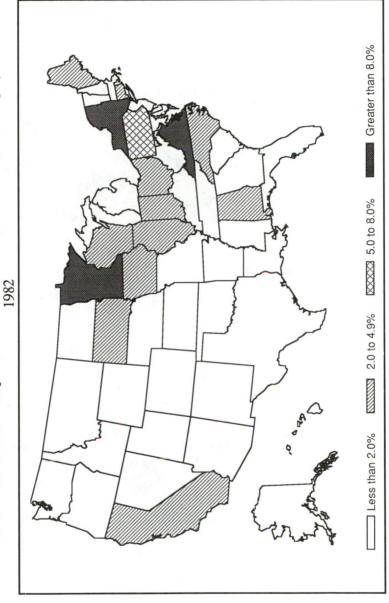

Less than 2.0%   2.0 to 4.9%   5.0 to 8.0%   Greater than 8.0%

FIGURE Q

States' Share of Rural Computer Electronics and Communications Sector Plants

1982

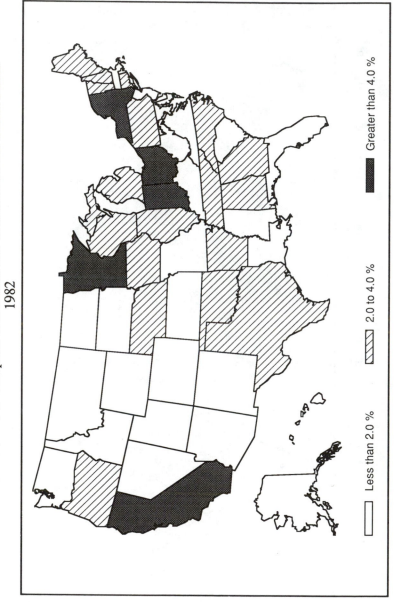

Less than 2.0 %   2.0 to 4.0 %   Greater than 4.0 %

centers. Minnesota's Control Data Corporation has a similar locational policy, placing plants in rural adjacent counties. As mentioned earlier, a company such as AMP explicitly followed a policy of locating production plants in small rural communities in Pennsylvania. The concentration of CEC employment in Virginia no doubt relates to the state's proximity to Washington, D.C., and its significant concentration of ammunition production plants.

Clearly, rural CEC employment and plants are not distributed randomly. In fact, this pattern suggests that existing policies to spread CEC employment more evenly across the nation have had little influence in the past and hold small chance of success in the future. Rural CEC location is tied either to unique circumstances of individual corporate decisions or to federal contractor installations. Both conditions are outside the domain of local policy.

Are there efforts local policymakers could undertake to attract employment in CEC sectors? It seems doubtful that many rural communities have the prerequisites to snare a high-tech CEC firm. However, communities can encourage local entrepreneurs such as Don Hamer of State of the Art, Inc. Support of local entrepreneurs and existing manufacturing may produce greater returns, resulting in employment growth and a stronger base for further development.

State Policies, Rural Realities:
High-Tech Development Policies

State governments are active participants in programs encouraging the formation and growth of high-tech industries. Almost every state has some type of high-tech program (Clarke 1986; Shapira 1989). Few, though, have high-tech development programs either targeted or applicable for rural economic development. In fact, as this analysis will suggest, state programs are normally biased *against* rural communities. If state-level programs are to address problems of rural economies, then they need to be significantly restructured to pay greater attention to improving the competitive position of *existing* rural industries. These provide the necessary foundation for further high-tech development in rural communities. The following section reviews state programs and identifies components of high-tech economic development efforts applicable for rural community development.

The information presented is based on a mail survey of state high-technology industry development programs. Responses to the survey were received from thirty states (see Table 6.2 for a condensed review of these programs).

Existing Programs

State technology programs generally serve to strengthen the existing technological infrastructure in three broad areas—education, research, and industrial facilities. More narrowly, programs are designed to further the development of existing high-technology industry and to integrate new technologies into existing industries (Plosila 1987; Rees 1987).

Development programs fall (according to emphasis) into seven categories:

Policy Development: Cultivating a plan to encourage technology-based industries to locate in an area.

Education and Training: Improving local educational facilities to prepare employees for technology-based jobs and to serve as centers of research.

Research and Development: Investing in either university-based or independent R and D facilities.

Entrepreneurship Training and Assistance: Developing local businesses through education or subsidization of their enterprise.

Assistance to Specific Firms: Investing in firms with desired qualities to encourage their location in the local community.

Technology and Information Transfer: Facilitating transfer of basic research techniques and information to the industrial arena so that it can be applied to production.

Research Parks and Incubator Facilities: Sponsoring industrial research parks and/or operating subsidized facilities to support businesses in their embryonic stages of growth. Creating an atmosphere attractive to technology-based firms.

TABLE 6.2

State High-Tech Development Programs

State	High-Tech Emphasis			Rural Emphasis		
	Policy	*Programs*	*Non-HT*	*HT Rural*	*HT Nonrural*	*Rural Non-HT*
CA		X			X	
GA		X			X	
HI		X			X	
ID			X			X
IL	X					X
IN		X			X	
LA	X					X
ME		X		X^1		
MD			X			
MA		X		X		
MI	X					
MN	X			X^1		
MO	X					X
MT	X					
NE	X					
NJ	X			X^1		
NY		X				
NC	X					X^2
ND	X				X	
OH	X				X	
OR	X				X	
PA			X		X	
PR	X			$X^{1,3}$		
TN			X			X
TX		X				X
VA			X			X^4
VT	X					X^4
WA			X			X^5
WV			X		X	
WI			X		X	

Notes: 1. Maine, Minnesota, New Jersey, and Puerto Rico have special programs to apply new technologies to agricultural and/or fishing or other nonurban industries.
2. North Carolina targets programs to "distressed counties"; programs are not necessarily rural or high tech in emphasis.
3. Puerto Rico also targets "high unemployment" areas, but programs have an agricultural versus high-tech emphasis.
4. Vermont and Virginia each have rural job development programs, but the programs are not high tech in emphasis.
5. The Washington State Legislature has directed the Community Development Agency to undertake a study of the feasibility of "office-intensive" industry in rural counties.

Survey Results

Most state funding for technology industry formation supports university-based research and new firm development. According to one estimate, in 1988, states spent almost half of allocated funds ($550 million) on advanced technology and research centers and an additional $150 million on research grants (Shapira 1989). Only a very small portion (less than 10 percent) of all funds went to upgrade existing manufacturing operations. Some critics argue that funds allocated to high-tech development represent little in the way of new resources. Most states are simply highlighting program funding that had been previously carried out under a variety of agencies and program titles. Others contend that even this effort represents significant potential payoffs as states rationalize existing programs and make easier identification of available resources for potential users.

While they may possess common objectives (such as encouraging high-tech development), programs differ in how they pursue goals. Some programs are designed to achieve long-range goals; others are of a more immediate nature (Rees 1987). In other words, program elements might seem similar, but their outcomes could be at odds. For example, shoring up areas that are experiencing a decline in manufacturing may have the unanticipated effect of further skewing economic development toward urban areas. Thus, programs designed to achieve short-run development goals may in fact be detrimental to rural areas' long-term economic viability.

The most common type of high-technology industry program consists of technology councils set up within state governors' offices, but the other six program areas were also found operating in a large number of states (see Clarke 1986 for a complete survey). Most programs currently receive only modest financial support through state governors' offices (Merrill 1984). Therefore, their success is significantly circumscribed by the availability of resources.

There is evidence that suggests other programs would prove beneficial for rural economic development. Recently created programs providing technical assistance to existing firms through industrial extension services are a case in point. Modeled on the agricultural extension service, these programs target existing small and medium-size firms and assist them in implementing new technologies in production facilities (see Shapira 1989 for a review of these programs).

Education and training, entrepreneurial training, and technology transfer programs hold significant potential for rural communities. However, important problems of rural economies place serious limitations on communities' ability to compete for inclusion in technology development programs (Rosenfeld 1987). Small and scattered rural communities lack necessary infrastructure and human capital resources. Case studies of successful plant attraction in rural southern communities note a major impediment is the low average level of education. Existing economic development policies emphasize low-wage, low-skill attributes of rural areas, further inhibiting their ability to attract more advanced manufacturing.

The costs of making rural communities competitive are particularly high. Case studies of new and expanding firms located in the rural South suggest just how expensive such efforts can be. Annville, Kentucky, successfully attracted a new plant of the Midsouth Electronics Company (Rosenfeld, Malazia, and Dugan 1988). The community provided an incentive package of loans and grants totaling more than $1.6 million that was used to purchase land and underwrite training costs. Annville was fortunate to have access to professionals and the support of influential community members who helped package the deal. It was also significant that Midsouth's chief executive officer (CEO) was from the region and had strong family ties. Although the CEO reported that incentives were not the deciding factor in the plant location decision, the large amount of funds expended in attracting the firm highlights the disadvantages faced by rural communities.

If the new high-tech employment attracted to rural areas does indeed largely reflect the mature phase of high-tech job growth, then many states should not woo high-tech differently than general manufacturing. Assumptions about the type of economic development that may accompany high-tech manufacturing foster mostly unachievable expectations of creating new industrial concentrations. Long-standing urban centers continue to dominate the high-tech landscape.

Most high-tech programs do not address rural economic development problems. The overwhelming majority of technology development initiatives are used to strengthen and retain established research facilities, not to develop new ones (Office of Technology Assessment, 1984). For this reason, rural communities (which usually lack sophisticated facilities) are not considered for funding.[19]

Rural Applicability

Recognizing the limitations of rural communities' infrastructure, a number of rural high-tech development programs might still prove useful:

- **Policy Development** program funding could be utilized to direct rural areas toward realistic goals for technology-based economic development.
- **Entrepreneurship Training and Assistance** programs hold potential for retaining local talent, avoiding the "brain drain" many rural communities suffer.
- **Education and Training** programs can help create a labor force attractive to industry as well as provide training for displaced workers.
- **Technology Transfer** programs can help upgrade existing firms to increase their competitiveness in their respective industries.

While these programs are appropriate for rural technology development, rural areas seldom participate. To be considered for a full spectrum of state program assistance, rural communities need to strengthen their hand by addressing fundamental deficiencies of size and lack of leadership and technological infrastructure. Acting alone and with severe limitations, rural communities have few options other than recruitment programs to garner technology-based industries, and these programs come with a price that is out of the reach of most rural communities. However, a number of existing high-tech development programs, with minor modifications, hold potential for rural areas.

Models of Rural Technology Development Programs

In this section, I will discuss the reality of state funding for rural technology development by highlighting state programs whose emphases are specifically "rural." The following is based on a review of high-technology program documentation provided by state economic development departments:

- **Washington State** passed House Bill 373 authorizing $42,000 to study the availability of its telecommunications system in rural areas. This program is designed to study the feasibility of introducing "office-intensive" industries to agriculture-based rural communities through the use of detariffing or complete deregulation of industries in certain regions. This type of program is characterized as "Financial Assistance to Firms" and "Policy Development."
- **California's Rural Economic Development Infrastructure Program** (REDIP; Senate Bill 2117) encourages the creation of permanent, private-sector jobs in manufacturing, service, R and D, production, assembly, warehousing, or industrial distribution facilities in rural areas. Incentives take the form of public infrastructure site development—water, wastewater, and storm sewer systems, bridges, and parking facilities. Development is restricted to new facilities; a firm may not relocate from another part of the state. This program is classified as "Financial Assistance to Firms" and "Entrepreneurship Assistance" (since a new firm must be established).
- **The State of Texas** has implemented the Industrial Development Loan Fund to encourage construction of manufacturing facilities in incorporated communities of 20,000 population or less. Up to 40 percent of a project's construction costs are loaned to a nonprofit organization, which builds a facility then leases or sells it to a manufacturer. This program is classified as "Financial Assistance to Firms."
- **Puerto Rico** has undertaken a full-fledged recruitment program aimed specifically at encouraging the location of high-technology firms in this basically rural territory. Among their offerings to high-tech firms are: training supervisory personnel; government salaries for instructors and technical personnel while production workers are trained; rent paid by the government during start-up; full or partial payment of freight on machinery and equipment shipped to Puerto Rico; and other negotiated costs.

- **The Southern Growth Policies Board** created a Southern States Technology Council to facilitate regional technology transfer and to develop the leadership capabilities of the region. Its stated purposes are: to act as a regional forum to share technology program information; to conduct feasibility studies; to initiate and manage cooperative technology arrangements; to better educate legislators about technology policy; to facilitate technology transfer to the private sector; to inventory state programs, policies, and activities; and to identify the impact of technology on education and training needs. This program can be classified as "Policy Development" and "Education and Training."

- **The Greater Minnesota Corporation** will form partnerships with education, business, labor, and agricultural entities to fund applied R and D projects in nonurban areas. The corporation provides matching grants to universities for research as well as contract research to impact growth of applied research. It constructs research facilities, currently participates in as many as four Regional Research Institutes located near major universities, and plans to take equity positions in new products and ventures researched and developed at the corporation's facilities. In addition, it provides loans to technology-oriented businesses. This program includes elements of "Education and Training," "Research and Development," "Research Parks and Incubator Facilities," and "Entrepreneurship Training and Assistance."

- **The State of Idaho** sponsors one program that has applicability and potential for enhancing rural high-tech development. The University of Idaho's Simplot/Micron Center has satellite up-link and video production facilities that have been used to develop advanced courses, such as calculus, for rural high schools. This example can be classified as improvements in "Education and Training."

- **The State of Michigan,** in conjunction with the state's premier university, created the Michigan Modernization Service program (MMS). MMS provides technical assistance to firms (primarily in the auto industry) to upgrade and rationalize existing production operations. The program relies on outside consultants whose expertise is highly tailored to individual plant operations. Although not specifically a program targeted either to high tech or to rural areas, current clients are predominantly located outside the state's major cities.

- **The State of Pennsylvania** pioneered technology transfer assistance through the PENTAP technical assistance program. Similar to Michigan's MMS, PENTAP provides limited consulting services, and companies can apply for assistance to resolve specific problems over a limited time period. The program is operated in conjunction with the state's universities and draws professionals from both the public and private sectors.

Summary

There are few state-administered high-technology industry programs targeted toward rural communities. Fewer still offer improvements to communities' underlying infrastructures. Some states are aware of the urban bias of high-tech programs and the need to better link high-tech policies to an existing industrial base rather than to attempt to create one anew. There does appear to be some correlation between the "ruralness" of a state and the presence of state policy emphasizing incorporation of high tech into traditional industries. Regional coalitions appear a worthy model for small states with small-size economies and limited resources for economic development. While such programs are a distinct minority in the overall policy environment encouraging high-tech development, they form important models for rural high-tech development.

That state high-tech development programs pay insufficient attention to rural problems may be symptomatic of their youthfulness. Many of these programs are less than five years old, and there has been little evaluation of their success. Studies that do exist indicate states copy one another; hence, few programs have distinguishing attributes (Feller 1988). State programs deemed most successful are now coming under greater scrutiny. Pennsylvania's Ben Franklin Partnership program is the dominant model for high-tech programs. However, recent evidence suggests that program results are overstated, leading government officials to erroneously expect large job increases and high new firm formation rates.

Policy duplication defines the nature of programs, limiting innovation. Fearing the political repercussions of breaking new ground in policy, governors hesitate to take the lead in establishing innovative programs. Resistance to risk-taking has resulted in program designs becoming increasingly conservative and homogenized. Few programs adequately address the problems of small entrepreneurial firms, regardless of program brochure rhetoric. While new developments in industrial services programs represent a positive step forward, resource commitments remain small. States should carefully evaluate existing program elements and match them to their particular situation rather than simply buying what consultants and other economic development practitioners find fashionable. Limitations of high-tech development programs should not deter remote communities from actively participating in their implementation. Rural communities must assert their voices to ensure that their concerns are represented in state program discussions. As economic development resources are now almost exclusively provided by state governments, available funds are extremely limited. Alone, rural communities may be ignored in the clamor of other needy locations. Communities should therefore consider the benefits of collaboration through formation of regional consortia. Models of this type of organization are now developing and must be strongly encouraged by rural economic development officials and state legislators.

In this chapter, I have argued that high-tech programs are largely oriented toward metropolitan areas where universities, research facilities, and high-tech employment are already concentrated. The conclusion was that present policy will have little impact on the distribution of high-tech jobs between urban and rural areas, but one way that metropolitan-adjacent rural areas might benefit is via the desirable spillover effects of urban high-tech activity.

To test this assertion, the metropolitan characteristics of two groups of cities (those boasting the largest concentrations of high-tech jobs and those having adjacent rural counties with the highest concentrations of rural high-tech jobs) can be compared. If the factors that characterize these high-tech concentrations and emerging centers are similar, then government policies might facilitate the dispersal of high-tech jobs to rural communities.

On the other hand, if characteristics that describe these high-tech growth experiences are dissimilar, then policy implications probably differ, too. One position might assert that the experiences that stimulate metropolitan high-tech growth in core areas may not be like those that affect the growth of rural adjacent high tech. While core cities thrive on product development and new firm formation, rural areas are receiving plants producing standardized products but still within the growth stage.

A second argument is that rural high tech and metropolitan high tech are more fundamentally dissimilar. High-tech plants in rural areas employ workers with substantially lower levels of skill than their urban counterparts. High tech in rural communities is also unlikely to foster spin-offs as new products are developed. This further signals that products being manufactured in rural areas are more advanced in the product cycle than those manufactured in core metropolitan areas. Thus, given that assistance programs are oriented toward new product development and new firm formation, we could conclude that existing public policy will have only minimal impact on the distribution of high tech in rural areas. Chapters 7 and 8 provide an empirical basis to determine just how public policies can influence the potential of high-tech jobs and plants in America's rural communities.

7

Factors Influencing Rural High-Tech Plant and Employment Location

Previous chapters alluded to the dual pattern of high-tech manufacturing decentralization—within regions from cities to their adjacent rural counties and, more recently, from long-standing northeastern and midwestern urban concentrations toward new markets and labor pools in the South and West.

These trends have obvious implications for rural communities. If the earlier rounds of high-tech growth indeed consisted of shifts from cities to adjacent rural counties in the industrial heartland, we should be able to determine the impacts of this development by examining the characteristics of the relationship between rural metropolitan-adjacent high-tech manufacturing and production in urban areas.[20] The industrial filtering/product-cycle model is central to this scrutiny.

Similarly, in more recent times, if labor quality and availability are determinants of high-tech location, then changes in the location of metropolitan-adjacent rural high-tech employment should reflect this. Insights from the spatial division of labor thesis would apply here.

The implications of such twofold development are straightforward. Employment that historically decentralized to rural areas fit an industrial filtering/product-cycle model of development. Firms initially sought low-wage, nonunion environments proximate to urban-centered manufacturing headquarters. For the most part, shifting jobs were in industries that had entered a phase of stable or declining demand. The composition of relocated jobs was importantly related to product maturation. Few technical skills were required because production processes were standardized and capital-intensive.

Still, even shifting jobs toward low-cost areas has not been enough to prevent further declines in the consumer and producer electronics, chemicals, and machinery industries. With today's increasing internationalization of manufacturing production, jobs that may have previously filtered into America's rural communities now bypass them and are shipped off to Third World countries where labor is cheaper and skill levels are higher. As seen in chapter 3, many rural communities in the Midwest and Northeast continue to lose high-tech jobs (*New York Times*, August 11, 1989). Given recent cost-cutting efforts (including automation) and resulting plant closures, there may now be even less employment decentralization to rural counties in the regions. Therefore, what drove high tech toward outlying counties in the postwar years may not continue to provide a flow of manufacturing jobs to rural communities of America's industrialized regions.

The emergence of microelectronics and the subsequent revolution in information technology precipitated a new industrial geography quite different from previous generations of manufacturing. Instead of relocation occurring at the late stages of a product's life, firms were creating a new spatial logic to counteract high domestic labor costs, to overcome shortages of technically trained labor in existing industrial concentrations, and to combat intense product competition. In this era, reductions in production costs, while still important, were counterbalanced by firms' needs to access appropriate pools of labor. Corporations were constrained by the very nature of new technology, which required the availability of engineering skills and high-quality social infrastructure.

High-tech industry location was also influenced by larger trends occurring in economic development. While decentralization of assembly jobs to Third World countries was a viable option for large multinational firms, it is not for small and medium-sized domestically headquartered corporations (Taylor and Thrift 1982). In the beginning stages of high-tech industry development, many firms were of modest size and nationally headquartered. Investing in productive capacity abroad was fraught with problems. Thus, many companies, particularly smaller ones, sought cheap locations at home. As firms' production processes reached a level of standardization, many jobs were filtered into the South, America's low-cost region.

Communities were not passive observers to this process of industrial geographic change (Cobb 1984). The South pioneered in industrial recruitment. Entrepreneurial state and local governments perfected enticing economic development packages. Not until the late 1970s did states and communities in the industrial heartland follow suit.

There was also a significant acceleration of job shifts to Third World countries. While maintaining technical production within the United States, large companies increasingly found that manufacturing costs in NICs could effectively halve product prices.

Therefore, the spatial structure of high-tech production within the United States has undergone rather dramatic change over the last forty years. Starting in the early postwar years, rural communities attracted manufacturing production that was cost sensitive but that could be decentralized away from major centers of manufacturing. A region's industrial base influenced the composition of manufacturing. In the Northeast and Midwest, rural manufacturing mirrored the regions' dominant industrial bases. In the South, traditional sectors, such as textiles and apparel and cost-sensitive facets of early technology-based products in electrical equipment, filtered into rural communities (Johnson 1988, 1989; Till 1974). The advent of microelectronic technology added another layer to high-tech industrial geography. Decentralization was influenced by both costs and the need to access labor. Rural communities received jobs that could be profitably undertaken within the shadow of metropolitan areas.

In this chapter, I developed a series of theoretical propositions about the spatial development path of high-tech industries in the United States. The first part of this chapter introduces a framework for understanding the historical distribution of rural and urban high-tech industries. The second presents a description of high-tech decentralization over the more recent period. Chapter 8 tests a set of propositions about high-tech location through a series of regression equations. Together, these results present an illuminating picture of high-tech industry location based on both conventional and uniquely high-tech locational attributes.

The Historical Basis of High-Tech Industries in Rural Areas

The creation of America's high-tech geography leading up to and following from the commercialization of microelectronics technology has been an evolutionary process. At different moments in the development of these industries, plants were constructed and the resulting industrial landscape formed. Therefore, any discussion of high-tech development in rural areas must take into account how the nation's high-tech geography evolved and the factors that were important at different stages of the industry's development.

The Premicroelectronics Era

In describing the premicroelectronics industrial geography of technology-intensive industries, it is necessary to differentiate among regional experiences and industrial heritage and the actual motives of firms that decentralized employment into rural areas. Post–World War II decentralization of manufacturing was governed first and foremost by cost and labor control factors. Firms shifted production to reduce labor costs where possible and to tap pools of workers who posed little resistance to industrialization (Erickson 1978; Hoover and Vernon 1959; Johnson 1988, 1989).

In considering this period, it is necessary to discuss the experience of America's rural high-tech prominent regions—the Northeast, Midwest, and South. While there are common factors among the regions' rural industrialization experiences (for example, agricultural bases and branch plants), each experienced a slightly different high-tech development path relating to its early industrial history.

The Northeast's settlement pattern is quite dense. Few rural areas are truly remote from population concentrations. Historically, waves of industry induced metropolitanization in much of the region. Thus, rural industrialization has been a component of the region's industrial geography for decades. It is also the case that industrialization often provided the basis for population growth in former rural communities.

Rural communities in the Northeast were early recipients of manufacturing employment that decentralized out of cities. For example, the radio assembly industry shifted from New York to rural Pennsylvania and electrical equipment assembly moved from Boston and surrounding suburbs into New Hampshire. Urban production costs and labor shortages contributed to these employment shifts. Indigenous companies headquartered in smaller cities, such as Harrisburg, Pennsylvania, and Corning, New York, also filtered employment into rural areas. Many times, as illustrated in the case study of AMP Corporation in chapter 3, it was corporate policy to keep plants small and isolated to minimize labor problems.

Additionally, companies in the Northeast that started out in electrical equipment evolved with the development of microelectronics. For example, early assembly operations in rural New Hampshire consisted of the wire wrapping of copper generators. Subsequent generations of electronics assembly, such as circuit-board stuffing for computers and communications equipment, incorporated new developments within the industry. Consequently, the composition of high-tech employment in rural communities of the Northeast included production of older technologies that were subsequently transformed as new innovations permeated the domestic electrical equipment industry.

Rural high tech in the Midwest complements the experience of the Northeast, yet its early roots are distinct. The Midwest is the nation's center for consumer electronics production. Televisions, communications equipment, and other consumer electronics were innovated and manufactured there. The Midwest has long been the nation's most integrated industrial complex. Component requirements and final assembly of these consumer electronics industries were served by manufacturers within the region. Midwestern rural communities were also dotted with small manufacturers that made parts and equipment for both regional and national markets. For many rural communities, these industries provided branch plant employment, a welcome antidote to agriculture.

A powerful factor shaping early rural high-tech employment in the Midwest was the geographic distribution of auto parts production and later assembly. Auto parts production, while confined to the midwestern region, was relatively dispersed among the Great Lakes states (Glasmeier and McCluskey 1987). Manufacturers consisted of a range of firms, including a few large multinational firms and thousands of parts subcontractors. Many rural communities are the homes of small, locally headquartered suppliers of the large-parts firms. The virtual total unionization of the industry prohibited auto assemblers and parts producers from escaping to lower cost regions. While companies could not evade wage rate schedules, by shifting production to rural communities they could gain greater control over their production processes. The mix of auto parts–producing firms in rural midwestern communities includes both locally headquartered parts makers as well as branch plants of larger firms. The integration phase of the 1950s also brought many auto parts producers under the ownership of the Big Three auto assemblers. Therefore, rural communities are often the sites of subsidiary plants of the major auto assembling firms.

Prior to World War II, the Midwest also had its share of firms on the cutting edge of technology. Minneapolis was the locus of hearing aid and environmental control manufacturing. Both industries pioneered premicroelectronic component miniaturization. Chicago was the headquarters for Motorola, and Dayton, Ohio, was the early home of National Cash Register Corporation. Firms headquartered in these cities went on to become major participants in microelectronic technology. Out of hearing aids and environmental controls arose a complex surrounding Control Data Corporation, a mainframe computer manufacturer. Motorola became one of the nation's largest communications and electronics firms and is the third largest domestic semiconductor manufacturer. Finally, NCR remains a powerhouse in the field of electronic calculation and data storage equipment. These firms maintained a policy of production decentralization both within and outside the region, occasionally favoring the placement of plants within rural counties.

Unlike the Northeast and Midwest, premicroelectronics manufacturing in the rural South did not represent an extension of the region's industrial complex into rural communities. Instead, postwar electronics location in rural southern communities reflected the introduction of branch plants of firms headquartered in industrial regions of the United States. As early as the late 1950s, researchers identified the dual development of branch plant location in the electrical equipment industry (Johnson 1988, 1989; Till 1974). Branch plant penetration was partly in response to concerted efforts by state and local officials to bring industrialization to the South. In his tightly argued book, *The Selling of the South* (1984), James Cobb illustrates how forty years of industrial recruitment using enticements such as low wages and inexperienced and unsophisticated work forces effectively bought manufacturing plants from firms headquartered in the Northeast and Midwest. The vast majority of this employment consisted of low-wage, low-skilled work. Occasionally, however, firms located branches that engaged in R and D. The early siting of IBM's plant in rural Research Triangle Park in Raleigh-Durham, North Carolina, was an exception to the persistent location of plants searching for low wages.

However, rural high-tech industrialization in the South is not monolithic. There have been waves of plant location that have alternately sought remote low-wage environments and resided in and around metropolitan areas where skilled labor and markets are found. Johnson's (1988, 1989) research in three southern states (Georgia, Mississippi, and South Carolina) highlights this dual trend. Using factor analysis, he identifies three labor environments: counties that had well-educated and well-paid populations and were urban, a manufacturing environment characterized by high levels of manufacturing jobs but not necessarily urbanized and well-educated workers, with a significant female manufacturing population, and a black labor environment. He then correlated the distribution of employment in the electronics industry with the three labor environments and found that jobs were associated with both well-educated metropolitan labor environments and the manufacturing-textile–dominated environments that also exhibited a significant female labor force. This dual distribution reflects two opposing tendencies in this sector. On one hand, employment locates in and around metro areas to access markets and pools of technically trained labor. On the other hand, employers in rural counties with some history of industrialization are seeking low-cost locations with a work force that is schooled in the ways of tedious and repetitive industry. Rather than finding the dual results in conflict, this research directly supports arguments made in this book about the evolving spatial division of labor in high-tech industries and the need for both skilled and unskilled labor pools.

As illustrated in chapter 3, the historical accumulation of high-tech jobs in rural areas consists of industries that demonstrated either slow or even negative job growth between 1972 and 1982. In the Midwest and the Northeast (to a lesser extent), the industries that form the base of rural high tech have experienced some recovery since their low point in the early 1980s, yet the industries that experienced recent brief reprieves from continual job loss (autos and consumer electronics) can still leave their host communities vulnerable to downturns in product markets. Industry analysts predict overcapacity in U.S. auto production by the early 1990s. Foreign auto assembly and parts firms now manufacturing in the United States are beginning to intrude on American firms' markets. Consumer electronics producers continue to shift production to cheap labor locations (increasing existing import orientation). Rural communities of the South have not escaped the effects of trade-related job declines in mature high-tech industry. The South's industrial base, heavily laden with branch plants, is predicted by some to be most vulnerable to future restructuring. In a study of the southern economy, Glickman and Glasmeier (1989b) showed that industries in the South were highly vulnerable to import penetration. While southern rural counties were once able to attract branch plants, developments in the Third World undermine any hope that labor-intensive jobs in electronics industries will repatriate to U.S. shores.

It is impossible to describe the geography of high tech in America without referencing the powerful influence of defense spending (Markusen et al. 1991). The regional experience with high tech has been underwritten by policies of the DOD. The early emergence of the aircraft industry in California led to the development of a technology complex spanning the northern and southern regions of the state. Northeastern metropolitan areas centering on Boston but stretching through upstate New York and Pennsylvania benefited from procurement and research policies of the DOD in the 1950s. Starting in the 1940s under the war relocation program, key southern and western states such as Colorado and Texas gained aircraft and missile manufacturing plants that moved inland, away from established East and West Coast military hardware manufacturing centers.

Rural America benefited little from this industrial stimulus. As pointed out earlier, there is almost no defense-dependent high-tech employment in rural communities. Jobs that do exist tend to be dirty and based on antiquated technology. These results come as no surprise, however. Unlike consumer-based manufacturing, weapons manufacturing and procurement have been immune to cost concerns, obviating the need to shift jobs to rural areas in search of low-cost production environments.

The Microelectronics Era

The dawn of microelectronics changed the nature of manufacturing forever. Technical skills replaced manual labor. Low-cost labor inputs were replaced by the need to be near technically trained labor pools. Markets became more important and more geographically select. Like the chemicals industry of the last century, the microelectronics industrial revolution is impacting virtually every facet of the national economy.

The microelectronics era of high-tech development involved a small subset of the industries studied. Communications, electronic components, and computers form the core of this group. These CEC industries were responsible for the creation of almost half of high-tech job growth during the 1970s. They created a spatial mosaic that reinforced but nevertheless was a substantial deviation from past experience.

Based initially around technological hegemony and dominance of key markets, the U.S. microelectronics industry has gone through numerous phases to the most recent intense competition with the Japanese (and increasingly the NICs) for market share. As thresholds were reached, geographic layers of manufacturing capacity were laid down. The resulting distribution represents the contemporary pattern of high-tech location. While at certain moments in the development of these industries there were prevailing trends, deviations always existed. These inhibited the development of a single static model explaining high-tech location.

In the early years of development, American firms producing components and microelectronic-based products were still learning by doing. Thus, they maintained technical production close to headquarters' engineering staff. This precipitated a spatial pattern of intensive high-tech agglomeration in close proximity to corporate headquarters. In regions in which these industries concentrated, poles of growth were clearly forming (Dorfman 1983; Saxenian 1985b).

Phoenix, Arizona, illustrates this early pattern. As Motorola expanded production of semiconductors and other component devices, new production facilities were added within the metropolitan area. Over time, as space limitations became a thorny problem, the company located plants within the surrounding suburbs and eventually into suburban areas of other regions.

Unlike previous eras of high-tech development, microelectronics-based products lent themselves to fragmentation (depending upon the phase in the production process). For example, in the semiconductor industry, R and D and fabrication remained onshore while companies broke off assembly as a discrete task and shifted this more labor-intensive activity to low-cost Asian locations.

By the late 1960s, even as domestic high-tech manufacturing employment was growing rapidly, many firms were shifting production to low-cost Third World locations. America's low-cost rural areas were largely overlooked as firms sought very low wage rates. Rural communities received very little benefit from this phase in the industry's development.

Price competition has always been a serious issue in high-tech industries. Japanese firms were important early players in high-tech product markets in both component and consumer electronic manufacturing (Grunwald and Flamm 1985). Thus, while U.S. firms took the lead in introducing new products, lower-cost competitors quickly gained market share as products became standardized. American firms moved assembly offshore in part to compete with low-cost Japanese production.

As high-tech products evolved, the manufacturing process became increasingly complex. Particularly with microelectronics, product innovation continually pushes the limit of existing manufacturing methods and requires ongoing advances in process technology. The manufacture of semiconductors is a case in point. With the advent of VLSI (very large-scale integration), semiconductors have become enormously complicated devices to produce. Their design is almost exclusively accomplished using computer-aided-design (CAD) systems. The use of this complex equipment in the development phase has pushed the price of designing a new chip to nearly $50 million, and the cost of production equipment has also increased astronomically, requiring increasing yields to rationalize large-scale investments. Construction of a complete manufacturing facility may cost as much as $500 million (Borrus 1988; *Dallas Morning News* 1989).

To achieve satisfactory product yields, firms have been required to almost completely automate production technology. As a consequence, additions to production capacity have taken the form of technical branch plants—stand-alone profit centers with product and process R and D attached. Where have these facilities located?

Technical Branch Plant Location Criteria

In the late 1970s, when high-tech manufacturers were deliberating whether to increase production capacity, they faced a choice of expanding within existing agglomerations or seeking new locations. Many firms decided to establish new plants outside core production regions, and as production capacity was added, they carved off self-contained operations and located them outside existing geographic industry clusters. While it was critical to maintain an R and D base in existing industry agglomerations, firms located new production facilities in cities where appropriate supplies of labor were available.

There were incentives for establishing new production locations. High-tech firms were increasingly landlocked in existing agglomerations in Santa Clara County's Silicon Valley and Boston's Route 128 area. In-place geographic expansion incurred high land and development costs. The intensity of these agglomerations had also resulted in high housing costs. Together with labor market competition, inflationary pressures drove wages sky-high and made it increasingly difficult to recruit new engineers not already living in the centers. In this environment, even low-skill production workers were commanding unprofitably high wages.

Another factor that influenced firms' decisions to locate outside existing core regions was the need to limit labor turnover, especially among professionals. Within existing agglomerations, workers could move freely between firms as new employment opportunities developed. While facilitating the formation of new firms in the complex, this resulted in labor force instability and the erosion of established firms' specific human capital investments. Firms were forced to continually increase benefits just to retain key personnel. By shifting process R and D and technical production facilities to areas with less-intense high-tech agglomerations, firms hoped to establish more stable employment relations. Importantly, wage rates for both professional and production employees were lower outside the high-tech centers (although the costs of attracting high-level professionals to these new locations were often prohibitively high). Extending Clark's (1981) original insight about high-tech industry's spatial division of labor, it eventually became necessary for high-tech firms to segment further R and D staff to ensure stability within production engineering.

Decentralization to the Third World quickly became a well-worn option as firms struggled to remain price competitive with the Japanese. In the early stages of the information revolution, product maturation sped up. New generations of technology making recent models obsolete were constantly introduced. Capital investment in automated assembly was risky and often impractical. Investments in new capital equipment required for subsequent generations of products were so costly that firms did not have the resources to invest in automated assembly, and while this characterization most clearly typifies the experience of the semiconductor industry, many different components and final assembly products evolved in the same fashion.

Government trade programs encouraged foreign manufacturing. Sections 706 and 708 of the U.S. trade code encouraged offshore assembly by requiring that firms pay tariffs only on the value added. By providing lucrative incentive packages, foreign governments also made it easy to establish offshore assembly operations. Given that wage rates in NICs were as low as $3 a day, the benefits of offshore assembly clearly greatly outweighed the costs of developing offshore production capacity.

In some instances, however, the relatively short life span of products made it impractical for firms to produce in offshore Asian locations. These high-tech producers set up branch plants within the United States. Because of higher labor costs, these domestic investments were often capital-intensive manufacturing plants (Hansen 1980). Thus, from the outer rings of cities where microelectronics-based technology was born, branch plants were first filtered close by and eventually to even lower-cost locations in the U.S. South and other rural areas.

Price competition was pervasive in many facets of high-tech manufacturing. Initially, American firms dominated high-tech manufacturing, which required some level of tailoring or after-sales service to specific market needs. In personal computers, American firms were able to stave off foreign competition for a considerable time primarily because of the relative newness of the product and the need for customer reassurance about the availability of after-sales service, but this did not mean that U.S. firms could sell high-priced products. Indeed, their only competitive edge was service. Therefore, they reduced prices to a minimum to maintain market share. Given that these products were rapidly changing in line with increased component capacity, American firms shifted assembly operations to low-cost locations within the United States and later to the Third World. Eventually, once they established distribution channels, foreign firms were able to compete head-to-head with American manufacturers.

The ultimate in penetration has now occurred. U.S. personal computer manufacturing now primarily consists of firms assembling components manufactured in the Third World. American producers of personal computers are no longer immune to competition. In many cases, American firms have ceded manufacturing to foreign producers, who ship assembled product into the United States under the name of the original equipment manufacturers. American firms have simply gotten out of the business of manufacturing (*Business Week* 1987). American hegemony in high-tech industry has been seriously eroded.

An aspect of rural high-tech geography consists of component manufacturers freed from the nation's high-tech agglomerations. Gore and Associates typifies this development. Because of rapid

product changes, domestically headquartered component industries needed to be near major markets, but they did not have to be
located within major metropolitan areas. Thus, an additional
source of high-tech plant location outside cities consisted of parts
plants with rapidly changing markets but technically stable products.

The Microelectronics Revolution Reconsidered

Starting in the late 1970s, a second round of decentralization
toward rural areas occurred. Compositional differences became
apparent in the high tech locating around metropolitan areas of
the southern and western United States. As microelectronics, computers, and information technology progressed, manufacturers felt
pressures to move—not so much in response to product maturation
as to market mandates and rising costs in traditional manufacturing locations. This second wave of decentralization was not entirely
footloose; manufacturers needed access to cities where process
engineering could be profitably carried out. So, as outlined in
chapter 4, new growth of employment and plants in rural areas
consisted of expansions in high-tech industries that were growing
nationally. To some extent, rural high tech began to reflect new
developments in technology, but as previous chapters point out,
this trend was minute compared with the vast majority of employment in the truly dynamic industries that have gone offshore in
search of even cheaper wages and more attractive manufacturing
conditions.

The Future of High Tech and Rural America

Rampant speculation exists about the eventual return of low-cost
manufacturing to the United States. As the dollar has declined
against foreign currencies (particularly the yen), there has been
intense speculation about the development of a reverse comparative
advantage that would bring assembly jobs back to the States. Much
of high-tech development between 1960 (the early era of chip pro-

duction and consumer electronics incorporation) and the late 1970s was based on low wages of the receiving country, but as products became more complex and the receiving countries saw the developmental significance of establishing a supplier base to service them (and support a nascent domestic industry), low-wage Asian NICS—South Korea, Taiwan, and Hong Kong—invested heavily in establishing a high-tech infrastructure. In a highly illuminating study, Sabina Deitrick (1990) dispels the hope that the declining value of the U.S. dollar will bring high-tech assembly—with jobs ripe for America's rural communities—home. From a nonexistent base in the mid-1970s, Taiwan, Singapore, South Korea, and, to a lesser extent, Hong Kong have established a technical supplier infrastructure that precludes any need for near-term repatriation of high-tech assembly jobs. In Asian countries, the supplier base has been developed to service both multinationals as well as domestic producers that now compete directly with American firms.

It seems no longer a question of whether or when U.S. high-tech industries will seek out the advantages of low-cost production locations available in America's rural communities. As for future capital investments, the declining dollar will make it possible for national and regional firms to selectively locate high-tech assembly operations in lower-cost regions of the United States; but with the declining importance of low-skilled assembly operatives in high-tech industry, wage differences are less important in the locational calculus of firms. Especially given that competition is not based on wage rates alone—a traditional strong suit of rural areas—but rather is defined by a combination of service capacity, markets, and low wages, it is unlikely that wage differences will ever be sufficient to bring back or maintain low-skilled assembly jobs at home. For rural communities to compete now, they must overcome not only wage differences but thirty years of production experience that give the NICs a decided edge on future high-tech manufacturing.

This development only underscores the point made throughout this book that the dynamic nature of high-tech industries makes it difficult to theorize a location or development theory that is static. The forces that shape the spatial distribution of these industries have altered through time, making strictly metropolitan evaluations suspect at best.

A Theoretical Restatement of High-Tech Location

In retesting the hypotheses posed in previous studies of high-tech location, I choose to both augment and dramatically depart from the traditional method of analysis by adding comparisons between rural and urban areas. In doing the two simultaneously, I hope to provide a piece of the puzzle that has historically been missing in explanations of the spatial evolution of high-tech industries.

Earlier the conclusion was that shifts across the regions constituted the maturation phase of product-cycle effects, but is it really these shifts that are so significant, or is it more important that we examine the different *types* of geographic spaces in which high technology moves? Relying solely upon the product-cycle model, without incorporating a division of labor element to the analysis of location, the tendency is to believe that any type of shift constitutes the maturation of industry, but what I will demonstrate here is that spatial evolution of high technology is a much more complicated process. There was an initial exodus from cities to rural hinterlands. However, as technology changed, the trend was to locate in metropolitan areas that possessed the technical capacity to support new, more infrastructure-dependent production.

As these original centers filled in, firms whose markets were more flexible began to decentralize proximately. This explains the spatial filtering within the immediate areas surrounding metropolitan areas of the West and South. Companies needed to be near cities to obtain engineering labor and maintain access to markets, but because the previous rapid rate of product change had slowed, there was little need for immediate face-to-face contact between product engineering and manufacturing processing. More remote locations became attractive for their pools of lower wage labor and less expensive facilities.

Thus, injection of the spatial division of labor theory permits analysis of firm locational decisions from a slightly different approach. In certain cases, a rural location could be acceptable if it was near a metropolitan area with a rapidly growing high-tech base to act as a market. Additionally, the unique characteristics of an R and D lab could permit a rural location. As long as companies were not forced to absorb the prohibitively high costs of creating new pools of skilled labor, these types of facilities (which are independent of markets) are more footloose geographically.

The overall distribution of high-tech jobs and plants reflects an historic accumulation of industries within a few areas. As shown in chapter 3, high-tech employment is a decidedly urban phenomenon reflecting both the long-standing role of major cities as seedbeds and the solidification of a few Sunbelt cities that have developed large concentrations of high-tech plants and employment, some with innovative capacity on their own. In the existing core centers, amenities and accessibility factors are well-developed and may have helped to maintain high tech locally, but in cities that have matured on high-tech, amenities and access, qualities have evolved as these agglomerations coalesced. Evolution was simultaneous. Therefore, evaluation of factors associated with this distribution requires the incorporation of a dynamic theory of high-tech location that can "accommodate historical change and which permits the 'dependent variables' of one era to become the independent forces for another" (Markusen et al. 1991).

We must further differentiate between the existence of industrial seedbed urbanizations and cities in which development was derived from the success of firms found in core centers of industrial activity. It would be a mistake to treat these two forms of development as one. The latter cities are dependent on and are derivative of successful industrial seedbeds. Independent core status is elusive for most areas that must be content to be secondary centers of modern high-tech development.

For high-tech employment and plants in rural areas, locational determinants must be viewed as resulting from a convergence of two eras of industrialization linked complexly with high-tech evolution. The earlier period of intraregional geographic decentralization began in the 1950s as branch plants sought low-skilled, cheap-labor locations. This pattern is manifest in the accumulation of high-tech jobs in adjacent rural counties and primarily occurred as firms spurned unions and high wages.

Predating the development of microelectronics and predictably based on the spatial filtering accompanying a product-cycle model explanation for employment decentralization, early high-tech jobs could shift about easily because they required little skill to either manage or execute the production process. Products were mature, and manufacturing technology, though still labor-intensive, had stabilized. Furthermore, prior to the 1970s economic crisis, markets were also established for many firms. Only those technical activities that required engineering oversight had to remain in cities where qualified labor was available.

With the evolution of microelectronics, communications, and computers, firm location decisions incorporated a new dimension. Low-wage jobs in these innovative industries shifted early to Third World countries where low-wage workers have more technical education than their more organized and higher-paid U.S. counterparts. Many aspects of high-tech manufacturing have never been attracted to domestic rural locations.

That which has remained in the United States has engendered a more complex location calculus. As the technology and production process evolved, high-tech industry was motivated to seek locations where low-skilled and high-skilled workers could be found or attracted jointly. Thus, the new model for location behavior must acknowledge firms' needs to access pools of skilled, technically trained labor and low-skilled production workers. It must explain high-tech location patterns among the nation's cities and rural areas dynamically, incorporating early periods of decentralization for cost reasons with those of more recent times that are also characterized by concerns about labor quality.

Therefore, this analysis attempts to discern the evolving tendency of decentralization by examining the geographic distribution of high-tech industries across both urban and rural areas. While employment and plants are examined in the regression study of metropolitan characteristics and rural adjacent high-tech development, I pay special attention to plant levels and changes over time. The following reports the results of a series of regressions of economic, social, and demographic characteristics of cities and their rural adjacent counties in relation to the distribution of high-tech employment and plants.

Description of the Analysis

As part of this analysis, I examined the attributes of cities that experienced increases in high-tech jobs between 1972 and 1982. These attributes are outlined in Appendix B. The summary of the relationship between metropolitan and nonmetropolitan high-tech growth for this period helps evaluate the effect particular policy-relevant variables (for example, the presence of two-year and four-year postsecondary institutions) might have on rural high-tech growth. The analysis also examines the metropolitan characteristics that describe the overall distribution of high-tech jobs and the changes in this pattern that occurred over the 1972–82 period.

Hypotheses Guiding the Analysis

The regression study is guided by the two central conclusions noted in previous chapters. Two periods of decentralization resulted in high-tech jobs locating in rural counties of the United States. In the first, an emphasis on minimizing labor and business costs led to *intra*regional shifts of high-tech jobs from metropolitan to non-metropolitan areas. The more recent period of decentralization was marked by the search for specific labor characteristics, both high and low skill.

Given early rounds of manufacturing decentralization *within* traditional manufacturing states, absolute levels of metropolitan to nonmetropolitan relationships would be expected to be character-ized by factors associated with the in-place costs of doing business—for example, levels of unionization.

At the same time, the analysis includes a variable measuring the attraction of metropolitan areas to in-migration from outside the state. This factor should be negatively correlated with the abso-lute distribution of high-tech employment and plants. That is, cities with large concentrations of high-tech jobs and plants in adja-cent rural areas were expected to have high relative levels of unioni-zation and experience slow or negative growth in population due to interstate migration.

Additionally, size of city—as measured by surrogates, such as air service or the availability of arts—might also be associated with rural adjacent high-tech jobs and plants. Given that the largest cities in the industrial heartland experienced manufacturing job loss—at least some of which is presumed to have decentralized to rural areas—high levels of rural high-tech jobs and plants should surround these cities.

The second decentralization trend, a shift toward new markets and labor supplies in the South and the West, corresponds to more recent rounds of high-tech development. These largely reflect *inter*regional shifts. In this instance, high-tech industries are constrained by labor requirements restricting location near cities where both skilled *and* unskilled labor are available. As high-tech companies in the West and Northeast reached a size where they considered expansion into new facilities, they followed broad manufacturing trends and shifted production toward the Sunbelt. Thus, more recent shifts have occurred in search of labor but also, importantly, as population and industry have migrated, in search of new markets.

TABLE 7.1
Adjacent Rural Counties:
Absolute Levels of Employment
1982

Top 20 MSAs[1]	1982
Binghamton, NY	10534.2
Milwaukee, WI	9905.0
Williamsport, PA	9096.6
Portland, ME	8960.7
Hartford–New Britain–Middletown–Bristol, CT	8092.0
Fort Pierce, FL	7901.8
Elmira, NY	7443.0
Erie, PA	7355.7
Manchester-Nashua, NH	7076.6
Aurora-Elgin, IL	6707.0
Syracuse, NY	6513.4
Hagerstown, MD	6294.0
Pittsburgh, PA	6136.9
Charlotte–Gastonia–Rock Hill, NC-SC	5771.4
Appleton–Oshkosh–Neenah, WI	5706.3
Asheville, NC	5445.2
Greenville-Spartanburg, SC	4843.9
Beaver County, PA	4402.7
Baton Rouge, LA	4251.5
Rochester, NY	3748.5

Note: 1. MSA = Metropolitan Statistical Area.

Source: Bureau of the Census, 1986, Census of Manufactures, *Plant Location Tape* (1972, 1977, 1982).

The dual shift can be partly seen by examining the regional location of metropolitan areas with metro-adjacent rural county high-tech jobs and plants. In absolute shares (Table 7.1), metropolitan areas in the Northeast and Midwest dominate the top twenty urban areas that have adjacent rural high-tech employment and plants. Manufacturing facilities in adjacent rural communities are even more concentrated, the majority located near Northeast and Midwest MSAs (metropolitan statistical areas; Table 7.2). In contrast, the top twenty cities—with high absolute differences indicat-

TABLE 7.2
Adjacent Rural Counties:
Absolute Employment Change
1982

Top 20 MSAs[1]	1982
Portland, ME	8960.70
Binghamton, NY	5392.84
Asheville, NC	4743.98
Milwaukee, WI	3304.93
Greenville-Spartanburg, SC	2676.69
Manchester-Nashua, NH	2478.72
Columbia, SC	2327.67
Eugene-Springfield, OR	1945.37
Baton Rouge, LA	1560.51
Atlanta, GA	1521.44
Akron, OH	1325.82
Charlotte–Gastonia–Rock Hill, NC-SC	1283.95
Santa Barbara, CA	1231.01
Hartford–New Britain–Middletown–Bristol, CT	1226.07
Oklahoma City, OK	1192.95
Hagerstown, MD	1141.36
Dayton-Springfield, OH	1100.68
Cincinnati, OH–KY–IN	1099.59
Elkhart-Goshen, IN	1088.15
State College, PA	1063.59

Note: 1. MSA = Metropolitan Statistical Area.

Source: Bureau of the Census, 1986, Census of Manufactures, *Plant Location Tape* (1972, 1977, 1982).

ing gains in high-tech plants and employment—are more recently concentrated in the South and West (Tables 7.3 and 7.4).

These contemporary trends—the search for lower-cost production and new markets—are visible in the changing distribution of plants and employment. Plant growth is an important indicator of larger trends in the economy, such as changes in population and the general movement of economic activity among regions. While

TABLE 7.3

Adjacent Rural Counties:
Absolute Levels of Plants
1982

Top 20 MSAs[1]	1982
Hartford–New Britain–Middletown–Bristol, CT	128
Erie, PA	106
Milwaukee, WI	76
Beaver County, PA	74
Manchester–Nashua, NH	55
Pittsburgh, PA	53
Kalamazoo, MI	45
Aurora-Elgin, IL	42
Binghamton, NY	40
Dayton–Springfield, OH	38
Grand Rapids, MI	37
Gary-Hammond, IN	37
Elkhart-Goshen, IN	36
Poughkeepsie, NY	34
Ann Arbor, MI	33
Cleveland, OH	32
Santa Barbara, CA	28
Portland, ME	28
Rochester, NY	25
Columbus, OH	25
Oklahoma City, OK	25
Albany–Schenectady–Troy, NY	25
La Crosse, WI	25

Note: 1. MSA = Metropolitan Statistical Area.

Source: Bureau of the Census, 1986, Census of Manufactures, *Plant Location Tape* (1972, 1977, 1982).

TABLE 7.4

Adjacent Rural Counties:
Absolute Plant Change
1982

Top 20 MSAs[1]	1982
Hartford–New Britain–Middletown–Bristol, CT	33
Erie, PA	31
Milwaukee, WI	26
Santa Barbara, CA	21
Binghamton, NY	19
Houston, TX	18
Sacramento, CA	16
Oklahoma City, OK	15
Manchester–Nashua, NH	14
Asheville, NC	13
Grand Rapids, MI	12
Eugene-Springfield, OR	12
Columbia, SC	12
Greenville-Spartanburg, SC	11
Columbus, OH	11
Dallas, TX	10
Atlanta, GA	10
Portland, ME	10
Salem, OR	10
Huntsville, AL	10

Note: 1. MSA = Metropolitan Statistical Area.

Source: Bureau of the Census, 1986, Census of Manufactures, *Plant Location Tape* (1972, 1977, 1982).

firms can shift employment relatively easily between production sites, opening a new plant signals much greater commitment to a location. Companies investing in a community expect that existing conditions (including labor market, business climate, and the state of the industry) will remain constant or expand in the near term.

8

Factors Governing the Spatial Distribution of High-Tech Jobs and Plants Among Cities and Rural Communities

The prospect of high-tech industries in rural areas of advanced industrial countries has only recently been the subject of academic discourse. Two strains of research emerge from this work. The first addresses the rural question from the standpoint of the labor process and employers' motivations for locating production facilities in rural communities. Prominent reasons included low wages, employee docility, and previous histories of factory labor. A second line of inquiry focuses on the characteristics of western U.S. counties where high-tech development has occurred. Rural communities most attractive to high-tech establishments had substantial population concentrations, high-quality amenities, and were located within the shadows of metropolitan areas.

Each of these research efforts has added important insights to our understanding of high-tech location. However, neither embeds rural high-tech development within a larger framework of modern industrialization. In this chapter, I situate the growth of high-tech industries in rural areas within a broader context by examining their spatial behavior within a theoretical model of contemporary high-tech development. Doing so requires that this inquiry blend an understanding of the urban and the rural dimensions of high-tech location.

In this final part of the analysis, I examine the dual pattern of high-tech decentralization suggested in earlier sections of this book.

Two sets of regressions are reviewed. The first set explains the characteristics of the cities associated with metropolitan-adjacent rural high-tech jobs and plants and changes in these cities over the 1972–82 period. A second set of regressions explains the metropolitan location of high-tech plants and employment and absolute changes in them over the study period. The analysis of high-tech location in 1982 reflects the historic accumulation of high-tech industries in metropolitan-adjacent rural counties. Certain locational features may differ from those that describe the change in high-tech location over the study period. When appropriate in the model construction discussion, I suggest instances where locational attributes are likely to differ. The chapter concludes with a discussion comparing rural and metropolitan high-tech experiences.

Model Construction and Variable Descriptions

The selection of variables used in the analysis is based on prior studies of high-tech industry location (Armington, Harris, and Odle 1983; Markusen, Hall, and Glasmeier 1986) and general industry locational behavior. In this research, Markusen et al. (1986) analyzed high-tech industry for 1977 and the change between 1972 and 1977 by examining four sets of factors. The first set consisted of labor market characteristics, including wage rates, the percentage of the manufacturing work force that is unionized, and unemployment rates. These measures are widely regarded as surrogates for measuring the costs of doing business in an area. Some analysts have argued that bad business climates effectively chased industry from traditional manufacturing centers where business costs and wages are high and unions are strong. The existence of bad business climates in cities is one reason plants moved to rural areas.

Based on notions of industrial filtering, rural high tech should be found contiguous with metropolitan areas where wage rates and unionization levels are high. Conventional analysis of metropolitan high-tech location would suggest that unemployment is associated with new high-tech development as firms seek areas with available labor, but because I am concerned with factors describing metropolitan areas with concentrations of metropolitan-adjacent rural high tech, it might be expected that labor shortages, hence low metropolitan unemployment rates, would characterize these cities. Given these competing views, the outcome on this variable is unpredictable.

Unlike previous analyses, I chose to include a measure of education in the labor force to determine whether proximity to pools of skilled labor increased the chances of rural areas gaining high-tech employment and plants. Firms could satisfy their needs for technical labor by locating in a metropolitan-adjacent rural county and drawing upon skilled workers available in the nearby city. Technical workers would commute from the urban area and lower-skilled workers would be attracted proximately. Thus, it would be expected that the growth of high-tech jobs and plants would occur in and near cities where high percentages of the population have sixteen years or more of education.

A second set of variables used in the earlier studies determined quality of life in metropolitan areas by measuring climate type and the availability of four-year colleges. Access to universities is important for a number of reasons. The inclusion of four-year colleges as possible locational determinants is based on the belief that technical and professional employees locate where there is access to colleges and other cultural factors.[21] In addition to providing pools of trained labor in technical and professional fields, universities sponsor cultural events, such as the ballet, the symphony, and the theater arts. Site location trade journals, anecdotal evidence, and comments from corporate interviews reveal firms' concerns about their ability to attract key personnel and to provide ongoing training for their workers. This factor is especially important for technical branch plants that conduct R and D and operate complex production processes. Metro-adjacent rural counties with proximity to a university would be expected to have a competitive edge over their rivals due to access to a ready supply of technically trained labor and the availability of educational institutions to provide ongoing employee training.[22] Amenities and access to higher education institutions are frequently cited as important prerequisites for attracting high-tech industry.

The general shift of population and jobs to more temperate locations has precipitated the regular inclusion of a climate measure in industrial location studies. Thus, a measure of mildness of climate was included in the analysis. Given the two periods of high-tech decentralization discussed in the previous chapter, it is impossible to predict the sign of the coefficient.[23]

I also incorporated a measure of local property taxes in the analysis. Again, drawing on the site location literature, it is hypothesized that firms might locate in a rural metro-adjacent county to avoid paying high taxes. Therefore, high urban property tax levels would be associated with metropolitan-adjacent rural high-tech jobs and plants.

Like the previous studies, I included a measure of housing costs in this analysis. Here housing prices are a surrogate for land values. In the case of the historic concentration of high-tech employment in rural areas, high-tech jobs and plants are prominently featured in rural communities surrounding older industrial cities (where restructuring and resulting slow population growth have depressed land and housing values). Therefore, it is expected that historic concentrations of plants and employment would be associated with low housing prices. Conversely, in the case of plant and employment change, the assumption was not that high-tech jobs would be plentiful in areas with low home values. Both industry agglomerative tendencies and the storm of branch plant chasing set off by the high-tech growth spurt of the late 1970s unleashed speculation in recipient locations. Given cost pressures, firms needing access but not requiring a location within a booming metropolitan area could locate plants in an adjacent rural county and avoid high housing costs, so I expected that change in high-tech employment and plants would be associated with high housing prices in the contiguous urban area.

The third type of variable measured access features of a local community. As in the previous studies, access was defined as availability of commercial air service. Interviews with branch plant managers indicate the importance of proximity to corporate headquarters. Many firms were concerned that their employees be able to travel to the branch plant and back to headquarters within one workday. Thus, air service should be positively associated with high-tech plant and employment distribution.[24]

The previous studies also included a fourth set of variables measuring agglomerative features of metropolitan areas. Unfortunately, when this analysis was undertaken, data for these variables were not available. In this analysis, I included 1982 high-tech employment in the surrounding metropolitan area to reflect the existence of agglomeration economies.

Like the previous analyses (Markusen, Hall, and Glasmeier 1986), a measure of federal government spending based on procurement contracts more than $10,000 was included. Concern with the role of defense/military expenditures in high-tech development stems from the early importance of government spending for cutting-edge technologies in electronics, computers, communications equipment, and aircraft production. More recently, some scholars (Markusen, Hall, and Glasmeier 1986) argue that a central variable shaping high-tech industry location is federal procurement contracts. Thus, it is expected that high levels of procurement contracts per capita would be positively associated with adjacent rural high-tech jobs and plants.

To capture product-cycle attributes of high-tech location, a measure of migration during the mid-1970 to early-1980 period was included. The hypothesis was that rural areas with large bases of high-tech jobs would be adjacent to cities that experienced low population change due to immigration. Conversely, more recent changes in rural high-tech employment would be closely associated with cities that experienced significant population increases. Following a model of industrial filtering, rural counties adjacent to rapidly growing metropolitan areas were expected to have the highest probability of receiving spillover development.

Finally, a variable was included that is of particular concern to rural areas: the percentage of the population living below the official poverty line. Many of the nation's poor live in urban areas. However, land values in urban areas have pushed poor residents to the edges of cities and beyond. In many instances, metro-adjacent rural counties are simply geographic extensions of their metropolitan counterparts. Therefore, it was hypothesized that high-tech industries would be averse to locating in areas of high economic deprivation. Including this variable was an indirect test of whether communities with high levels of poverty should anticipate relief through the location of high-tech jobs and plants.

I attempted to reproduce the structure of the earlier analyses of high-tech location. In part, this was to determine whether characteristics describing the recent historic pattern of high-tech location persisted during a period of rapid industry growth. A number of variables incorporated in the earlier analyses are not included. Some were found to be highly intercorrelated measures of city size, such as the arts, services employment, and federal employees; thus, they are measuring the same trend. These redundant variables were eliminated in early stages of the regression analysis. Table 8.1 summarizes the hypothesized signs of the thirteen independent variables tested in the alternative regression analysis of adjacent rural high-tech location.

I selected variables based both on standard firm location considerations—labor market, demographic and economic characteristics—and factors believed directly associated with the specific case of high-tech industry location.

Composition of the Analysis

This analysis is multilevel. The first level of analysis considers the overall relationships between metropolitan-adjacent rural high-tech employment and plants and the characteristics of adjacent cities. This was then compared with metropolitan high-tech development over the same period.

The analysis consists of four sets of dependent variables (two sets for adjacent rural high tech and two sets for metropolitan high tech, for a total of eight dependent variables) and thirteen independent variables. The first set of rural dependent variables is the absolute number of high-tech jobs and plants in metropolitan-adjacent rural counties. The second set of rural dependent variables reflects the absolute difference between rural employment and plants in counties adjacent to metropolitan areas over the 1972–82 period. The first set examines the cumulative distribution of high-tech employment and plants in rural adjacent counties. The second set of dependent variables explores the change in the distribution of high-tech employment and plants in adjacent counties over the ten-year period.

These results are then compared to regression analyses correlating metropolitan characteristics with the distribution of high-

TABLE 8.1

Expected Signs of Coefficients Indicating Spatial Location
of High-Tech Industries in Rural Adjacent and Metro Areas

	Log of Metropolitan Plants and Employment 1982	*Absolute Difference Metropolitan Plants[1] and Employment 1982*
Climate	+	+
Housing Costs	+	+
Property Taxes	+	+
Commercial Air Service	+	+
Four-Year College	+	+
Sixteen Years Education	+	+
Poverty	−	−
Unemployment in 1983	−	−
Wages	+	+
Interstate Migration	+	+
Manufacturing Union Representation	−	−
Defense Procurement Per Capita	+	+

	Log of Rural Adjacent Plants and Employment 1982	*Absolute Difference Rural Adjacent Plants and Employment[1] 1982*
Climate		
Housing Costs	−	+
Property Taxes	+	+
Commercial Air Service	+	+
Four-Year College	+	+
Sixteen Years Education	+	+
Poverty	−	−
Unemployment in 1983		
Wages	+	+
Interstate Migration	−	+
Manufacturing Union Representation	+	−
Defense Procurement Per Capita	+	+
Metropolitan High-Tech Employment	+	+

Note: 1. Logged.

tech jobs and plants among America's cities. The first set of metropolitan-dependent variables consists of absolute levels of plants and employment in metropolitan areas. The second set of metropolitan-dependent variables reflects the absolute difference between employment and plants over the ten-year study period.

Two hundred and forty-seven census-defined metropolitan statistical areas were included in the metropolitan-adjacent rural regression analysis. This includes all but two metropolitan areas with adjacent rural counties for which data were available. The definition of cities and their rural adjacent counties is based on 1980 urban-rural designations and 1983 MSA designations. The urban-rural classification is defined in Table 3.1 in chapter 3.

While I posit a series of expected relationships based on existing studies of high-tech location, my goal was to discern the evolving pattern of high-tech location — not to predict it outright.

Model Specification

There were a number of technical problems involved in analyzing the relationship between rural high-tech employment and plants and adjacent metropolitan characteristics. Perhaps the most critical problem is that many metropolitan-adjacent rural counties had no high-tech employment or plants during the study period. For example, out of the 247 metropolitan areas with adjacent rural counties for which I was able to gather data, only 130 rural counties had high-tech plants and employment. Thus, the dependent variable is censored. Linear regression analysis is inappropriate in this case because Ordinary Least Squares results in estimators that are inconsistent. While I could have chosen to model only instances where there were both employment and plants in adjacent rural counties, the absence of high tech in these counties is itself useful information.

The presence of censored dependent variables is a common problem in studies of rural industrial location. Research by Barkley, Dahlgran, and Smith (1988) and Barkley and Keith (1990) on high-tech location in the western United States had been particularly sensitive to this problem. In modeling high-tech location in the western United States, Barkley and Keith employ the Tobit procedure to model rural high-tech location. As they note, "The Tobit procedure recognizes the special nature of threshold values of independent variables and makes use of the information contained in counties with zero employment by first analyzing the difference between zero and nonzero values and then differentiating, on the basis of explanatory variables, between varying nonzero levels of employment." Based on Barkley and Keith's experience, I chose to use the Tobit procedure to evaluate the relationship between rural high-tech employment and plants and adjacent metropolitan area characteristics.[25]

Several variables were transformed to take account of heterogeneous variance in the largest cities.[26] Procurement contracts were divided by the resident population to generate a measure of per capita defense spending. In addition, the dependent variable for metropolitan-adjacent rural employment and plants and rural adjacent employment difference, the dependent variables for metropolitan plants and employment, and changes in metropolitan plant location were logged. As outlined previously, in the earliest stages of the studies, a number of variables were examined and discarded due to multicolinearity. This was especially prevalent among variables that are surrogates for city size, such as services employment, the arts, and numbers of federal employees. Residual plots were rigorously analyzed in each step of the analysis to uncover statistical problems, but even with this effort, multicolinearity could not be totally eradicated from the analysis. Nevertheless, every effort was made to minimize this problem.[27]

There also may have been variables left out of the analysis. In some instances, this was due to missing data for a specific time period. Tobit analysis is particularly sensitive to problems of model specification. To the extent possible, this problem was minimized based on theoretical and empirical observations of industrial location in the United States in the late 1970s and early 1980s. Autocorrelation (the interdependence of two adjacent metropolitan areas) may also be a problem. Unfortunately, there is no satisfactory way to resolve this effect.

Estimation Results

The Tobit analysis for high-tech plant and employment and the absolute difference in plants and employment are presented in Tables 8.2, 8.3, 8.4, and 8.5, respectively. Maximum likelihood estimations were used for the Tobit analysis and provide consistent and efficient estimators. The following discussion first reviews the results of Tobit analyses of metropolitan-adjacent rural high-tech employment and plants in 1982. This is followed by a discussion of the Tobit results based on the absolute difference in high-tech employment and plant levels over the 1972–82 period.

Tobit Analysis of Metropolitan-Adjacent Rural High-Tech Employment and Plants

The results of the Tobit analysis confirm a number of the relationships stated at the introduction of this chapter. Assessing the importance of the relationship of explanatory independent variables to observed values of plants and employment requires a detailed discussion. I will review first the results for high-tech employment followed by the results for plants.

In the case of employment concentrations, five of the thirteen variables were statistically significant (using a one-tailed t test). Rural communities with large concentrations of high-tech jobs were adjacent to metropolitan areas with mild climates, large airports, low rates of poverty, high levels of unionization, and large concentrations of high-tech employment. Although not statistically significant, the signs of the remaining variables were consistent with the earlier discussion.

There were a few important exceptions. The presence of four-year colleges and wage rates were negatively associated with adjacent high-tech employment. The negative relationship between employment levels and the presence of four-year colleges may signify that premicroelectronics age high tech was not dependent upon access to local educational facilities for reasons of future labor supply or labor attraction. However, as originally hypothesized, an educated population was positively related to adjacent rural high-tech employment. Markusen, Hall, and Glasmeier (1986) and oth-

TABLE 8.2
Tobit Analysis of
Metropolitan-Adjacent Rural High-Tech Employment
1982

	Standard Error	*T Ratio*	*Significance Level*
Intercept	−2.26818	−.613	(.54005)
Climate	.627111^{e-2}	2.106	(.03521)
Housing	−.138933^{e-2}	−.389	(.69764)
Property Tax	.104545^{e-2}	1.051	(.29326)
Air Service	.725616	1.861	(.06269)
Four-Year College	−.655453^{e-1}	−.832	(.40514)
Sixteen Years Education	.313509^{e-1}	.347	(.72842)
Poverty	−.158486	−1.448	(.14765)
Unemployment	.561685^{e-2}	.038	(.96990)
Procurement	150.659	.449	(.65356)
Wages	−.113592^{e-3}	−1.112	(.26615)
Migration	−.672324^{e-3}	−1.201	(.22984)
Unionization	.536004^{e-1}	1.663	(.09638)
Employment in 1982	.407670	1.654	(.09810)
Sigma	4.12114	9.776	(.00000)

F Statistic (13,233)	5.78124
Significance of F Test	.00000
Chi Squared (13)	68.643
Significance Level	.93332^{e-11}

ers have noted that in the early days of high-tech development, firms had to construct their own technical labor pools. Over time, as university research became more oriented toward microelectronics, colleges began to play a more important role as both the source of and prerequisite for labor attraction. Thus, the historic concentration of metropolitan-adjacent rural high-tech employment and plants may be a result of a preexisting labor force constructed by firms originally located in metropolitan areas that filtered standard production operations to adjacent rural counties.

A second deviation from original expectations was the positive relationship between high-tech employment and unemployment rates. Though not statistically significant, this result may indicate that rural high-tech employment was concentrated around metropolitan areas that had experienced job loss due to industrial restructuring in traditional manufacturing.

TABLE 8.3

Tobit Analysis
Metropolitan-Adjacent Rural High-Tech Plants
1982

	Standard Error	*T Ratio*	*Significance Level*
Intercept	−1.83467	−1.172	(.24133)
Climate	.219571^{e-2}	1.861	(.06277)
Housing	−.417279^{e-3}	−.324	(.74569)
Property Tax	.578519^{e-3}	1.440	(.14985)
Air Service	.373683	2.480	(.01315)
Four-Year College	−.219698^{e-1}	−.735	(.46226)
Sixteen Years Education	.169161^{e-1}	.445	(.65659)
Poverty	−.521753^{e-1}	−1.175	(.23996)
Unemployment	.855921^{e-2}	.147	(.88294)
Procurement	19.8642	.180	(.85745)
Wages	−.305844^{e-4}	−.739	(.46019)
Migration	−.404857^{e-1}	−1.805	(.07107)
Unionization	.260652^{e-1}	2.006	(.04490)
Employment in 1982	.152555	1.624	(.10427)
Sigma	1.63524	.1513	(.00000)

F Statistic (13,233)	7.92631
Significance of F Test	.00000
Chi Squared (13)	90.040
Significance Level	.32173^{e-13}

A similar interpretation can be made regarding factors associated with adjacent rural high-tech plants. Metropolitan areas with significant levels of adjacent rural high-tech plants had similar characteristics as those with concentrations of rural high-tech employment. Plant concentrations were found near cities with mild climates, large airports, high levels of unions, large concentrations of metropolitan high-tech jobs, and low rates of population change due to migration.

That rural high-tech employment is found near places with moderate climates may signify that the early and later periods of high-tech decentralization were not entirely separate or distinct. That is, over the ten-year period, there was a blurring of the shifts both within and among regions. Most likely, this indicates that con-

TABLE 8.4

Tobit Analysis
Metropolitan-Adjacent Rural High-Tech Plants Change
1972–1982

	Standard Error	*T Ratio*	*Significance Level*
Intercept	−8.93990	−1.090	(.27577)
Climate	.101341^{e-1}	1.797	(.07233)
Housing	.415060^{e-2}	.786	(.43215)
Property Tax	.256544^{e-2}	1.369	(.17102)
Air Service	.193524	.233	(.81586)
Four-Year College	.841776^{e-1}	.663	(.50757)
Sixteen Years Education	−.954212^{e-2}	−.052	(.95817)
Poverty	−.222067	−.928	(.35356)
Unemployment	.100203	.341	(.73318)
Procurement	230.336	.352	(.72519)
Wages	−.339029^{e-3}	−1.591	(.11162)
Migration	−.714139^{e-1}	−.600	(.54827)
Unionization	.815617^{e-2}	.134	(.89302)
Employment in 1982	.678531	1.383	(.16663)
Sigma	7.23560	19.615	(.00000)

F Statistic (13,233)	3.17220
Significance of F Test	.00023
Chi Squared (13)	39.841
Significance Level	.14663^{e-3}

ditions applicable to both shifts were operating simultaneously, and it was only over the long run that the emphasis was on interregional decentralization. It is also the case that the climate measure reflects only the absence of extreme weather and therefore may not be precise in capturing intraregional differences. Additional research and more complex modeling would be necessary to confirm this hypothesis.

The negative correlation between adjacent rural high tech and positive interstate migration confirms that rural high tech was not found in abundance in rapidly growing American cities. During the period for which these data apply (1975 through 1980), America was experiencing rapid migration to states outside the industrial core. Given the preexisting concentration of metropolitan-adjacent

TABLE 8.5

Tobit Analysis
Metropolitan-Adjacent Rural High-Tech Employment Change
1972–1982

	Standard Error	T Ratio	Significance Level
Intercept	−1.22923	−.244	(.80704)
Climate	.981113^{e-2}	2.398	(.01650)
Housing	.213643^{e-2}	.479	(.63164)
Property Tax	−.670961^{e-3}	−.534	(.59317)
Air Service	.613151	1.161	(.24572)
Four-Year College	.516508^{e-1}	.497	(.61902)
Sixteen Years Education	−.417849^{e-2}	−.039	(.96893)
Poverty	−.119938	−.814	(.41582)
Unemployment	−.217012	−1.156	(.24767)
Procurement	237.995	.703	(.48175)
Wages	−.134879^{e-3}	−1.056	(.29083)
Migration	−.468510^{e-1}	−.614	(.53948)
Unionization	.158168^{e-1}	.418	(.67626)
Employment in 1982	.215718^{e-1}	.067	(.94687)
Sigma	4.86914	6.725	(.00000)

F Statistic (13,233)	3.23085
Significance of F Test	.00018
Chi Squared (13)	40.527
Significance Level	.11368^{e-3}

rural high tech around cities in the Midwest (and secondarily in the South), we interpret these results to mean that cities with adjacent rural high-tech concentrations were found in states with a history of manufacturing. These places also were growing slowly through immigration.

Earlier analysis by Markusen, Hall, and Glasmeier (1986) indicated a significant statistical relationship between defense spending and high-tech location in 1977. The study results failed to confirm any statistically significant relationship to adjacent rural high-tech location. Nonetheless, the sign of the coefficient was positive, as expected. Perhaps the lack of a significant relationship is due to the overall distribution of defense spending, which is highly skewed toward the largest northeastern and western cities. A second explanation may be that a majority of metro areas share no borders with rural counties. Whatever the explanation, this finding indicates that neither increases nor decreases in defense spending had much effect on historic concentrations of adjacent rural high-tech development.

Metropolitan Characteristics and Changes in Rural High-Tech Employment and Plants

The second set of Tobit analyses reflects the absolute change in rural high-tech plant and employment levels over the study period. These dependent variables characterize more recent rounds of high-tech decentralization that I have suggested were motivated by firms' labor requirements. Tables 8.4 and 8.5 present the results of the Tobit procedure.

Metropolitan characteristics associated with growth in metropolitan-adjacent rural high-tech employment and plants were in part similar to the historic concentration of plants and employment previously discussed. Nonetheless, a number of exceptions are noteworthy. In the case of plant differences, changes in adjacent rural plants were significantly associated with metropolitan areas with mild climates, low wages, high property taxes, and 1982 metropolitan high-tech employment levels. Plant changes were positively associated with high housing prices. This provides modest evidence for the premise that rural high-tech growth was in part a response to rising land costs in cities where high-tech industry was growing rapidly over the decade. At the same time, high tech was growing around metropolitan areas where unemployment rates were high, signifying labor availability and, in extreme cases, labor redundancy. Importantly, high-tech plant change was positively associated with four-year colleges.

Although not statistically significant, the signs of the remaining variables were as expected — with two important exceptions. Plant growth was positively associated with high levels of unionization and low levels of residents with college educations. A possible explanation for these results is that in the case of unionization rates, plant additions may still have been occurring in places with existing concentrations of rural plants. The negative association between plant change and the percentage of the population with a college education may reflect the fact that high-tech firms were shifting plants to city environs where prerequisite educational facilities were found in abundance. In this instance, four-year colleges may have become important for firms recruiting technically trained workers outside core high-tech areas. It may still be the case that high-tech firms are engaged in creating their own labor markets rather than relying strictly on local supply of college-educated residents, but in recent times, creating labor pools requires access to institutions of higher learning as both sources of labor supply and amenities. Finally, procurement levels (although not statistically significant) were positively associated with plant change.

Rural employment change was similarly associated with characteristics of metropolitan areas surrounded by existing concentrations of high-tech employment and plants. However, mildness of climate was the only statistically significant variable in explaining the spatial characteristics of adjacent rural employment change. Unlike plant change, employment change was negatively associated with property tax levels and unemployment rates. In the case of unemployment rates, metropolitan-adjacent rural employment growth could have been occurring in response to firms' needs to tap adjacent rural labor markets for routine assembly and production workers.

Metropolitan Analysis

To understand the significance of rural high-tech development, it is important to contrast the results with analysis of what motivates the majority of these industries and their location decisions. Thus, I turn to examination of metropolitan high tech. This analysis used Ordinary Least Squares regression estimators. No metropolitan areas in the analysis lacked high-tech employment and plants over the study period. This analysis does not include a variable measuring metropolitan high-tech employment.

The first set of regressions estimates the model for 1982 for both plant and employment distributions. The results are quite distinct. Tables 8.6 and 8.7 list the parameter estimates with their signs, t statistics, and symbols indicating their level of significance. The F value shows that we can reject the hypothesis that the

TABLE 8.6
Metropolitan Area Employment
Absolute Values
1982

Variable	B Statistic	Beta Weight	T Statistic
Manufacturing Unions	−.004095	−.033509	(−.569)
Air Service	.518934	.389502	(7.430)[1]
Federal Procurement	235.927645	.174441	(4.081)[1]
Sixteen Years Education by Population	−.004122	−.015257	(−.276)
Climate	.001840	.136997	(2.865)[1]
Four-Year College Education by Population	.043774	.229332	(4.719)[1]
Poverty	−.080352	−.199733	(−3.558)[1]
Wages	-1.61754^{e-5}	−.033954	(−.627)
Migration	−.052850	−.216827	(−4.096)[1]
Property Taxes	2.79792^{e-5}	.007383	(.135)
Unemployment in 1983	−.056706	−.122844	(−2.030)[2]
Housing	-8.50640^{e-4}	−.100657	(−1.628)[3]

Notes: 1. Denotes significance at .01 level.
2. Denotes significance at .05 level.
3. Denotes significance at .10 level.

N = 316
R^2 = .49542
F = 24.79131

independent variables are jointly equal to 0 at the 1 percent level of significance. The models explained .49 and .65 of the variation in the distribution of high-tech employment and plants in American cities. I begin this discussion by reviewing the results of high-tech employment levels followed by that of plants.

A large subset of the twelve variables were important contributors to the explanation of metropolitan high-tech employment concentrations. Eight of the twelve variables were significant at the .10 level and nine had signs in the hypothesized direction.

Certain labor market characteristics were significant in explaining the distribution of metropolitan high-tech employment. Low unemployment rates characterize cities with large concentrations of high-tech employment. Therefore, cities with substantial

TABLE 8.7
Metropolitan Area Plants
Absolute Values
1982

Variable	B Statistic	Beta Weight	T Statistic
Manufacturing Unions	-4.28151^{e-4}	$-.004263$	$(-.087)$
Air Service	.537689	.491044	$(11.271)^1$
Federal Procurement	104.921965	.094390	$(2.657)^1$
Sixteen Years Education			
by Population	$-.012447$	$-.056061$	(-1.220)
Climate	6.84998^{e-4}	.062070	(1.562)
Four-Year College Education			
by Population	.045932	.292788	$(7.250)^1$
Poverty	$-.042249$	$-.127778$	$(-2.739)^1$
Wages	-1.78947^{e-5}	$-.045704$	(-1.015)
Migration	$-.031947$	$-.159472$	$(-3.625)^1$
Property Taxes	1.96722^{e-4}	.063157	(1.391)
Unemployment in 1983	$-.018873$	$-.049746$	$(-.989)$
Housing	1.88811^{e-4}	.027184	$(.529)$

Note: 1.   Denotes significance at .01 level.

N = 316
R^2 = .65154
F   = 47.21067

concentrations of high-tech employment may face full employment conditions. Wage rates were negatively associated with large concentrations of high-tech employment, perhaps reflecting the wholesale regional shift of high tech out of high labor cost cities in the Midwest (and secondarily in the Northeast). Levels of unionization (although not statistically significant) were negatively associated with the distribution of employment.

Selected amenity factors were significant in explaining high-tech employment concentrations. High-tech employment was found in metropolitan areas with mild climates and access to four-year colleges. Access to four-year colleges was the second most important variable in explaining high-tech job concentrations. A one-standard-deviation change in the number of four-year colleges in a community is associated with a .229-standard-deviation change in high-tech employment. Property taxes were positively associated with employment concentrations. Interestingly, the share of population with a college education was negatively associated with metropolitan high-tech employment. Firms may be more concerned about being able to attract a requisite labor force than locating where a large concentration of educated persons is found. It is also the case that large concentrations of high-tech employment are found in metropolitan areas with relatively diversified economic bases.

Access to good air service was the major explanatory variable important in defining both employment and plant location. A one-standard-deviation change in commercial air service resulted in a .389-standard-deviation change in high-tech employment distributions.

From earlier studies of high tech in the United States, defense spending was known to be an important determinant of high-tech location. Our results confirm that levels of federal defense procurement were positively associated with metropolitan high-tech employment. The consistency of these results over numerous studies and time suggests the undeniable importance of federal policy in shaping the spatial distribution of metropolitan high-tech industry in the nation.

Metropolitan employment location was negatively associated with high rates of interstate migration. This result suggests that high tech does not concentrate in small, rapidly growing metropolitan areas. High tech needs instead an established industrial economy and labor market.

Metropolitan high-tech employment distribution was strongly negatively correlated with poverty in the population. Cities with high rates of poverty tend to be concentrated in America's southern states (80 percent of cities with poverty rates above 15 percent were located in the South). These results suggest that high poverty communities stand little chance of benefiting from local economic development policy emphasizing high-tech industry. Given that high tech is a major component of local economic development programs, and that we are experiencing an era of static or declining federal funding for community assistance, this possibility is especially ominous for poor communities.

A detailed discussion of plant concentrations reveals strong similarities with the distribution of high-tech employment. Air service was very important in explaining the distribution of plants. A one-standard-deviation change in air service leads to a .491-standard-deviation change in plants. Availability of four-year degree-granting institutions was also important in explaining metropolitan plant location. A one-standard-deviation change in plants leads to a .292-standard-deviation change in the number of four-year colleges. Defense spending was also significant in explaining plant location. Mild climate was positive in explaining the distribution of plants, although the coefficient was only significant at the .15 level. Like high-tech employment, plants were negatively associated with high rates of poverty and immigration.

Changes in Metropolitan High-Tech Employment and Plants

The second set of regressions estimates the changes in high-tech plants and employment over the 1972–82 study period. Although there are some significant differences, the results share similarities with cities boasting large concentrations of high-tech jobs and plants in 1982. Tables 8.8 and 8.9 list the parameter estimates with their signs, t statistics, and symbols indicating their level of significance. The F values are highly significant, indicating we can reject the hypothesis that the independent variables are equal to 0 at a 1 percent significance level. The models explained .27 and .54 of the variation in the change in high-tech employment and plants in American cities. A subset of the variables was significant, and the signs were generally in the predicted direction. Again, I begin with a discussion of jobs followed by that of plants.

Cities that experienced the greatest increases in their base of high-tech employment are characterized by high housing costs and high procurement contract levels per capita. Access to four-year colleges (although positive) was not a statistically significant determinant of employment change. As with the overall distribution of high-tech employment, fast-growing cities proved unattractive to high-tech industry employment change.

Labor market variables performed as predicted. Both low wages and the absence of unions were important predictors of high-tech employment growth (although wage levels were not statistically significant).

TABLE 8.8
Metropolitan Area Employment
Absolute Change
1972–1982

Variable	B Statistic	Beta Weight	T Statistic
Manufacturing Unions	–99.892549	–.121588	(–1.715)[2]
Air Service	766.656839	.085596	(1.357)
Federal Procurement	1680790.4174	.184858	(3.593)[1]
Sixteen Years Education			
by Population	–.652815	-3.595^{e-4}	(–.005)
Climate	7.491505	.082990	(1.442)
Four-Year College			
Education by Population	17.646221	.013752	(.235)
Poverty	–44.877579	–.016593	(–.246)
Wages	–.019739	–.006163	(–.095)
Migration	–174.372712	–.106415	(–1.670)[2]
Property Taxes	–.648512	–.025454	(–.387)
Unemployment in 1983	–221.510343	–.071380	(–.980)
Housing	19.134990	.336809	(4.526)[1]

Note: 1. Denotes significance at .01 level.
2. Denotes significance at .10 level.

N = 316
R^2 = .26904
F = 9.29357

With some important exceptions, results for plant change are quite similar to those of employment. Plant growth was associated with communities boasting good air service. Air service was the second most important explanatory factor in the distribution of plant change. A one-standard-deviation change in air service leads to a .219-standard-deviation change in plant additions. Although not statistically significant, like employment change, growth in plants was negatively associated with unions.

Interestingly, plant change was strongly negatively associated with four-year degree-granting colleges while positively associated with the share of population with a college education. This may signify that the formation of new plants was more responsive to the composition of the local labor market than the supply of available college-level educational options. It is also the case that large concentrations of four-year colleges are found in relatively few major

TABLE 8.9

Metropolitan Area Plants
Absolute Change
1972–1982

Variable	B Statistic	Beta Weight	T Statistic
Manufacturing Unions	–.076690	–.039895	(–.708)
Air Service	4.609328	.219947	(4.386)[1]
Federal Procurement	1204.914107	.056638	(1.385)
Sixteen Years Education			
by Population	.279917	.065876	(1.245)
Climate	.009870	.046731	(1.022)
Four-Year College			
Education by Population	–2.336446	–.778187	(–16.740)[1]
Poverty	–.626452	–.098997	(–1.843)[2]
Wages	-2.37106^{e-4}	–.031641	(–.611)
Migration	–.465689	–.121464	(–2.399)[1]
Property Taxes	–.008458	–.141882	(–2.715)[1]
Unemployment in 1983	–.550386	–.075801	(–1.310)
Housing	.005164	.038846	(.657)

Note: 1.   Denotes significance at .01 level.
        2.   Denotes significance at .05 level.

N = 316
R^2 = .53826
F = 29.43427

American cities. Given that high tech was decentralizing over the period studied, these results may not be entirely unexpected.

Finally, procurement levels were not significant in explaining plant change. Evidently, high-tech plant growth was not occurring in communities that were recipients of large government procurement contracts.

Comparisons Between Metropolitan and Rural High-Tech Regions for 1982 Plant and Employment Distributions

In comparing the two groups of cities, both similarities and differences are apparent in the factors that explain metropolitan and rural high tech. Both groups share an aversion to areas with high levels of poverty. They also sport good air services. Interstate migration rates were uniformly low.

The distinct features that describe the two groups of cities are

also noteworthy. Colleges were important determinants of metropolitan high-tech plant and employment location (except those
with historic concentrations of high tech in adjacent rural areas).
In contrast, the percentage of population with a college education
was positively related to cities with surrounding concentrations of
rural high-tech employment and plants. Levels of defense procurement were also statistically significant in explaining the existing
concentration of high tech in metropolitan areas but not those with
adjacent rural high-tech plants and employment.

The second set of regressions measuring change over time also
shared a number of similarities between the two groups of cities.
For both, changes in high-tech job levels are positively associated
with mild climates and high housing prices while access to four-year
colleges was important in explaining variation in employment levels. Cities with significant changes in adjacent rural county employment and plants were positively associated with unionization rates
while the opposite was true for metropolitan high-tech employment
and plant change.

These two distinct results deserve comment. It may be that
metropolitan employment and plant change reflect a tilt toward the
Sunbelt, where climates are milder and unionization rates are
lower. This conforms to our original model of early-stage, high-
tech decentralization. Similarly, that employment change is concentrated in and near cities with access to four-year colleges and
high housing prices may reflect the selective growth of employment
in communities especially endowed with educational resources.
Relatively few locations emerged in the 1970s as attractive to high-
tech industry. These communities experienced rapid population
growth, which often resulted in inflationary pressure on housing
prices. Clearly, these results beg further analysis of specific rural
community experiences, and yet they largely confirm the
hypotheses outlined in chapter 7.

Limitations to the Methodology

Admittedly, this exercise has limitations. Spillover effects can be
directly measured only by identifying firms that shifted employment from metro to rural areas. The data used in these studies provide both a cross-sectional view of the historic accumulation of
high-tech industry at one point in time and the net change in the

distribution of high-tech jobs and plants in rural and metropolitan areas over the 1972–82 period. Because the second measure simply accounts for net changes in employment and plants, it is indeterminable whether rural jobs and plants originated in adjacent cities or in locations outside the local areas.

A second limitation relates to the composition of the variables. With few exceptions, the variables reflect their value in the year 1982; but some of the variables (two-year and four-year colleges, unemployment, federal procurement, and property taxes) are 1983 values and a number of other variables were collected in 1980 (such as housing prices, percentage of population with twelve and sixteen or more years of education, and poverty in the population). Additionally, one variable—the percentage of unionized workers in manufacturing—was available on only a state basis. In most states, these rates reflect conditions found in metropolitan areas. Unionization rates probably vary within states, especially between urban and rural areas. Nevertheless, even with this limitation, this variable was an important business climate feature, so it remained in the analysis.

Finally, there are a number of ways bias could have entered into the analysis. Numerous metropolitan areas are contiguous. In such cases, it is possible that high-tech location is a function of the joint effects of more than one metropolitan area. Access to amenities and services in a coterminous urban area may boost the attraction of a metropolis in excess of its own local characteristics. This is particularly likely when considering a pair of metropolitan areas of which one member is substantially larger.

The problem of adjacency also arises in allocating rural areas to a metropolitan counterpart. In constructing the data base, it was necessary to allocate rural counties to specific cities. This was accomplished by using unpublished census "journey to work" data. A rural county was allocated to a metropolitan area based on the metropolitan work destination of the largest percentage of the county's commuting population. A rural county could have been incorrectly allocated to a city, causing an underestimation or overestimation of an urban area's adjacent rural employment and plants, but recognizing these caveats, it was still possible to examine the relationship between urban and adjacent rural high-tech employment for all counties in the country. The data base included a number of variables that have come to be synonymous with high-tech development. By comparing the two groups of cities, I am able to make limited statements about the likely impact of recent policy innovations on rural high-tech development.

Summary

Previous regression analyses of rural high-tech location probably did not behave as predicted because they attempted to place known historical outcomes within the contemporary phenomena of high-tech development. At the time these studies were conducted, the reality of tremendous new growth had not yet caught up with the image of what high tech was believed to be and the outcomes it was thought to cause.

In searching for a location in which to reproduce the Silicon Valley phenomenon, firms considered places where they believed they could attract the human component that makes up high tech, and economic development officials and chambers of commerce representatives of such places as Denver, Research Triangle Park, and Austin touted their cities as heirs to the next high-tech agglomeration. It was thought that if the template from Silicon Valley and Route 128 was laid over another location with matching strategic amenities, a new center of innovation could be created.

Firms *were* searching for a midplace to park production. Financial constraints necessitated that they take advantage of existing labor pools, and some industries had matured to the point where they had produced labor markets within specific locations. For example, in central Texas, the University of Texas at Austin and Texas A&M University in College Station were producing engineers to support new demand from area high-tech firms.

However, in studying these phenomena, previous research did not acknowledge that in existing cores, such as Boston, the features identifiable as high-tech–conducive had traditionally been available. Thus, new development really just grafted itself onto the existing amenity agglomeration. In new high-tech centers, it was a simultaneous process of development in which growth of high tech created the enthusiasm that perpetuated the expansion of amenities. So in the former case, the goods were there, but in the latter, there was more of an evolution in amenities that occurred to match the rhetoric of the popular image.

Drawing upon earlier sections of this book, I suggest that the historic accumulation of high-tech jobs largely reflects firms' efforts to shift high-tech jobs and plants toward metropolitan-adjacent rural counties near established manufacturing cities. More recent shifts to metropolitan-adjacent rural counties reflect firms' searches for locations close to metropolitan areas where suitable pools of technical labor and markets can be found.

9

Prospects for Rural High-Tech Development

High-tech industry development beckons as a prospect for future manufacturing growth in America's rural communities. Over a period of rapid national high-tech growth, rural counties had some success attracting high-tech industries. Though growth rates were less than the national average, both new jobs and plants were added to the existing rural base.

In light of our findings, it is important to consider the composition of rural high-tech employment and plants. Both absolutely and in terms of new growth, rural high-tech development is significantly tied to the fortunes of traditional rural industries. Thus, growth in one should clearly stimulate the other. The reverse is also likely to be true; declines in traditional rural industries will most likely lead to negative changes for rural high-technology production.

Although rural high-tech industry development exhibits more variety than the present industrial base, it is still not without problems. Growth of employment and plants has been quite concentrated in only a few industries. Lack of diversity increases a county's vulnerability to industry changes at national and, increasingly, global levels. A more favorable distribution, one that includes many different industries, would insulate a community from the negative effects of decline in a single sector, but diversity itself is not enough. Rural communities have traditionally attracted slow-growing industries. Future increases in jobs through diversification efforts need to be in industries with some prospects for growth.

Growth of high-tech industries is not distributed evenly across all rural counties. The most isolated rural areas have simply not benefited from high-tech growth over the study period. Real winners are those rural counties with small but significant urban centers of their own, located both adjacent and nonadjacent to larger metropolitan counties. This departs from the experiences of traditionally rural industries that demonstrate a significant presence (such as textiles) and past successes in the smaller, more isolated rural counties.

Since the early 1970s, high-tech industry location has followed the shifts in population and total manufacturing already under way among U.S. regions. The Midwest has declined in shares of the nation's population, manufacturing, and high-tech jobs. Redistribution appears to have benefited the South and, to a lesser extent, the West. Manufacturing in the Northeast has become more high tech as the region has shed its older industries. This pattern is also evident in the Northeast's rural areas.

The West is clearly the most polarized region, given its large share of total national high-tech employment relative to population and overall manufacturing, yet has a modest presence of high-tech jobs in rural counties. Although rapidly growing in the urban West, the meager presence of high-technology industries underscores their limited importance to most rural communities in the region. As in the Northeast, the persistence of this pattern is noteworthy.

The similarity in the trends of high-tech location and other regional aggregates, such as population and manufacturing, has significant implications for rural areas. Conditions that sparked the initial redistribution of economic activity among America's regions may have largely subsided. Manufacturing employment has to some extent stabilized among regions; firms are no longer setting up branch plants at the pace characteristic of the 1970s, and even high-tech industry growth has slowed dramatically. This implies that the circumstances that unleashed the subsequent pattern of high-tech location are no longer operative; thus, future rural gains in high-tech employment will likely be modest.

The dynamic CEC high-tech sectors and those most influenced by national policies (DDS) contribute little to development of a technological base of employment in rural counties. While there have been modest increases in the presence of these industries within the nation's rural communities, shares of CEC and DDS sectors in rural areas are still substantially below comparable figures for the nation. All regions show small amounts of this type of rural employment, but it is doubtful that these dynamic sectors will play a significant role in changing the long-standing composition of high-tech jobs in rural areas (that is, the concentration of rural high-tech jobs in metropolitan-adjacent counties and their ties to traditional rural industries).

At least for rural areas of the South, high-tech job growth has brought mixed blessings. New employment is never discounted, but its composition should not be expected to deviate from existing rural industries. Other research indicates high-tech industries differ imperceptibly from traditional rural manufacturing comprised of low-skilled blue-collar jobs (Falk and Lyson 1988). Most new employment is found in branch plants. High tech is concentrated in establishments owned by firms headquartered outside local communities. Major metropolitan areas of the South remain only regional control centers of production plants in their rural hinterlands. R and D is still concentrated in the nation's premier high-tech center of the West and Northeast. Case studies of selected rural high-tech plants indicate a strong emerging pattern of new technology applications. In some cases, this means new skills for local workers. Over the long term, though, job displacement remains a distinct possibility, and many rural high-tech plants upgrade production to compete more effectively with their international counterparts. This often results in job loss and skills reduction in existing plants. Clearly, communities must remain aware of the types of jobs they attract and vigilantly monitor prospects for long-term employment stability.

Rural counties in the United States have very modestly benefited from the growth of high-tech jobs and plants at a national level. The Midwest and the South have been the almost exclusive winners in rural high-tech growth at the regional level. As I have tried to argue, this pattern reflects a dual decentralization tendency both in earlier and more recent periods—to regional hinterlands within the Midwest and toward rural areas of the South. In the case of the Midwest, rural high-tech growth corresponds to early efforts by companies to escape metropolitan areas where manufacturing workers were highly unionized. In contrast, the South reflects a blending of the two periods, with early branch plants seeking strictly low-cost locations and a more recent shift of high tech to large market locations and toward rural areas surrounding cities where both high-skilled and lower-skilled labor can be found.

These two tendencies—the shift to the hinterlands for lower-cost labor and to the South toward markets and appropriate labor pools—were tested in a series of regression analyses. This exercise related rural adjacent county employment and plants with metropolitan characteristics. Rural counties with high absolute levels of plants and employment are adjacent to MSAs, where union levels are high and population growth through migration is slow. Additionally, high levels of air service signify that absolute levels of high-tech jobs and plants in adjacent rural counties occurred near larger metropolitan areas as opposed to smaller ones. In contrast, rural counties that experienced absolute gains in plants were adjacent to MSAs with proximity to four-year colleges.

The findings of the regression analyses present some indications of how existing high-tech development policy will influence further growth of these industries in rural areas. The results suggest that rural high-tech location is influenced by larger economic trends associated with the costs of doing business in manufacturing. There are only a few state programs designed to increase the quality of the labor force, thus reducing the costs of production, while accelerating the development of new products and processes.

The nation's implicit industrial policy of defense-led industrialization presents few opportunities for rural communities. Defense spending levels per capita were not important in explaining rural adjacent high-tech development. This comes as little surprise because defense industries are largely insensitive to costs and have little incentive to seek out low-cost production locations.

Many states with more enlightened programs do not have an explicit rural focus to their high-tech efforts. Therefore, the most rural communities can expect is that benefits of high-tech policy will trickle down over time as a state's manufacturing base becomes more competitive. A process of industrial filtering is essential in this case, but as we have suggested, filtering of particular high-tech jobs to rural areas is tied to labor characteristics and firms' needs to find suitable pools of both low-skilled and higher-skilled, well-educated workers. Few rural communities outside the influence of metropolitan areas meet these requirements. This returns us to long-standing problems of rural economic development.

Defects in rural economies keep rural communities from full participation in state programs. Rural areas tend to depend on a single source of economic development, such as agriculture or mining. These basic sectors do little to broaden the skill base of rural communities. Lack of adequate basic infrastructure—constant electricity sources, digital telecommunications, high-quality roads, and airports—also limits the type of industry that can successfully operate in rural communities. Low levels of general skill in the population and small numbers of technically trained personnel further restrict high-tech location.

Programs that do target rural areas are predominantly of the recruitment type. Limited economic development resources and short-term horizons of local politicians reinforce industrial recruitment as the major option for rural economic development.[28] Other riskier efforts, such as local support for small firms and entrepreneurship training, are viewed as costly and the payoff too long term to be effective in rural locations, but it is these programs that present rural areas with the greatest opportunities. Narrow economic bases, limited infrastructures, low levels of skills in the population, and dependence on industrial recruitment simply preserve the cycle of nonparticipation by rural communities. Given that cities are currently the most likely location where new technologies and industries will develop, state high-tech development programs may, in fact, be far more necessary and important for rural areas than they are for metropolitan.

Although there is no magic formula to guarantee a share of future high-tech jobs, one can glean from the case studies outlined here the factors that, in combination, produce high-tech success stories in rural communities. The characteristics of individual place were key determinants of successful rural high-tech companies. The presence of universities in rural communities is important, not because they necessarily create the seeds of rural high-tech firms but because they exist in economic and social climates—economies of agglomeration—conducive to successful firm growth. University towns tend to have higher quality educational systems at primary and secondary levels. It is from this pool of individuals that high-tech firms will draw their labor. Universities are also important because they increase the availability of cultural and retail options for local consumers. Many of these same benefits can be had by firms operating in rural counties adjacent to metropolitan areas with their own distinct characteristics.

The role of the entrepreneur is also a critical component of positive high-tech development. While rural communities have had success in attracting high-tech branch plants, there are a number of reasons to believe that this source of economic development may be unstable. Our example of successful cases concluded that corporate policy and enlightened management are important ingredients. As a branch plant, Gore and Associates is relatively unique in this regard. Branch plants are not widely associated with the staying qualities that an entrepreneur often has in his or her local community.

Traditional location factors such as access to markets or material inputs do not appear to limit rural high-tech development. This probably means that rural high-tech firms function as freestanding operations independent of other local firms; the absence of these locational constraints increases the potential for rural high-tech development. Lack of interfirm links is importantly tied to the type of product successfully produced in rural locations. In both cases, interregional and international trade, rather than local exchange, is important, if not *key* to firm success.

The reality of rural high tech is that there just isn't much. It tends to follow existing patterns rather than setting new trends and is almost always found in slower growing industries than its urban counterparts.

Thus, in formulating high-tech development policy to benefit rural areas, high-tech industries should be treated as any other manufacturing sector. Policymakers should take care not to buy into the idea that these industries are somehow more stable or enduring. Rather than glamorizing the idea of attracting high technology, communities must negotiate for these new branch plants as they would a furniture manufacturer or a machining facility. Incentives should be offered more warily, always considering how a particular firm will benefit the community. A high-tech facility should not receive concessions based solely on its industry classification. Witness Crystalis Semiconductors in Albuquerque,

New Mexico, which was spawned in the community, took advantage of a myriad of incentive programs, and when it became successful, moved on to Silicon Valley, where its markets were geographically concentrated. Rural areas usually have a finite amount of funding available, so they must make choices about the composition of industries they wish to attract. Recognizing that new industrial bases usually do not differ much from those of the past, communities should not rule out more nontraditional assistance, such as funding for local entrepreneurs.

Government at the national level can also implement policies to decant federally funded high-tech activities that are now mostly concentrated in urban high-tech agglomerations. For example, the economic development wealth associated with research labs should be more evenly distributed. Rural communities are the home for a number of the nation's R and D labs, yet there has been little attendant development found in these communities. Efforts should be made to stimulate local business development around these installations, and similar to guidelines already in place to protect minority-owned and small businesses' supplier positions, procurement and contracting policies could be designed to spread federal government spending geographically.

Rural areas should also bargain harder about the types of activities going on in their facilities. For example, if a community is compiling an incentive package that will benefit a company financially (for example, land, tax concessions, utility infrastructure, and so on), it should also negotiate with the firm to take more responsibility for training its labor force. Firm surveys indicate that companies rate training as an important location factor (Glickman and Glasmeier 1989a). Thus, communities must develop a heightened consciousness about the longevity of the effects of packages they develop. Firms that locate in an area and implement educational programs that *create* skills serve to enhance the existing labor pool, making it more attractive in subsequent rounds of competition for industry.

However, the only way that rural areas will begin to be competitive over the long run in the race for high-tech industrial development will be to take a very realistic assessment of their basic deficiencies now. This would include not only utility, access, and services infrastructure but also local people and the base of existing industries. As long as these are unyielding to new technology, slow to react to market changes, and unresponsive to consumer demands, the overall view of a community's business environment will be similar.

An aggressive rural-based agenda would address these long-standing deficiencies but also realize that a remote community's chances of becoming a high-tech agglomeration are slim. Thus, in order to increase the stability of existing economies, there should be a new mandate for programs that upgrade existing industries. The previous push for high-tech branch plants has left many rural communities disappointed. Since 1984, after the initial high-tech golden period, many of these facilities have closed down or moved to foreign locations. Lobbyists should urge a softening of state high-tech policy so that process-oriented innovations can be adopted in existing facilities. Becoming high tech *users* may make firms more competitive, perhaps preserving existing establishments. As technical capacities of plants are upgraded, improved production techniques may also provide new market opportunities.

Whether peripheral areas of advanced economies are still competitive compared to their Third World, low-wage, high-skilled counterparts should be the subject for future serious debate. Even urban workers in industrialized nations can no longer compete with comparably trained foreign labor. More remote communities have labor bases that are deficient in the skills needed to function in this age of high technology. We must recognize that national policies for improvements in education and various kinds of infrastructure upgrades do not "filter down" to rural areas of their own volition. Only in the rare instances in which a few insightful people have taken initiative have rural areas benefited.

We have yet to incorporate a fully elaborated understanding of rural areas in this new era of high tech. Therefore, the issue for rural America in the 1990s becomes one of survival. What is the niche in the new global system of production? Will the adjustment costs of industry relocation to foreign sites be less than the costs of investing in rural areas? The idea that high technology will follow traditional product-cycle model predictions of decentralization is not being manifested. Semiconductor plants moved elsewhere twenty years ago, and high-technology industry displays agglomerative, not decentralizing, tendencies. Places dominant in the 1970s remain dominant today.

Given the emphasis on technology in industry, our rural areas are more vulnerable now than ever, but we continue to enact policy that is metropolitan-oriented and decanted into rural areas. We must develop proactive rural development programs. Industry is no longer faced with clear-cut choices of capital or labor. Capital basically produces a better product. As the case study of State of the Art, Inc., showed, indigenous development provides good opportunities if rural areas can cultivate entrepreneurs. However, this implies complete reorientation of existing high-tech policy that is not small business-oriented but rather metropolitan R and D-oriented. A much greater amount of realism must be injected into the debate about what development means for rural areas and how rural communities will be incorporated into inevitable industrial changes due to advances in technology.

Appendix A

High-Tech Industry Growth Performance: 1972–1982

SIC	Establishments			Percent Growth			Employment			Percent Growth		
	1972	1977	1982	1972–77	1977–82	1972–82	1972	1977	1982	1972–77	1977–82	1972–82
2812	48.	49.	51.	2.1	4.1	6.3	13357.	11833.	8654.	-11.4	-26.9	-35.2
2813	503.	562.	563.	11.7	0.2	11.9	9863.	7398.	7538.	-25.0	1.9	-23.6
2816	114.	106	106	-7.0	0.0	-7.0	14904.	12000.	13116.	-19.5	9.3	-12.0
2819	384.	564.	645.	46.9	14.4	68.0	63808.	78203.	86464.	22.6	10.6	35.5
2821	323.	397.	440.	22.9	10.8	36.2	54612.	57107.	58925.	4.6	3.2	7.9
2822	59.	63.	78.	6.8	23.8	32.2	12589.	11545.	14712.	-8.3	27.4	16.9
2823	18.	25.	18.	38.9	-28.0	0.0	20508.	16229.	14679.	-20.9	-9.6	-28.4
2824	61.	66.	70.	8.2	6.1	14.8	79158.	74065.	63758.	-6.4	-13.9	-19.5
2831	182.	310.	370.	70.3	19.4	103.3	10959.	18468.	26905.	68.5	45.7	145.5
2833	140.	177.	228.	26.4	28.8	62.9	9440.	15725.	18124.	66.6	15.3	92.0
2834	756.	756.	683.	0.0	-9.7	-9.7	112100.	126400.	131905.	12.8	4.4	17.7
2841	642.	638.	723.	-0.6	13.3	12.6	31499.	32641.	38174.	3.6	16.9	21.2
2842	1108.	1022.	807.	-7.8	-21.0	-27.2	26080.	22920.	25961.	-12.1	13.3	-0.5
2843	178.	175.	210.	-1.7	20.0	18.0	6957	6839.	9309.	-1.7	36.1	33.8
2844	645.	693.	639.	7.4	-7.8	-0.9	48134.	50800.	68519.	5.5	34.9	42.3
2851	1599	1579.	1441.	-1.3	-8.7	-9.9	66901.	61297.	57306.	-8.4	-6.5	-14.3
2861	139.	119.	92.	-14.4	-22.7	-33.8	6039.	4721.	4554.	-21.8	-3.5	-24.6
2865	174.	191.	189.	9.8	-1.0	8.6	28087.	35514.	29983.	26.4	-15.6	6.7
2869	514.	569.	688.	10.7	20.9	33.9	101994.	112400.	118682.	10.2	5.6	16.4
2873	73.	152.	143.	108.2	-5.9	95.9	9563.	12447.	11227.	30.2	-9.8	17.4
2874	145.	91.	110.	-37.2	20.9	-24.1	15801.	15706	15561.	-0.6	-0.9	-1.5
2875	627.	673.	544.	7.3	-19.2	-13.2	11415.	12489.	9849.	9.4	-21.1	-13.7
2879	388.	409.	330.	5.4	-19.3	-14.9	12575.	15168.	17804.	20.6	17.4	41.6
2891	463.	573.	684.	23.8	19.4	47.7	15053.	16672.	20260.	10.8	21.5	34.6

2892	92.	97	114.	5.4	17.5	23.9	16998.	11549.	15155.	-32.1	31.2	-10.8
2893	407.	446.	467.	9.6	4.7	14.7	9701.	10100.	10021.	4.1	-0.8	3.3
2895	37.	31.	25.	-16.2	-19.4	-32.4	3017.	2600.	2318.	-13.8	-10.8	-23.2
2899	1606.	1639.	1443.	2.1	-12.0	-10.1	37885.	35299.	44464.	-6.8	26.0	17.4
2911	323.	349.	433.	8.0	24.1	34.1	100543.	102399.	120856.	1.8	18.0	20.2
3031	20	21.	25.	5.0	19.0	25.0	1115.	1007.	780.	-9.7	-22.6	-30.0
3482	62.	65.	0.	4.8	-100.0	-100.0	13867.	12187.	0.	-12.1	-100.0	-100.0
3483	95.	81.	0.	-14.7	-100.0	-100.0	54992.	20581.	0.	-62.6	-100.0	-100.0
3484	82.	112.	0.	36.6	-100.0	-100.0	16000.	17500.	0	9.4	-100.0	-100.0
3489	76.	89.	0.	17.1	-100.0	-100.0	25407.	19037.	0	-25.1	-100.0	-100.0
3511	75.	83.	88.	10.7	6.0	17.3	46286.	40964.	36394.	-11.5	-11.2	-21.4
3519	178.	232.	253.	30.3	9.1	42.1	69947.	88800.	84566.	27.0	-4.8	20.9
3531	748.	922.	939.	23.3	1.8	25.5	133700.	155199.	127548.	16.1	-17.8	-4.6
3532	240.	344.	369.	43.3	7.3	53.8	21700.	31299.	28262.	44.2	-9.7	30.2
3533	315.	478.	1015.	51.7	112.3	222.2	35872.	58499.	106270.	63.1	81.7	196.2
3534	154.	152.	165.	-1.3	8.6	7.1	15839.	10201.	13869.	-35.6	35.9	-12.4
3535	492.	616.	699.	25.2	13.5	42.1	27138.	32927.	39940.	21.3	21.3	47.2
3536	188.	242.	276.	28.7	14.0	46.8	17168.	15800.	16779.	-8.0	6.2	-2.3
3537	380.	475.	489.	25.0	2.9	28.7	25901.	28386.	27924.	9.6	-1.6	7.8
3541	894.	919.	942.	2.8	2.5	5.4	56960.	59463.	60196.	4.4	1.2	5.7
3542	383.	426.	452.	11.2	6.1	18.0	24095.	23145.	21143.	-3.9	-8.6	-12.2
3544	6616.	7152.	7255.	8.1	1.4	9.7	97807.	106108.	110875.	8.5	4.5	13.4
3545	1231.	1412.	1620	14.7	14.7	31.6	46572.	54257.	61656.	16.5	13.6	32.4
3546	88.	124.	203.	40.9	63.7	130.7	22926.	27676.	24411.	20.7	-11.8	6.5
3547	47.	63.	63.	34.0	0.0	34.0	9232.	8530.	6115.	-7.6	-28.3	-33.8
3549	393.	534.	446.	35.9	-16.5	13.5	13937.	19141.	24052.	37.3	25.7	72.6
3561	559.	613.	626.	9.7	2.1	12.0	55718.	63055.	76908.	13.2	22.0	38.0
3562	135.	149.	162.	10.4	8.7	20.0	50830.	50288.	47742.	-1.1	-5.1	-6.1
3563	84.	175.	282.	108.3	61.1	235.7	22373.	31900.	35343.	42.6	10.8	58.0

Appendix A (Continued)
High-Tech Industry Growth Performance: 1972–1982

SIC	Establishments			Percent Growth			Employment			Percent Growth		
	1972	1977	1982	1972–77	1977–82	1972–82	1972	1977	1982	1972–77	1977–82	1972–82
3564	396.	482.	502.	21.7	4.1	26.8	24202.	28430.	34728.	17.5	22.2	43.5
3565	1021.	1002.	996.	-1.9	-0.6	-2.4	8502.	9399.	11387.	10.6	21.1	33.9
3566	346.	327.	309.	-5.5	-5.5	-10.7	27059.	24547.	26148.	-9.3	6.5	-3.4
3567	266.	327.	353.	22.9	8.0	32.7	14692.	16263.	18265.	10.7	12.3	24.3
3568	155.	226.	293.	45.8	29.6	89.0	27353.	32559.	30976.	19.0	-4.9	13.2
3569	901.	1646.	1458.	82.7	-11.4	61.8	38441.	58554.	67346.	52.3	15.0	75.2
3573	602.	932.	1739.	54.8	86.6	188.9	144661.	192514.	348821.	33.1	81.2	141.1
3574	79.	64.	70.	-19.0	9.4	-11.4	19365.	15460.	17874.	-20.2	15.6	-7.7
3576	97.	103.	128.	6.2	24.3	32.0	7154.	6712.	7141.	-6.2	6.4	-0.2
3579	217.	218.	232.	0.5	6.4	6.9	34501.	42412.	50895.	22.9	20.0	47.5
3612	216.	279.	293.	29.2	5.0	35.6	45900.	43360.	41567.	-5.5	-4.1	-9.4
3613	568.	668.	649.	17.6	-2.8	14.3	69412.	72225.	75671.	4.1	4.8	9.0
3621	425.	447.	472.	5.2	5.6	11.1	90241.	96971.	96191.	7.5	-0.8	6.6
3622	590.	726.	913.	23.1	25.8	54.7	51006.	56428.	69989.	10.6	24.0	37.2
3623	166.	176.	182.	6.0	3.4	9.6	15233.	17400.	16865.	14.2	-3.1	10.7
3624	72.	74.	90.	2.8	21.6	25.0	11683.	12083.	13559.	3.4	12.2	16.1
3629	58.	223.	323.	-13.6	44.8	25.2	20127.	16475.	18281.	-18.1	11.0	-9.2
3651	372.	581.	458.	56.2	-21.2	23.1	86500.	74601.	52012.	-13.8	-30.3	-39.9
3652	567.	709.	574.	25.0	-19.0	1.2	21221.	23102.	18295.	8.9	-20.8	-13.8
3661	203.	264.	333.	30.0	26.1	64.0	74068.	124310.	146442.	67.8	17.8	97.7
3662	1773.	2121.	2388.	19.6	12.6	34.7	317556.	332923.	491821.	4.8	47.7	54.9
3671	25.	146.	102.	484.0	-30.1	308.0	10515.	36800.	36469.	250.0	-0.9	246.8
3672	75.	0.	0.	-100.0	0.0	-100.0	15211.	0.	0.	-100.0	0.0	-100.0

3673	53.	0.	0.	-100.0	0.0	-100.0	20285.	0.	0.	-100.0	0.0	-100.0
3674	327.	545.	766.	66.7	40.6	134.3	97389.	114001.	184019.	17.1	61.4	89.0
3675	113.	118.	130.	4.4	10.2	15.0	27568.	28643.	32930.	3.9	15.0	19.5
3676	86.	101.	103.	17.4	2.0	19.8	20264.	24923.	19929.	23.0	-20.0	-1.7
3677	248.	294.	386.	18.5	31.3	55.6	24326.	22425.	24245.	-7.8	8.1	-0.3
3678	91.	133.	198.	46.2	48.9	117.6	19648.	26013.	44967.	32.4	72.9	128.9
3679	1844.	3118.	3770.	69.1	20.9	104.4	98340.	125966.	226362.	28.1	79.7	130.2
3721	168.	176.	165.	4.8	-6.3	-1.8	231919.	222800.	264295.	-3.9	18.6	14.0
3724	232.	269.	340.	15.9	26.4	46.6	95563.	106200.	134530.	11.1	26.7	40.8
3728	694.	728.	966.	4.9	32.7	39.2	102414.	101934.	137201.	-0.5	34.6	34.0
3743	163.	201.	200.	23.3	-0.5	22.7	50859.	56399.	33225.	10.9	-41.1	-34.7
3761	70.	40.	29.	-42.9	-27.5	-58.6	118309.	93929.	112417.	-20.6	19.7	-5.0
3764	29.	26.	27.	-10.3	3.8	-6.9	21018.	17014.	26276.	-19.1	54.4	25.0
3769	48.	42.	49.	-12.5	16.7	2.1	20952.	10193.	21981.	-51.3	115.6	4.9
3795	22.	24.	44.	9.1	83.3	100.0	5319.	12120.	16753.	127.9	38.2	215.0
3811	739.	786.	771.	6.4	-1.9	4.3	36482.	42197.	47448.	15.7	12.4	30.1
3822	131.	201.	245.	53.4	21.9	87.0	30600.	39100.	30361.	27.8	-22.3	-0.8
3823	187.	426.	627.	127.8	47.2	235.3	35446.	46499.	66223.	31.2	42.4	86.8
3824	61.	111.	145.	82.0	30.6	137.7	8271.	16019.	13440.	93.7	-16.1	62.5
3825	645.	671.	749.	4.0	11.6	16.1	55232.	66601.	96100.	20.6	44.3	74.0
3829	595.	670.	717.	12.6	7.0	20.5	26480.	32200.	40206.	21.6	24.9	51.8
3832	494.	545.	638.	10.3	17.1	29.1	19637.	29906.	53348.	52.3	78.4	171.7
3841	506.	651.	859.	28.7	32.0	69.8	34873.	43226.	63069.	24.0	45.9	80.9
3842	872.	1154.	1167.	32.3	18.5	56.8	40545.	53991.	75998.	33.2	40.8	87.4
3843	429.	550.	485.	28.2	-11.8	13.1	12609.	16637.	17544.	31.9	5.5	39.1
3861	627.	780.	795.	24.4	1.9	26.8	95903.	111557.	112335.	16.3	0.7	17.1
Total	44147.	52101.	56131.	18.0	7.7	27.1	4379777.	4760507.	5601503.	8.7	17.7	27.9

Appendix B

1. Climate

The climate score is a variable indicating the mildness or harshness of an MSA's climate. A low score indicates a harsh climate; a high one indicates a mild climate. The score, found in *Places Rated Almanac*, is computed beginning at 1,000 points and subtracting for each of the following climatological factors: 1. very hot and cold months; 2. seasonal temperature variation; 3. heating- and cooling-degree days; 4. freezing days; 5. zero-degree days; and 6. ninety-degree days. Some figures are referred to as 30-year normals (averages); others are the means of annual records kept for periods ranging from a few years to more than 100 years. The data on each of these factors comes from the National Oceanic and Atmospheric Administration (NOAA), the National Climatic Center in Asheville, North Carolina, and its two-volume publication, *Local Climatological Data*. NOAA does not provide information on all MSAs: in these cases, scores are provided from the nearest substation, as reported in NOAA Series 20. Richard Boyer and David Savageau, *Places Rated Almanac: Your Guide to Finding the Best Places to Live in America*, Second Edition (Chicago: Rand McNally, 1985), chapter 1.

2. Housing Prices, in $000s

The second variable refers to the average price of a single-family residence in the MSA. The prices, found in *Places Rated Almanac*, come ultimately from the U.S. Department of Commerce, Bureau of the Census, *1980 Census of Population and Housing*, adjusted for inflation with 1984 regional data from the National Association of Realtors.

3. Property Taxes

Property tax bills are estimates from *Places Rated*, based on average market values multiplied by each state's average effective property tax rate for residences as reported by the Advisory Commission on Intergovernmental Relations, *Significant Features of Fiscal Federalism* (1984).

4. Air Service

Places Rated lists the FAA's hub classification for all metropolitan areas: large hub, medium hub, small hub, and non-hub. We gave these classifications numerical scores of 4, 3, 2, and 1, respectively. In some cases, the MSA neither has an airport nor shares one with other members of a CMSA. These MSAs received zeros for their airport scores.

5. Number of Four-Year Colleges

This variable comes from the National Center for Education Statistics, *Education Directory, Colleges and Universities, 1983–1984* (1984) via *Places Rated*.

6. Percent of the Population Aged 25 Years and Over With 16 Or More Years of Education, 1980

Item A156 in U.S. Department of Commerce, Bureau of the Census, *State and Metropolitan Area Data Book 1986* (Washington, DC: U.S. Government Printing Office, 1986). Ultimate source: U.S. Department of Commerce, Bureau of the Census, *1980 Census of Population and Housing*, Summary Tape File 3C.

7. Percent of Individuals Living Below the Federally Determined Poverty Threshold, 1980

Item A166 in U.S. Department of Commerce, Bureau of the Census, *State and Metropolitan Area Data Book 1986* (Washington, DC: U.S. Government Printing Office, 1986). Ultimate source:

U.S. Department of Commerce, Bureau of the Census, *1980 Census of Population and Housing*, Summary Tape File 3C.

8.   Unemployment, 1983

Percent of the civilian labor force unemployed and looking for work within the previous four weeks during the survey week. Item A191 in U.S. Department of Commerce, Bureau of the Census, *State and Metropolitan Area Data Book 1986* (Washington, DC: U.S. Government Printing Office, 1986) via U.S. Bureau of Labor Statistics *Employment and Unemployment for States and Local Areas*, 1983.

9.   Procurement Contract Awards from the Federal Government

Item A210 in U.S. Department of Commerce, Bureau of the Census, *State and Metropolitan Area Data Book 1986* (Washington, DC: U.S. Government Printing Office, 1986). Ultimate source: U.S. Department of Commerce, Bureau of the Census, *Consolidated Federal Funds Report, Fiscal Year 1984*, Vol. I, *County Areas*. Statistics were obtained from the U.S. Postal Service for Postal Service procurement and from the federal procurement Data Center for procurement actions of all other federal agencies, including DOD.

10.   Manufacturing Wages, 1982

This figure represents the average compensation paid to production workers. Source is Item A240, U.S. Department of Commerce, Bureau of the Census, *State and Metropolitan Area Data Book 1986* (Washington, DC: U.S. Government Printing Office, 1986). Ultimate source: U.S. Department of Commerce, Bureau of the Census, *1982 Census of Manufactures, Geographic Area Statistics* (series MC82-A).

11.   Migration from Another State

This figure represents the percent of the population living in a different state on April 1, 1975 than on April 1, 1980. Item A26 in U.S. Department of Commerce, Bureau of the Census, *State and Metropolitan Area Data Book 1986* (Washington, DC: U.S.

Government Printing Office, 1986). Ultimate source: U.S. Department of Commerce, Bureau of the Census, *1980 Census of Population and Housing*, Summary Tape File 3C.

12.   *Percent of the State Manufacturing Labor Force in Unions, 1984*

This variable comes from Alexander Grant and Company, *The Sixth Annual Study of General Manufacturing Climates of the Forty-eight Contiguous States of America* (Los Angeles: Alexander Grant & Co., June 1985), p. 64. The ultimate source is listed as a "Special study conducted by Leo Troy, Ph.D., Professor of Economics, Rutgers University, March 1985."

Notes

1. **Data Sources.** The analysis presented throughout this manuscript is derived from a data base consisting of industry plant counts and employment estimates. The data base was developed using the Census of Manufactures plant location file, which consists of four-digit industry plant counts for all counties in the United States. Plants are arrayed in employment-size categories and are used to construct employment estimates.

The results reported in this manuscript represent aggregations of high-tech employment for regions, states, and rural counties. The data span ten years and are reported in five-year intervals from the 1972, 1977, and 1982 Census of Manufactures.

An obvious limitation of the data base is the terminal date, 1982. The recession of 1982 was the most severe since the Great Depression of 1929. Unfortunately, due to the reporting requirements of the census, more recent data were unavailable. Readers should be advised that there could be some bias, particularly as it relates to regional conditions, in this analysis. However, it is important to note that the low point in high-technology industry growth did not occur until 1983–84. Therefore, to the extent that there is a downward bias in the employment figures, this is somewhat mitigated by the fact that high-tech job growth remained strong during the intense downturn of 1982.

The data used in the regression analysis reported in Chapter 7 are taken from two sources—the Census of Population and Housing and *Places Rated*. A more complete description of the independent variable construction is found in Appendix B.

2. Although previous studies have treated urban-adjacent rural areas separately from their more remote rural counterparts, this study makes no such conceptual distinction. Thus, the terms nonmetropolitan and rural will be used interchangeably throughout this book.

3. See Barkley (1988) for a recent exception.

4. Industrial filtering refers to the process whereby industries of increasingly mature and stable varieties move plants from metropolitan to rural areas.

5. Personal conversation with Sabina Deitrick, BRIE Project, University of California, Berkeley, 1988.

6. As most researchers in the field of urban and regional economic development will admit, this working definition is not without flaws, a few of which should be pointed out. First, the definition concentrates on industries that produce high-tech products. Thus, the economic benefits of high-tech production processes are unaccounted for.

Second, data limitations associated with occupational employment statistics require that selection of industries occur at a three-digit industry level, but the majority of industries popularly considered high tech and ultimately analyzed in this study are actually distinguishable at finer levels of disaggregation.

Finally, a definition of high tech ideally should be based on firm-level data that identify what is being done in individual establishments. Otherwise, it is possible to identify plants at a local level that produce a product called "high tech" that actually represents a more mature product within a larger group of products (for example, the difference between discrete semiconductor devices and microprocessors).

Lacking a solution to these three major problems, researchers have settled on a working definition of high tech based on the human capital component of the labor process. This study conforms to that definition.

7. See Rosenfeld, Malazia, and Dugan (1988), for pros and cons on this issue.

8. States in the Deep South continued to suffer enormous out-migration due mostly to changes in agriculture.

9. Employment filtering refers to the process whereby as manufacturing processes become mature and stable, other cost considerations, such as land and labor, become important facets of location decision making. Consequently, companies filter employment and select locations that reduce land and labor costs.

10. The urban-rural continuum is a geographic system that classifies counties on the basis of population size and population commuting patterns. The scale has become somewhat of a standard in rural research using counties as the basic unit of analysis. It was developed by Calvin Beale of the U.S. Department of Agriculture. Table 3.1 provides a detailed accounting of the continuum.

11. This method results in a hierarchy of counties, ranging from those with a million or more in population to rural counties not adjacent

to urban areas and containing no significant urban settlement. Because the definition is based on a single point in time, it ignores changes in population densities over the study period. In some cases, urban counties (particularly those adjacent to metropolitan areas) may have actually been rural earlier in the period. Unfortunately, to make the research manageable, studies like this must accept such limitations while noting their existence.

12. Los Angeles stands out as the quintessential city of high-tech industry. In this huge metropolis, all ninety-four identified high-tech industries are present, and they contribute in excess of 500,000 jobs to the region's economic base.

13. The discussion of the AMP Corporation is based on personal interviews with AMP personnel.

14. This information is based on personal interviews with Mark Glasmeier, a prototype machinist who builds automated machinery for firms in the connector industry, including AMP and its competitors.

15. This is becoming true for northeastern firms as well.

16. Goretex — the preferred material for many types of outdoor gear — was invented by a scientist and former employee of the Dupont Chemical Company in Maryland. Wilbert Gore developed the product in his basement and then set up business in the late 1950s. Goretex's applicability goes far beyond outdoor equipment. It is used in a variety of products, ranging from medical products to materials used in space flights.

Gore and Associates grew rapidly from a small basement-based company to a multimillion-dollar corporation. In 1985 — deliberating a production location to serve the western United States — the company looked specifically at Texas, a large market for their products.

17. Gore and Associates anticipated considerable expansion of the southwestern electronics market, but wildly over-optimistic projections have not materialized. Like other high-tech firms located in and around Austin, Gore has settled in for the long haul in hopes that the regional electronics industry will eventually recover.

18. Two other sectors, Communications Equipment, SIC 3662, and Computers, SIC 3573, also sell a substantial part of their output to the DOD. SIC 3662 is a defense-dependent sector; however, it is also part of the computer-electronics complex and is therefore discussed in these sections.

19. This section does not detail the common use of Community Development Block Grants for rural infrastructure development. Numerous states indicated in the study that they used this program for rural development. In addition, no mention is made here of services provided by the Agricultural Extension Service, although there is certainly potential

for collaboration between this long-standing extension program and other technology development programs.

20. **Determining Rural-Adjacent Counties.** This analysis uses Calvin Beale's urban-rural continuum. Using this classification scheme, all 3,140 counties were classified as either adjacent or nonadjacent. To proceed with the current analysis, rural-adjacent counties had to be teamed up with appropriate metropolitan areas. To determine adjacent counties (using 1985 definitions), maps were used to initially identify them.

As part of the identification process, I also had to contend with instances where counties were adjacent to more than one metro area. Again, as with adjacent counties, those bordering one metropolitan area, coterminous counties were identified using maps. Once coterminous counties were identified, unpublished census intercounty commuting data were obtained and dominant metropolitan areas identified on the basis of the metro area to which a majority of rural-adjacent county workers commuted.

Out of the 1,673 rural-adjacent counties, 331 shared boundaries with more than one metropolitan area. These counties were selected out and then attached to the corresponding metropolitan area.

21. There is, however, an element of follow-the-leadership; thus, the importance of amenities as a primary determinant for location is still open to debate. Even companies that are *not* high tech are now saying amenities are important to attract nontechnical employees. In other words, amenities have simply become indiscriminately used buzzwords and are part of the pervasive jargon of local economic development.

22. Interviews were conducted with officials from several corporations. At their request, I do not disclose their identities.

23. The climate measure in this analysis reflects the absence of extreme variations in temperature and precipitation and is not absolute "pleasantness" of climate as perceived by individuals.

24. Unlike the previous study, I was not able to develop a measure of freeway density comparable to that used in the previous analysis. While the absence of this variable is unfortunate, it was highly correlated with size of metropolitan area, and in that sense, other variables (including air service) captured this metropolitan feature.

25. For readers wishing a technical description of the Tobit procedure and other methods developed for the case of limited dependent variables, see G. S. Maddala, *Limited Dependent and Qualitative Variables in Econometrics* (New York: Cambridge University Press) 1983.

26. There was more than proportionate change in a number of the variables as city size increased.

27. Readers should note that the use of regression analysis in this study does not constitute an analysis of structural economic relationships as considered in econometrics. As noted here, in reporting significant coefficients and accompanying statistics, I am not implying a cause-and-effect relationship between the dependent and independent variables. Rather, I am simply saying that the occurrence of rural high-tech plants and employment is correlated with certain metropolitan-area characteristics.

In this study, regression analysis is used to identify characteristics describing metropolitan areas with either large concentrations of high-tech jobs and plants in contiguous rural areas or where large positive changes occurred in the number of high-tech jobs and plants in adjacent rural counties. Given that I am using adjacent rural county measures of high tech as the dependent variable, it is unlikely that the analysis is plagued by problems of simultaneity wherein the dependent variable determines the value of the independent variable.

28. See Feller (1984) for a critique of high-tech programs.

Bibliography

Armington, C., C. Harris, and M. Odle. *Formation and Growth in High-Tech Businesses: A Regional Assessment.* Washington, DC: Brookings Institution, Micro Data Project, 1983.

Barkley, D. L. "The Decentralization of High-Technology Manufacturing to Nonmetropolitan Areas," *Growth and Change,* 1988; 19(1, Winter):13-30.

Barkley, D. L., and J. E. Keith. "The Locational Determinants of Western Nonmetro High-Tech Manufacturers: An Econometric Analysis." Unpublished paper, 1990.

Barkley, D., R. Dahlgran, and S. Smith. "High-Technology Manufacturing in the Nonmetropolitan West: Gold or Just Glitter?" *American Journal of Agricultural Economics,* 1988; 70(3):560-571.

Barkley, D. L., S. M. Smith, and R. H. Coupal. "High-Tech Entrepreneurs in the Nonmetro West: Who Is Starting What?" *Community Economics.* Western Rural Development Center, January 1990, 116.

Blakely, E., and T. Bradshaw. *Rural Communities in Advanced Industrial Society.* New York: Praeger, 1979.

Bloomquist, L. "Performance of the Rural Manufacturing Sector." In *Rural Economic Development in the 1980s: Preparing for the Future.* Washington, DC: U.S. Department of Agriculture, Economic Research Service, 1987, pp. 3.1-3.31.

Borrus, M. *Competing for America's Stake in Microelectronics Control.* Boston: Ballinger, 1988.

Browne, L. "Can High Tech Save the Great Lakes States?" *New England Economic Review.* Boston: Federal Reserve Bank of Boston, November/December 1983, pp. 19-33.

Browne, L. "Shifting Regional Fortunes: The Wheel Turns," *New England Economic Review*. Boston: Federal Reserve Bank of Boston, May/June 1989.

Business Week. "The Hollow Corporation," September 4, 1987, p. 51.

Business Week. "Rural Areas Fall Behind," June 21, 1986, p. 23.

Campbell, S. Personal Conversation, Research Triangle Park, North Carolina, 1989.

Capellin, R. *The Diffusion of Producer Services in the Urban System.* Paper presented at the Regional Science Association European Summer Institute, Arco, Lake of Garda, Italy, 1988.

Castells, M., and L. Tyson. "High-Technology Choices Ahead." In John W. Sewell and Stuart K. Tucker, eds., *Growth, Exports and Jobs in a Changing World Economy.* New Brunswick, NJ: Transaction Books, 1988.

Center on Budget and Policy Priorities. "Laboring for Less" by I. Shapiro. Washington, DC, 1989.

Clark, G. "The Employment Relation and the Spatial Division of Labor: A Hypothesis," *Annals of the Association of American Geographers,* 1981; 71:412–424.

Clarke, M. *Revitalizing State Economies, A Review of State Development Policies and Programs.* Washington, DC: Center for Policy Research and Analysis, National Governors' Association, 1986.

Cobb, J. *The Selling of the South: The Southern Crusade for Industrial Development, 1936–1980.* Baton Rouge: University of Louisiana Press, 1984.

Cohen, R. "The New International Division of Labor, Multinational Corporations, and Urban Hierarchy." In Michael Dear and Allen Scott, eds., *Urbanization and Urban Planning in Capitalistic Society.* London: Mathuen, 1981, pp. 287–315.

Dallas Morning News, July 23, 1989.

Deitrick, S. *Industrial Linkages and Services in Newly Industrializing Countries.* Unpublished Ph.D. dissertation. Berkeley: Department of City and Regional Planning, University of California, 1990.

Deutermann, E. "Seeding Science-based Industry," *The Federal Reserve Bank of Boston Business Review,* December 1966, pp. 7–15.

Dicken, P. *Global Shift: Industrial Change in a Turbulent World.* London: Harper & Row, 1986.

Dorfman, N. "Route 128: The Development of a Regional High-Technology Economy," *Research Policy,* 1983; 12:181–197.

Erickson, R. "The Industrial Filtering Process," *Earth and Minerals Science Bulletin.* University Park, PA: Pennsylvania State University, 1978.

Estall, R. *A Modern Geography of the United States: Aspects of Life and Economy.* London: Penguin, 1972.

Falk, W., and T. Lyson. *High Tech, Low Tech, No Tech: Recent Industrial and Occupational Change in the South.* Buffalo: University of New York at Buffalo Press, 1988.

Feller, I. "Political and Administrative Aspects of State High-Technology Programs," *Policy Studies Review,* May 1984; 3(4):460–466.

Feller, I. *Positive and Negative Knowledge: An Interim Critique of Assessment of State Advanced Technology Programs.* Paper presented to the Association for Public Policy Analysis and Management, Annual Research Conference, October 1988. Graduate Program in Policy Analysis, Pennsylvania State University.

Freeman, C. *The Economics of Industrial Innovation.* Cambridge, MA: MIT Press, 1982.

Garnick, W. "Patterns of Growth in Metropolitan and Nonmetropolitan Areas: An Update," *Survey of Current Business.* Washington, DC: Bureau of Economic Analysis, 1985.

Glasmeier, A. *The Structure, Location, and Role of High-Technology Industries and U.S. Regional Development.* Unpublished Ph.D. dissertation. University of California: Department of City and Regional Planning, 1986a.

Glasmeier, A. "High Tech and the Regional Division of Labor," *Industrial Relations,* 1986b; 25(2):197–211.

Glasmeier, A. "When the Well Runs Dry: Regional Analysis of the Southwest Central States." Paper presented to the 1987 Association of Collegiate Schools of Planning, Los Angeles, California, 1987a.

Glasmeier, A. Telephone interview with AMP production manager, 1987b.

Glasmeier, A. "Factors Governing the Development of High-Technology Industry Complexes: A Tale of Three Cities," *Regional Studies,* 1988; 22(4):287–301.

Glasmeier, A. *The Missing Link: The Role of Merchant Wholesalers in U.S. Regional Development.* Working Paper 1. University of Texas, Austin: Graduate Program of Community and Regional Planning, 1989.

Glasmeier, A., and G. Borchard. "From Branch Plants to Back Offices: Service Sector Growth and Rural Economic Development," *Environment and Planning A,* 1989; 21:1565–1583.

Glasmeier, A., and R. McCluskey. "U.S. Auto Parts Production: An Analysis of the Organization and Location of a Changing Industry," *Economic Geography,* Spring 1987; 63:2.

Glasmeier, A., and K. Patrizi. *U.S. Auto Parts Industry: A Technical*

Report on the Spatial Location of Production Facilities. Working Paper 411. University of California, Berkeley: Institute of Urban and Regional Development, 1985.

Glasmeier, A., P. Hall, and A. Markusen. *Defining High-Technology Industries.* Working Paper 407. University of California, Berkeley: Institute of Urban and Regional Development, 1983.

Glasmeier, A., R. Pendall, M. Crowley, S. Ko, D. Rothchild, K. Safer, and F. Smith. "Industrial Linkages and Complex Analysis Survey Results." Unpublished manuscript of survey results from CRP 384 1987 Research Seminar, 1987.

Glickman, N., and A. Glasmeier. *Foreign Direct Investment, Industrial Linkages and Regional Development.* Washington, DC: Final Report to the Ford Foundation and Economic Development Administration of the U.S. Department of Commerce, 1989a.

Glickman, N., and A. Glasmeier. "The International Economy and the American South." In Lloyd Rodwin, ed., *Deindustrialization of the U.S. and Japan.* London: Allen and Hyman, 1989b.

Gordon, R., and L. Kimball. "The Impact of Industrial Structure on Global High-Technology Location." In Peter Hall and Michael Breheny, eds., *The Geography of High Technology: An Anglo–American Comparison.* London: Allen and Hyman, 1987.

Grunwald, J., and K. Flamm. *The Global Factory.* Washington, DC: Brookings Press, 1985.

Hansen, N. "Dualism, Capital-Labor Ratios and the Regions of the U.S.: A Comment," *Journal of Regional Science,* 1980; 20:401–403.

Haren, C., and R. Holling. "Industrial Development in Non-Metropolitan America: A Locational Perspective." In R. E. Lonsdale and H. L. Seyler, *Non-Metropolitan Industrialization.* New York: Wiley & Sons, 1979, pp. 13–46.

Harrison, B. "The Tendency Toward Instability and Inequality Underlying the 'Revival' of New England," *Papers of the Regional Science Association,* 1982; 50:41–65.

Hekman, J. "The Product Cycle and New England Textiles," *The Quarterly Journal of Economics,* 1980; 94(4):697–717.

Henderson, J. *The Globalisation of High-Technology Production: Society, Space, and Semiconductors in the Restructuring of the Modern World.* London: Routledge, 1989.

Henderson, J. "The Political Economy of Technological Transformation in Hong Kong." In Michael Peter Smith, ed., *Pacific Rim Cities in the World Economy: Comparative Urban and Community Research.* New Brunswick, NJ: Transaction Publishers, 1988.

Henry, D. "Defense Spending: A Growth Market for Industry," U.S. *Industrial Outlook,* 1983; 39:67–84.

Hoover, E., and R. Vernon. *The Anatomy of a Metropolis.* Boston: Cambridge University Press, 1959.

Hounshell, D. *From the American System to Mass Production.* Baltimore: Johns Hopkins University Press, 1984.

Hymer, S. "The Multinational Corporation and the Spatial Division of Labor." In Robert Cohen, ed., *The Multinational Corporation: A Radical Critique.* Cambridge, MA: Harvard University Press, 1979, pp. 140–207.

Johnson, M. "Industrial Transition and the Location of High-Technology Branch Plants in the Nonmetropolitan Southeast," *Economic Geography,* January 1989; 65:1.

Johnson, M. "Labor Environment and the Location of Electrical Machinery Employment in the U.S. South," *Growth and Change,* Spring 1988; 19:2.

Lichter, D. "Race, Underemployment, and Inequality in the American Rural South, 1970–1985." Working Paper No. 1988-28. Pennsylvania State University, University Park: Population Research Center, Institute for Policy Research and Evaluation, 1988.

Lonsdale, R., and H. Seyler. *Non-Metropolitan Industrialization.* New York: Wiley & Sons, 1979.

Maddala, G. S. *Limited Dependent and Qualitative Variables in Econometrics.* New York: Cambridge University Press, 1983.

Malecki, E. "Corporate Organization of R and D and the Location of Technological Activities," *Regional Studies,* 1980; 14:219–234.

Malecki, E. "High Technology for Local Economic Development," *Journal of the American Planning Association,* 1984; 50:262–269.

Malecki, E. "Industrial Location and Corporate Organization in High-Technology Industries," *Economic Geography,* 1985; 61:345–369.

Malecki, E. "Technological Imperatives and Modern Corporate Strategy," *Production, Work, Territory: The Geographical Anatomy of Industrial Capitalism.* London: Allen and Hyman, 1986, pp. 67–79.

Markusen, A. *Defense Spending: A Successful Industrial Policy?* University of California, Berkeley: Institute of Urban and Regional Development, 1985.

Markusen, A., and V. Carlson. "Deindustrialization and Regional Economic Transformation: Deindustrialization in the American Midwest–Causes and Responses." In Lloyd Rodwin, ed., *Deindustrialization of the U. S. and Japan.* London: Allen and Hyman,

Markusen, A., and K. McCurdy. *Chicago's Defense-Based High*

Technology: A Case Study of the "Seedbeds of Innovation" Hypothesis. Working Paper. Evanston, IL: Center for Urban Affairs and Policy Research, 1988.

Markusen, A., P. Hall, and A. Glasmeier. *High-Tech America: The What, How, Where and Why of the Sunrise Industries.* Winchester, MA: Unwin Hyman, 1986.

Markusen, A., P. Hall, S. Campbell, and S. Deitrick. *The Rise of the American Gunbelt: The Geography of U.S. Defense Spending.* To be published by Oxford University Press, 1991.

Massey, D. *Spatial Divisions of Labor: Social Structures and the Geography of Production.* New York: Macmillan, 1984.

McCluskey, R., T. Jagger, and R. Dahl. *New Hampshire.* Paper prepared for ComS 498. University Park, PA: Pennsylvania State University, 1985.

McWilliams, C. *California: The Great Exception.* New York: Current Books, 1949.

Merrill, S. A. "The Politics of Micropolicy: Innovation and Industrial Policy in the United States," *Policy Studies Review,* 1984; 3(4):445–451.

Mollenkopf, J. *Contested City.* Princeton, NJ: Princeton University Press, 1984.

New York Times. "The Defense Advanced Research Projects Agency," March 5, 1989.

New York Times. "The Maturing of Route 128," August 11, 1989.

Norton, R., and J. Rees. "The Product Cycle Model and the Spatial Decentralization of American Manufacturing," *Regional Studies,* 1979; 13:141–151.

Noyelle, T., and T. Stanback. *Cities in Transition.* Totowa, NJ: Allanheld and Osmun, 1982.

Office of Technology Assessment. *High-Technology Industries and Regional Development.* Washington, DC: U.S. Congress, 1984.

O'Hare, W. *The Rise of Poverty in Rural America.* Population Trends and Public Policy Reports, Number 15. Washington, DC: Population Reference Bureau, July 1988.

Park, S., and J. Wheeler. "The Filter Down Process in Georgia: The Third Stage in the Product Life Cycle," *Professional Geographer,* 1983; 35:18–31.

Parker, E., H. Hudson, D. Dillman, and A. Roscoe. *Rural America in the Information Age: Telecommunications Policy for Rural Development.* London: University Press of America, 1989.

Perloff, H., L. Wingo, R. Lampard, and L. Muth. *Regions, Resources, and Economic Growth.* Lincoln: University of Nebraska, 1960.

Phillips, B., B. Kirchoff, and H. S. Brown. "Formation, Growth and

Mobility of Technology-Based Firms in the U.S. Economy." Paper presented at the tenth annual Babson Entrepreneurship Research Conference, Babson College, Wellesley, Massachusetts, April 4-6 1990.

Plosila, W. "State Technical Development Programs," *Forum for Applied Research and Public Policy,* Summer 1987, pp. 30-38.

Porterfield, S., and G. Pulver. "The Export Potential of Service-Producing Industries, Survey Results." Agricultural Economics Staff Papers No. 284, 1988.

Prestowitz, C. *Trading Places: How the Japanese Took the Technological Lead.* New York: Basic Books, 1988.

Pudup, M. "Appalachia and the Regional Question." Paper presented to Department of City and Regional Planning, University of California, Berkeley, 1988.

Pudup, M. *Informal Work and Rural Poverty in Appalachia: An Intensive Field Study of West Virginia Household Strategies.* A research proposal submitted to the Rural Economic Policy Project, Ford Foundation, 1989.

Pudup, M. "Packers and Reapers, Merchants and Manufacturers: Industrial Restructuring and Location in an Era of Emergent Capitalism." Unpublished master's thesis. University of California, Berkeley: Department of Geography, 1986.

Rand, C. *Cambridge, U.S.A.: A Hub of a New World.* New York: Oxford University Press, 1964.

Rees, J. "State Technology Development Programs in the United States: A Perspective on Evolution and Evaluation." Unpublished preliminary report. Greensboro: University of North Carolina, Department of Geography, 1987.

Rees, J. "Technical Change and Regional Shifts in American Manufacturing," *Professional Geographer,* 1979; 31:45-54.

Resek, R., and R. Kosobud, eds. *The Midwestern Economy: Issues and Policy.* Bureau of Economic and Business Research, College of Commerce and Business Administration. Chicago: University of Illinois, Champaign-Urbana, 1982.

Richie, R., D. Hecker, and J. Burgan. "High Technology Today and Tomorrow: A Small Slice of the Employment Pie," *Monthly Labor Review,* 1983; 106:50-58.

Rosenfeld, S. "Southern Strategies for Economic Development," *Forum for Applied Research and Public Policy,* Summer 1987, pp. 48-56.

Rosenfeld, S., E. Malazia, and M. Dugan. *Reviving the Rural Factory: Automation and Work in the South.* Vol. 2: The Case Studies. Research Triangle Park, NC: Southern Growth Policies Board, 1988.

Safer, K., T. Leaf, and J. McCaine. *Phoenix, Arizona.* Unpublished paper. University of Texas, Austin: Graduate Program in Community and Regional Planning, 1986.

Saxenian, A. *Silicon Chips and Spatial Structure: The Urban Development of Santa Clara Valley, California.* Unpublished master's thesis. University of California, Berkeley: Department of City and Regional Planning, 1981.

Saxenian, A. "Silicon Valley and Route 128: Regional Prototypes or Historical Exceptions?" In Manuel Castells, ed., *High Technology, Space and Society.* Newbury Park, CA: Sage Publications, 1985a.

Saxenian, A. "The Genesis of Silicon Valley." In Peter Hall and Ann Markusen, eds., *Silicon Landscapes.* Winchester, MA: Unwin Hyman, 1985b.

Sayer, A. "Industry and Space: A Sympathetic Critique of Radical Research," *Environment and Planning D: Society and Space,* 1984; 3:3-29.

Schlessinger, T., J. Gaventa, and J. Merrifield. *Our Own Worst Enemy: The Impact of Military Production on the Upper South.* New Market, TN: Highlander Research and Education Center, 1983.

Scott, A. "Industrial Organization and the Logic of Intra-Metropolitan Location II: A Case Study of the Printed Circuits Industry in the Greater Los Angeles Region," *Economic Geography* 1983; 59:343-367.

Scott, A., and D. P. Angel. "The U.S. Semiconductor Industry: A Locational Analysis," *Environment and Planning D,* 1987; 19:875-912.

The Semiconductor Industry Association. *Two Years of Experience Under the U.S.-Japan Semiconductor Agreement.* Cupertino, CA: Semiconductor Industry Association, 1989.

Shapira, P. *Industrial Services Programs.* Morgantown: University of West Virginia, Regional Research Institute, 1989.

Shapiro, A. *The Structure and Dynamics of the Defense R&D Industry.* Stanford, CA: Stanford Research Institute, 1964.

Sieling, M. "Strong Gains in Semiconductor Productivity Tied to Innovation," *Monthly Labor Review,* April 1988; 111(4), U.S. Department of Labor, Washington, D.C.

Smith, S. M., and D. L. Barkley. "Labor Force Characteristics of 'High Tech' vs. 'Low Tech' Manufacturing in Nonmetropolitan Counties in the West," *Journal of the Community Development Society,* 1988; 19(1):21-36.

Smith, S. M., and D. L. Barkley. "Local Impacts of High-Technology Manufacturing in the Nonmetropolitan West." *Community Economics.* Western Rural Development Center, March 1989, 98.

Starr, A. "Small Business and Midwest Revitalization." In Richard Robert and Richard Kosobud, eds., *The Midwestern Economy: Issues and Policy.* Chicago, IL: University of Illinois, 1982.

Stone, C. *The Impact of Trade and Macroeconomic Policy Developments on the Rural Economy, 1972–1984.* Washington, D.C.: Urban Institute, 1986.

Storper, M. "Oligopoly and the Product Cycle, Essentialism in Economic Geography," *Economic Geography,* July 1985; 61:3.

Storper, M. *The Spatial Division of Labor: Technology, the Labor Process and the Location of Industries.* Unpublished Ph.D. dissertation. University of California, Berkeley: Department of Geography, 1982.

Taylor, M. "The Product Cycle Model: A Critique," *Environment and Planning A,* 1986; 18:751–761.

Taylor, M., and N. Thrift. "Industrial Linkage and the Segmented Economy: Some Theoretical Proposals," *Environment and Planning A,* 1982; 14(12):1601–1613.

Till, T. "Industrialization and Poverty in Southern Nonmetropolitan Labor Markets," *Growth and Change,* January 1974; 5:1.

U.S. Department of Commerce. *State and Metropolitan Data Book.* Washington, DC: Bureau of the Census, 1986.

U.S. Department of Commerce. *U.S. Industrial Outlook.* Washington, DC: Government Printing Office, 1988.

Vance, J. *The Merchant's World: The Geography of Wholesaling.* Englewood Cliffs, NJ: Prentice Hall, 1970.

Vinson, J., and M. Harrington. *Defining High-Technology Industries.* Working Paper. Boston: Massachusetts Department of Manpower Development, 1983.

Weinstein, B., H. Gross, and J. Rees. *Regional Growth and Decline in the United States.* 2d ed. New York: Praeger, 1988.

Wilson, R., and J. Schmandt. *High-Technology Industries and State Policy.* Boulder, CO: Westview Press, 1987.

Wright, G. *Old South, New South: Revolutions in the Southern Economy Since the Civil War.* New York: Basic Books, 1986.

Index

Advisory Commission on Intergovernmental Relations, 199
Aerojet General, 109–110, 119
Aerospace industry, 26, 31, 77, 97, 109, 110
Agriculture industry, 1, 13, 39, 59, 91, 189
  extension service, 126, 204
  Midwest, 72–74, 82, 139
  South, 75, 203
Air service availability
  influence on high-tech location, 162, 170, 177, 178, 179, 180, 188, 199, 205
Aircraft engines industry, 97
Aircraft industry, 30, 62, 77, 97, 107, 142–143, 163
Alabama, 107
Albuquerque, New Mexico, 34, 190–191
AMP Corporation, The, 68–69, 123, 139, 204
Annville, Kentucky, 127
Appalachia, 48
Apparel industry, 13, 137
  impact of global competition, 49
Arizona, 33, 37, 77, 115, 144
Artificial intelligence, 96
Asheville, North Carolina, 198
Assistance to specific firms' development programs, 124, 126–127, 189

California, 129
Texas, 129
Washington, 129
Atlanta, Georgia, 33
Austin, Texas, 37–41, 43, 90, 183
  IBM branch plant, 40, 44
Auto electronics industry, 4, 81, 95, 115
Auto parts industry, 74, 79, 139–140
Automation, 13, 15, 45, 49, 67–68, 69, 87, 111, 136, 145, 204
Automobile industry, 24, 35–36, 115, 139–140
  Michigan Modernization Service, 130–131
  overproduction, 142
  semiconductor consumer, 95

Baltimore, Maryland, 35
Barkley, D. L., 101, 203
Barkley and Keith, 166–167
Barkley and Smith, 68
Barkley, Dahlgran, and Smith, 38, 39, 110, 166–167
Barkley, Smith, and Coupal, 64, 110
Bastrop County, Texas, 90–91
Beale, Calvin, 203, 205
Bell Labs, 41
Ben Franklin Partnership program, 131–132
Boca Raton, Florida, 40
Boeing Aircraft, 119

Boston, Massachusetts, 16, 24, 27, 145
  DOD policies, 142
  electrical industry, 139
  key high-tech center, 49-50, 183
Boyer, Richard, 198
Branch plants
  See High-tech plants
Burlington, Vermont, 37

California, 16, 24, 27, 30, 31, 38, 41, 49-50, 77, 83, 84, 145, 203
  aerospace industry, 109, 119
  aircraft industry, 142
  CEC sectors, 119
  defense-dependent sectors, 119
  entrepreneurship assistance, 129
  financial assistance to firms, 129
Capital flight, 74
CEC sectors, 54, 95, 98-103, 115-123, 143-148, 186-187, 204
  Also see Computer industry; Electronics industry; Communications equipment industry
Census of Manufactures, 25, 200, 202
Census of Population and Housing, 198, 199, 200, 201, 202
Centre County, Pennsylvania, 110
Champion, 81
Chemical industry, 2, 9, 19, 22, 24, 63
  declines in, 136
  employment concentrations, 61, 75-76
  employment loss, 25
  in the South, 75
  plant concentrations, 61, 79
  SIC code, 23
Chicago, Illinois
  Motorola headquarters, 140
Chinese labor, 77
Chrysler, 80, 115
Clark, G., 146
Climatic factors
  influence on high-tech location,

161, 162, 168, 170, 171, 173, 174, 176, 178, 181, 198, 205
Cobb, James, 88, 141
College Station, Texas, 183
Colorado, 37, 43, 77, 84, 107, 183
  aircraft industry, 142
  missile manufacturing, 142
Colorado Springs, Colorado, 37, 43
Communications equipment industry, 2, 15, 64, 93-95, 98-103, 115-123, 143-148, 163
  employment, 50-52, 54
  growth in, 26, 62
  SIC code, 23, 204
  Also see CEC sectors
Communications industry, 4, 6
Community Development Block Grants, 204
Competition, 7, 67, 68, 69, 136, 188
  defined by, 148
  in computer and component-related industries, 83
  price, 144, 146, 147
  qualities in rural communities, 90-91, 127, 191-192
  Also see International competition
Computer industry, 4, 6, 19-22, 63, 82, 93-95, 98-103, 115-123, 143-148, 163
  competition, 83, 146-147
  Control Data Corporation, 123, 140
  employment, 25, 50-52, 54
  SIC code, 204
  Also see CEC sectors
Computer-aided design (CAD), 145
Connecticut, 8
Consolidated Federal Funds Report, 200
Construction equipment industry, 62, 66
Consumer electronics industry, 72, 81, 139, 149
  location shifts, 142
Consumer goods industry, 4, 96, 115
  impact of global competition, 49

location of, 79
Control Data Corporation, 123, 140
Corning, New York, 139
Corporate headquarters, 42, 77, 88,
    101
County Business Patterns, 38
Crystalis Semiconductors, 190–191

Dale Corporation, The, 50
Dallas–Fort Worth, Texas, 16, 33
    defense industry in, 107
    job growth, 54
Data General, 41
Dayton, Ohio
    National Cash Register Corpora-
        tion headquarters, 140
Defense-dependent sectors (DDS),
    103, 115–123, 143, 186–187,
    188
Defense industry, 4, 6, 15, 16, 38, 39,
    93, 96–98, 103–110, 115–123,
    188
    employment, 50–52, 97
    focus on South and West, 30, 31,
        77
    growth, 54
    location of, 97
    Also see Defense-dependent sec-
        tors; Defense spending; Pro-
        curement contracts
Defense spending, 41, 72, 75, 96, 142,
    188
    influence on high-tech location,
        163, 172, 177, 178, 180, 181
    Also see Defense-dependent sec-
        tors; Defense industry; Procure-
        ment contracts
Deitrick, Sabina, 149, 203
Delco, 81
Denver, Colorado, 183
    defense industry in, 107
Detroit, Michigan, 24
Digital Equipment Corporation, 24,
    41
Dun and Bradstreet, 13, 24, 55
Dupont Chemical Company, 204

Durham, North Carolina, 141

Education
    See Population, education
Education and training development
    programs, 124, 127, 128, 130
*Education Directory, Colleges and
    Universities,* 199
Electrical industry, 2, 9, 137, 139
    SIC code, 23
Electronics components industry, 93–
    95, 96, 98–103, 143
Electronics industry, 4, 6, 24, 26, 63,
    93–95, 115–123, 143–148, 163
    declines in, 136
    employment, 50–52, 54, 93, 141,
        142
    Gore and Associates, 90–91
    growth in, 62
    in the Northeast, 71
    location of, 31, 41
    National Cash Register Corpora-
        tion, 140
    new plants, 66, 67
    State of the Art, Inc., 110–112
    Also see CEC sectors
Employment
    changes in, 173–184
    concentrations, 7, 42, 61, 79–86,
        93, 135–159, 206
    decentralization, 39, 50, 136, 151
    distribution, 44, 71, 98–103, 103–
        110, 156–157
    estimates, 202
    growth, 1, 3, 6, 8, 13, 19, 25, 54,
        63–66, 98, 185–193
    levels, 154
    loss, 13, 49, 54, 187
    low-wage, 10
    shifts, 15, 32, 43, 51–54, 59–66,
        80–86, 113–133, 135, 151, 155
    spatial distribution of, 2, 3, 4, 5,
        95, 113–133, 159–184
    Also see Labor
*Employment and Unemployment for
    States and Local Areas,* 200

Energy prices, 47
Engineering and scientific instruments industry, 23
Entrepreneurial ventures, 64, 76, 190, 191, 193
Entrepreneurship training and assistance development programs, 124, 128, 130, 189
in California, 129
Environmental controls manufacturing, 140
Environmental Protection Agency, 109
Environmentally damaging industries, 4
Erie, Pennsylvania, 111
Erie-Murata, 111
Explosives industry, 62, 109
Export markets, 30

Fabricated metal products industry, 9
Fair Labor Standards Act, 75
Fairchild Semiconductors, 41
Falk, William, 88, 91
Farm equipment industry, 62, 66
Farm foreclosures, 13
Federal Aviation Administration, 199
Feller, I., 206
First World countries, 11
Florida, 31, 40, 75
defense-dependent sectors, 115
Food-processing industry, 13, 72
Ford Aerospace, 42
Ford Motor Company, 24, 81, 115
Foreign investment, 11
Furniture industry, 9, 74

General Motors, 24, 81, 115
Geneva, Switzerland, 35
Georgia, 33, 75
aircraft production in, 107
defense-dependent sectors, 115
skilled labor and markets, 141
Glasmeier, Mark, 204
Global production, 3, 8, 27, 49, 136, 192

Gore, Wilbert, 204
Gore and Associates, 90, 147-148, 190, 204
Goretex, 204
Government trade programs, 146-147
Gray, John, 40
Great Depression, 75, 202
Greater Minnesota Corporation, The, 130

Hamer, Don, 111, 112, 123
Harrisburg, Pennsylvania, 68-69, 139
Hearing aid manufacturing, 140
Hewlett-Packard, 50
High Tech, Low Tech, No Tech, 88, 91
High-tech industry
characteristics, 14-16, 17
definition, 5, 19-24
development prospects, 2, 24-27, 185-193
employment. *See* Employment, shifts
future, 148-157
growth, 5, 24-31, 57, 183, 185-193
historical basis, 138-145, 173, 181, 184
limits to, 16-17
location of, 2-6, 7, 9, 16, 28-45, 49-69, 71-92, 93, 110-112, 113-133, 159-184
spatial distribution, 4, 6, 10, 12, 14, 32-39, 47-69, 71, 135-157, 159-184
state development programs, 123-133
Also see high-tech plants
High-tech plants, 7, 27, 34, 48, 133
effect on employment, 83, 87, 90
changes in, 173-184
closures of, 13-14, 49, 54, 72, 136
concentrations, 61, 93
distribution of, 71, 86-87, 91-92, 98-103, 104-110, 156-157, 159-184

growth of, 57–68, 185–193
location of, 38–39, 59–69, 79, 84–
    86, 95, 98, 101, 115, 127, 135–
    159, 206
organizational structure, 41–45
survival, 56
High-tech services, 23
Hispanic labor, 77
Hong Kong, 11, 69, 149
Housing costs, 162, 173, 178, 181,
    198–199

IBM, 40, 82, 119, 141
Idaho, 130
Illinois, 8
integrated economy, 82
manufacturing industry, 115
Motorola, 115, 140
Import penetration, 13
impact on South, 142
Income growth, 12
Indiana, 8
integrated economy, 82
manufacturing industry, 115
Industrial Development Loan Fund,
    129
Industrial filtering, 15, 16, 60, 64,
    135, 160, 163, 188, 203
Industry. See specific industry
Innovativeness, 23, 30, 33, 41, 43, 74,
    95, 111, 192
levels of, 65
limitations on, 132
Intel, 24, 41
Intermetropolitan decentralization, 2
Intermountain West (United States),
    13
    Also see West (United States)
International competition, 1, 3, 14,
    24, 26, 27, 49, 136, 143, 187,
    192
Iowa, 48
outmigration, 48

Japan
auto industry, 143

microelectronics industry, 143,
    144, 146
Job generators, 63–66, 94
Job growth
    See Employment, growth
Johnson, M., 141
Jura Mountains, 35

Kentucky, 127
Korea, 15

Labor
cost, 3, 4, 39, 136, 138
impact of microelectronics on,
    143, 152
low-cost, 15, 16–17, 49, 50, 67, 68,
    87, 91–92, 112, 127, 143, 149
market characteristics, 160, 174,
    175
minimizing costs of, 153
quality, 16–17, 135
shortages, 139, 161
skill level, 3, 7, 16–17, 36, 39, 44–
    45, 65, 69, 87, 88–92, 101, 111,
    127, 145–146, 149, 161, 188
spatial division of, 37, 43, 44, 135,
    146, 150
    Also see Employment
Lawrence, Massachusetts, 72
Limited Dependent and Qualitative
    Variables in Econometrics, 205
Local Climatological Data, 198
Lockheed, 42
Los Angeles, California, 16, 30, 31,
    204
job growth, 54
Louisiana
growth of, 79
Lowell, Massachusetts, 72
Lyson, Thomas, 88, 91

Machinery industry, 13, 19, 22, 66–
    67, 95
declines in, 136
employment loss, 25
growth of, 58

Maddala, G.S., 205
Maine, 115
Manufacturing, 1, 2, 3, 39, 62, 113,
    127
    changing composition, 82
    decentralization of, 13, 43, 59, 91,
        135, 137
    employment, 5, 6, 32, 86, 141, 186
    growth of, 57, 92
    high-tech industries versus, 14,
        28-31
    problems of, 24, 49
    return of, 148
    spatial distribution of, 8, 155-156
Markusen, Hall, and Glasmeier, 172
Maryland, 35, 204
Massachusetts, 8, 16, 24, 27, 49-50,
        82-83, 139, 142, 145, 183
    strategic planning complex in, 109
    unemployment rate, 72
    Also see Route 128
Medical equipment industry, 64
Michigan, 8, 24
    integrated economy, 82
    technology and information
        transfer, 130-131
Michigan Modernization Service
        (MMS), 130-131
Microchip development, 94-95
Microelectronics industry, 4, 5, 6, 7,
        19, 36, 136
    AMP Corporation, The, 68-69
    era, 143-148
    Also see Premicroelectronics; Post-
        microelectronics
Microprocessors industry, 203
    SIC code, 66
Midsouth Electronics Company, 127
Midwest (United States), 4, 5, 28-31,
        172
    agricultural equipment industry,
        72, 139
    auto parts industry, 139-140
    automobile industry, 140
    CEC sectors, 101
    corporate headquarters, 42, 88,

101
    economic factors, 48, 72-74
    employment concentration, 79-
        86, 104-110, 113-133, 135,
        154, 155, 176
    industrial complex, 2, 139
    industrialization of, 138-143
    job loss, 14, 136, 186
    labor force, 73
    manufacturing employment, 8,
        73-74, 78, 137, 186
    metal fabricating, 72
    plant distribution, 86-87, 91-92,
        113-133, 139, 187
    population, 77, 78, 79, 186
Military-industrial complex, 103-110
Mining equipment industry, 62, 66
Mining industry, 13, 59, 83, 189
Minneapolis, Minnesota
    environmental control manufac-
        turing, 140
    hearing aid manufacturing, 140
Minnesota, 140
    CEC sectors, 119, 123
Missile manufacturing, 107, 142-143
Mississippi, 144
Motorola, 77, 115, 140, 144

National Association of Realtors, 199
National Center for Education Statis-
        tics, 199
National Climatic Center, 198
National Electronic Corporation
        (NEC), 50
National Industrial Relations Act, 75
National Oceanic and Atmospheric
        Administration, 198
New Deal, 75, 109
New England, 71-72
    branch plants in South and Asia,
        84
    Also see Northeast (United States)
New firm development, 43, 126, 129
New Hampshire, 82
    electrical industry, 139
New Jersey, 8

New Mexico, 34, 190-191
  defense industry in, 108
New product development, 2
New York, 8, 82, 139
  CEC sectors, 119
  DOD policies, 142
  job growth, 54
  manufacturing industry, 139
Newly industrializing countries
    (NICs), 4, 5, 11, 16-17, 137,
    143, 146, 149
Nittany Lions, 110
Nonagricultural industry, 25
Nonelectrical machinery industry
  new plants, 66
  SIC code, 23
North Carolina, 40, 141, 183, 198
Northeast (United States), 6, 28-31,
    74, 77
  CEC sectors, 101
  corporate headquarters, 42, 101
  defense industry, 97
  economy, 71-72, 73
  employment concentration, 79-
    86, 88, 104-110, 113-133, 135,
    154, 155, 176
  industrialization of, 138-143
  labor force, 71-72
  large-scale job loss, 14, 136
  manufacturing industry, 8, 78, 82,
    91, 137, 186
  new firm formation rates, 43
  plant distribution, 86-87, 113-
    133, 154
  population, 77, 78, 79
  research and development, 71-72,
    187
  single-location firms, 42
  technical education, 71-72

Oak Ridge National Laboratory, 112
Occupational data, 65-66, 88-91
Office of Management and Budget,
    23
Ohio, 8, 140
  integrated economy, 82

manufacturing industry, 115
Oil prices, 13, 47-49, 79
Oklahoma, 79
Oregon, 37, 50
  defense-dependent sectors, 119
Outmigration, 12, 31, 48
  Also see Population

Pennsylvania, 8, 35, 110-112, 123,
    139
  Ben Franklin Partnership pro-
    gram, 131-132
  defense-dependent sectors, 115,
    142
  manufacturing industry, 143
  technology and information
    transfer, 131
Pennsylvania State University, 110
PENTAP, 131
Peripheral regions, 11-12
Philadelphia, Pennsylvania, 35
Phillips, Kirchhoff, and Brown, 13,
    24, 55-56
Phoenix, Arizona, 33, 77
  Motorola, 115, 144
Photographic equipment industry, 63
Places Rated Almanac, 198, 199, 202
Population
  concentrations, 4, 77-80, 159, 177
  decentralization, 30
  demographic changes, 48
  education, 161, 168, 169, 173-
    174, 179, 181, 189-190, 199
  migration, 12, 13, 48, 153, 163,
    170, 171, 177, 178, 180, 200
  regional shares, 28, 77, 86
  shifts, 5, 6, 12, 80, 204
  trends, 31
Portland, Oregon, 37
Postmicroelectronics production, 2, 3
Poverty level, 12
  influence on high-tech location,
    163, 177, 178, 180, 182, 199
Premicroelectronics production, 2, 3,
    138-143
Price competition

See Competition, price
Procurement contracts, 191
    influence on high-tech location,
        163, 167, 174, 177, 178, 180,
        181, 182, 199
    Also see Defense spending
Product-cycle model, 135, 151, 192
Production techniques, 192
Property taxes
    influence on high-tech location,
        162, 173, 174, 176–177, 182,
        199
Public policy, 6, 8, 10, 12, 14, 17, 62,
        112, 123–133, 186, 190, 192,
        193
    development programs, 123–133,
        129, 130, 189, 191
Puerto Rico
    new firm development, 129

Raleigh, North Carolina
    IBM computer manufacturing
        plant, 40
    Research Triangle Park, 141
Recruitment, 14
Research and development, 2, 3, 12,
        43, 69, 71, 101, 107, 141, 144,
        187, 193
    contracts, 72, 77, 96
    development programs, 124, 130
    spending, 19
    state investments in, 5
Research parks and incubator facili-
    ties
    development programs, 124, 127–
        128, 130, 132, 191
Research Triangle Park, 141, 183
Rhode Island, 115
Rosenfeld, Malazia, and Dugan, 203
Route 128 (Massachusetts), 9, 27, 33,
        41, 42, 72, 145, 183
Rural America
    description of, 47–49, 71
    locational boundaries of, 50–57
    survival of, 192–193
    transformation of, 47, 77–80

Rural Coalition, 12
Rural economics, 16, 71–92
    collapse of, 12
    defects in, 189
    development, 13, 126–128, 132,
        177, 189
    impact of new plants on, 66–69,
        87, 88
    international impacts on, 47
Rural industrialization, 71–92
Rural renaissance, 12, 47
Rutgers University, 201

Sacramento, California, 119
San Diego, California, 119
San Francisco Bay Area, 38, 41
San Jose, California, 24
Sandia National Laboratories, 112
Santa Clara County, California, 27,
        34
    branch plants, 84, 145
    key high-tech center, 49–50
    Also see Silicon Valley
Satellite industry
    State of the Art, Inc., 110–111
Savageau, David, 198
Schaumsburg, Illinois, 115
Schockley Semiconductor, 41
Scientific instruments industry, 95, 97
Semiconductor industry, 9, 15, 17,
        22, 64, 93–95, 96, 98–103, 203
    job growth in, 26
    location of, 31, 34, 41, 77, 192
    Motorola, 115, 140, 144
    SIC code, 23, 66
    Spatial division within, 37
Service industries, 23
Shoe industry, 72, 74
Siemens, 50
*Significant Features of Fiscal Federal-
    ism,* 199
Silicon Valley, 9, 27, 31, 33, 38, 41,
        42, 183, 191
    branch plants, 84, 145
    Also see Santa Clara County, Cali-
        fornia

Singapore, 11, 15, 16, 69, 149
*Sixth Annual Study of General
    Manufacturing,* 201
Smith and Barkley, 64, 84, 88, 110
South (United States), 3, 4, 6, 28–31,
    69, 72, 172
  agricultural industry, 75, 203
  auto parts industry, 79
  CEC sectors, 101
  chemical industry, 75–76, 79
  computer industry, 84
  defense industry, 75, 76
  economic factors, 48, 74–76, 142
  educational system, 75
  employment concentration, 43,
    79, 80–86, 104–110, 135, 137,
    155–156, 187
  exploitation of, 49, 74, 88, 141
  import penetration, 142
  industrialization of, 140–143
  labor pool, 74–75, 88, 101, 153–
    154, 188
  manufacturing, 8, 74, 78
  plant distributions, 86–87, 88,
    91–92, 101, 155–156, 186, 187
  population, 77, 78, 79
  poverty levels, 177
  spatial filtering, 150
  Also see Sunbelt
South Korea, 11, 17, 149
Southern Growth Policy Board, 62,
    130
Southern States Technology Council,
    130
Spatial economy, 10–11
Standard Industrial Classification
    (SIC) code, 23, 204
  inadequacies in, 66
  reclassification of, 26
*State and Metropolitan Area Data
    Book,* 1986, 199, 200
State College, Pennsylvania, 110–112
State of the Art, Inc., 110–112, 123,
    193
Steel industry, 24
Sunbelt, 6

buildup of industries in, 33, 45,
    79, 151, 154, 181
  composition of, 74
  Also see South; West
Superfund sites, 109
Switzerland, 35

Taiwan, 15, 17, 149
Tax incentives, 88
Technology and information transfer
    development programs, 124,
    128, 130–131
Technology diffusion, 11
Telecommunications industry
    deregulation of, 26
Tennessee, 109–110
Tennessee Valley Authority (TVA), 31
Texas, 16, 31, 33, 37–41, 43, 44, 54–
    55, 75, 90, 183
  aircraft production, 107, 142–143
  defense-dependent sectors, 115
  financial assistance to firms, 129
  Gore and Associates, 90–91, 147–
    148, 190, 204
  growth of, 79
  missile manufacturing, 107, 142–
    143
Texas A&M University, 183
Textile industry, 9, 13, 61–62, 74,
    137, 186
  employment, 141
  impact of global competition, 49,
    62
  production shifts, 72
The Selling of the South, 141
Third World countries, 8, 10, 11, 13,
    15, 192
  production shifts to, 49, 67, 136,
    142–147
Timber industry, 9, 61, 83
Tobit procedure, 167–174, 205
Transportation equipment industry,
    23
Troy, Leo, 201
Tucson, Arizona, 37
  defense industry in, 107

Unemployment rates, 12, 72
  influence on high-tech location,
    160–161, 169, 173, 174, 175,
    182, 200
Unions, 7, 30, 88, 151, 153
  in automobile industry, 140
  influence on high-tech locations,
    160, 170, 173–174, 176, 178,
    179, 181, 182, 187, 201
U.S. Air Force, 30–31
U.S. Armed Forces, 30–31
U.S. Bureau of Labor Statistics, 200
U.S. Department of Agriculture, 203
U.S. Department of Commerce, 198,
    199, 200, 201
U.S. Department of Defense (DOD),
    15, 31, 38, 96, 111, 142, 200,
    204
U.S. Postal Service, 200
Universities
  influence on high-tech location,
    161, 169, 173–174, 176, 178,
    179, 180, 181, 182, 188, 189–
    190, 199
University-based research, 72, 126,
    130, 132
University of California, 203
University of Idaho, 130
University of Texas, 90, 183
Utah, 77

Venture financing, 14
Vermont, 37, 82
  defense-dependent sectors, 115
Very large-scale integration (VLSI),
    144–145
Virginia, 75
  CEC sectors, 119, 123

Wages, 10, 11, 30, 151

  influence on high-tech location,
    160, 173, 176, 178, 200
Waltham Watch Company, 72
War Industry Board, 109
Washington, 77
  defense-dependent sectors, 119
  financial assistance to firms, 129
  policy development, 129
Washington, D.C., 123
Watch industry, 72
West (United States), 4, 6, 28–31,
    76–77, 159
  aerospace industry, 77
  branch plants, 76, 91–92
  CEC sectors, 101
  Coast area, 31
  corporate headquarters, 77
  defense industry, 77
  economic factors, 48, 83
  employment concentrations, 79–
    86, 104–110, 112, 135
  entrepreneurial ventures, 64, 76
  in-place capital reinvestment, 76
  labor pool, 153–154
  manufacturing employment, 8, 78
  mineral resources, 76
  mining industry, 83
  new firm formation rates, 43
  plant distribution, 86–87, 154, 186
  population, 78, 79
  R&D, 187
  single location firms, 42
  spatial filtering, 150
  timber industry, 83
  wages, 83
  Also see Sunbelt
Wisconsin, 8
Works Progress Administration, 75

Zurich, Switzerland, 35